ISBN 0-8373-2644-3

C-2644   CAREER EXAMINATION SERIES

This is your PASSBOOK® for...

Principal Financial Analyst

Test Preparation Study Guide

Questions & Answers

NLC

NATIONAL LEARNING CORPORATION

Copyright © 2017 by

National Learning Corporation

212 Michael Drive, Syosset, New York 11791

All rights reserved, including the right of reproduction in whole or in part, in any form or by any means, electronic or mechanical, including photocopying, recording, or by any information storage and retrieval system, without permission in writing from the Publisher.

(516) 921-8888
(800) 632-8888
(800) 645-6337
FAX: (516) 921-8743
www.passbooks.com
info @ passbooks.com

PRINTED IN THE UNITED STATES OF AMERICA

PASSBOOK®
NOTICE

This book is SOLELY intended for, is sold ONLY to, and its use is RESTRICTED to *individual*, bona fide applicants or candidates who qualify by virtue of having seriously filed applications for appropriate license, certificate, professional and/or promotional advancement, higher school matriculation, scholarship, or other legitimate requirements of educational and/or governmental authorities.

This book is NOT intended for use, class instruction, tutoring, training, duplication, copying, reprinting, excerption, or adaptation, etc., by:

(1) Other publishers

(2) Proprietors and/or Instructors of "Coaching" and/or Preparatory Courses

(3) Personnel and/or Training Divisions of commercial, industrial, and governmental organizations

(4) Schools, colleges, or universities and/or their departments and staffs, including teachers and other personnel

(5) Testing Agencies or Bureaus

(6) Study groups which seek by the purchase of a single volume to copy and/or duplicate and/or adapt this material for use by the group as a whole without having purchased individual volumes for each of the members of the group

(7) Et al.

Such persons would be in violation of appropriate Federal and State statutes.

PROVISION OF LICENSING AGREEMENTS. — Recognized educational commercial, industrial, and governmental institutions and organizations, and others legitimately engaged in educational pursuits, including training, testing, and measurement activities, may address a request for a licensing agreement to the copyright owners, who will determine whether, and under what conditions, including fees and charges, the materials in this book may be used by them. In other words, a licensing facility exists for the legitimate use of the material in this book on other than an individual basis. However, it is asseverated and affirmed here that the material in this book *CANNOT* be used without the receipt of the express permission of such a licensing agreement from the Publishers.

NATIONAL LEARNING CORPORATION
212 Michael Drive
Syosset, New York 11791

Inquiries re licensing agreements should be addressed to:
The President
National Learning Corporation
212 Michael Drive
Syosset, New York 11791

PASSBOOK® SERIES

THE *PASSBOOK® SERIES* has been created to prepare applicants and candidates for the ultimate academic battlefield – the examination room.

At some time in our lives, each and every one of us may be required to take an examination – for validation, matriculation, admission, qualification, registration, certification, or licensure.

Based on the assumption that every applicant or candidate has met the basic formal educational standards, has taken the required number of courses, and read the necessary texts, the *PASSBOOK® SERIES* furnishes the one special preparation which may assure passing with confidence, instead of failing with insecurity. Examination questions – together with answers – are furnished as the basic vehicle for study so that the mysteries of the examination and its compounding difficulties may be eliminated or diminished by a sure method.

This book is meant to help you pass your examination provided that you qualify and are serious in your objective.

The entire field is reviewed through the huge store of content information which is succinctly presented through a provocative and challenging approach – the question-and-answer method.

A climate of success is established by furnishing the correct answers at the end of each test.

You soon learn to recognize types of questions, forms of questions, and patterns of questioning. You may even begin to anticipate expected outcomes.

You perceive that many questions are repeated or adapted so that you can gain acute insights, which may enable you to score many sure points.

You learn how to confront new questions, or types of questions, and to attack them confidently and work out the correct answers.

You note objectives and emphases, and recognize pitfalls and dangers, so that you may make positive educational adjustments.

Moreover, you are kept fully informed in relation to new concepts, methods, practices, and directions in the field.

You discover that you are actually taking the examination all the time: you are preparing for the examination by "taking" an examination, not by reading extraneous and/or supererogatory textbooks.

In short, this PASSBOOK®, used directedly, should be an important factor in helping you to pass your test.

PRINCIPAL FINANCIAL ANALYST

DUTIES:
An employee in this class conducts statistical analysis of information affecting an investment or revenue program on a Countywide or departmental basis. Depending upon the location of the position, work may involve planning for future bond offerings, debt service, cash management, and/or determining future sources of revenue. The incumbent reports to an administrative supervisor through frequent conferences and written reports. This position differs from those in the Budget Examiner and Budget Analyst class in that, in addition to any budget responsibilities, the incumbent develops financial policies and plans, presents these plans to the appropriate administrator or outside agency and plans and prepares the necessary statements and materials to implement the program. Supervision will be exercised over a professional and support staff as necessary. Does related work as required.

SCOPE OF THE EXAMINATION
The written test will cover knowledge, skills, and/or abilities in such areas as:
1. Evaluating conclusions in light of known facts;
2. Fiscal management;
3. Preparing written material;
4. Supervision;
5. Understanding and interpreting tabular material; and
6. Understanding and interpreting written material.

HOW TO TAKE A TEST

I. YOU MUST PASS AN EXAMINATION

A. *WHAT EVERY CANDIDATE SHOULD KNOW*

Examination applicants often ask us for help in preparing for the written test. What can I study in advance? What kinds of questions will be asked? How will the test be given? How will the papers be graded?

As an applicant for a civil service examination, you may be wondering about some of these things. Our purpose here is to suggest effective methods of advance study and to describe civil service examinations.

Your chances for success on this examination can be increased if you know how to prepare. Those "pre-examination jitters" can be reduced if you know what to expect. You can even experience an adventure in good citizenship if you know why civil service exams are given.

B. *WHY ARE CIVIL SERVICE EXAMINATIONS GIVEN?*

Civil service examinations are important to you in two ways. As a citizen, you want public jobs filled by employees who know how to do their work. As a job seeker, you want a fair chance to compete for that job on an equal footing with other candidates. The best-known means of accomplishing this two-fold goal is the competitive examination.

Exams are widely publicized throughout the nation. They may be administered for jobs in federal, state, city, municipal, town or village governments or agencies.

Any citizen may apply, with some limitations, such as the age or residence of applicants. Your experience and education may be reviewed to see whether you meet the requirements for the particular examination. When these requirements exist, they are reasonable and applied consistently to all applicants. Thus, a competitive examination may cause you some uneasiness now, but it is your privilege and safeguard.

C. *HOW ARE CIVIL SERVICE EXAMS DEVELOPED?*

Examinations are carefully written by trained technicians who are specialists in the field known as "psychological measurement," in consultation with recognized authorities in the field of work that the test will cover. These experts recommend the subject matter areas or skills to be tested; only those knowledges or skills important to your success on the job are included. The most reliable books and source materials available are used as references. Together, the experts and technicians judge the difficulty level of the questions.

Test technicians know how to phrase questions so that the problem is clearly stated. Their ethics do not permit "trick" or "catch" questions. Questions may have been tried out on sample groups, or subjected to statistical analysis, to determine their usefulness.

Written tests are often used in combination with performance tests, ratings of training and experience, and oral interviews. All of these measures combine to form the best-known means of finding the right person for the right job.

II. HOW TO PASS THE WRITTEN TEST

A. NATURE OF THE EXAMINATION

To prepare intelligently for civil service examinations, you should know how they differ from school examinations you have taken. In school you were assigned certain definite pages to read or subjects to cover. The examination questions were quite detailed and usually emphasized memory. Civil service exams, on the other hand, try to discover your present ability to perform the duties of a position, plus your potentiality to learn these duties. In other words, a civil service exam attempts to predict how successful you will be. Questions cover such a broad area that they cannot be as minute and detailed as school exam questions.

In the public service similar kinds of work, or positions, are grouped together in one "class." This process is known as *position-classification*. All the positions in a class are paid according to the salary range for that class. One class title covers all of these positions, and they are all tested by the same examination.

B. FOUR BASIC STEPS

1) Study the announcement

How, then, can you know what subjects to study? Our best answer is: "Learn as much as possible about the class of positions for which you've applied." The exam will test the knowledge, skills and abilities needed to do the work.

Your most valuable source of information about the position you want is the official exam announcement. This announcement lists the training and experience qualifications. Check these standards and apply only if you come reasonably close to meeting them.

The brief description of the position in the examination announcement offers some clues to the subjects which will be tested. Think about the job itself. Review the duties in your mind. Can you perform them, or are there some in which you are rusty? Fill in the blank spots in your preparation.

Many jurisdictions preview the written test in the exam announcement by including a section called "Knowledge and Abilities Required," "Scope of the Examination," or some similar heading. Here you will find out specifically what fields will be tested.

2) Review your own background

Once you learn in general what the position is all about, and what you need to know to do the work, ask yourself which subjects you already know fairly well and which need improvement. You may wonder whether to concentrate on improving your strong areas or on building some background in your fields of weakness. When the announcement has specified "some knowledge" or "considerable knowledge," or has used adjectives like "beginning principles of…" or "advanced … methods," you can get a clue as to the number and difficulty of questions to be asked in any given field. More questions, and hence broader coverage, would be included for those subjects which are more important in the work. Now weigh your strengths and weaknesses against the job requirements and prepare accordingly.

3) Determine the level of the position

Another way to tell how intensively you should prepare is to understand the level of the job for which you are applying. Is it the entering level? In other words, is this the position in which beginners in a field of work are hired? Or is it an intermediate or advanced level? Sometimes this is indicated by such words as "Junior" or "Senior" in the class title. Other jurisdictions use Roman numerals to designate the level – Clerk I, Clerk II, for example. The word "Supervisor" sometimes appears in the title. If the level is not indicated by the title, check the description of duties. Will you be working under very close supervision, or will you have responsibility for independent decisions in this work?

4) Choose appropriate study materials

Now that you know the subjects to be examined and the relative amount of each subject to be covered, you can choose suitable study materials. For beginning level jobs, or even advanced ones, if you have a pronounced weakness in some aspect of your training, read a modern, standard textbook in that field. Be sure it is up to date and has general coverage. Such books are normally available at your library, and the librarian will be glad to help you locate one. For entry-level positions, questions of appropriate difficulty are chosen – neither highly advanced questions, nor those too simple. Such questions require careful thought but not advanced training.

If the position for which you are applying is technical or advanced, you will read more advanced, specialized material. If you are already familiar with the basic principles of your field, elementary textbooks would waste your time. Concentrate on advanced textbooks and technical periodicals. Think through the concepts and review difficult problems in your field.

These are all general sources. You can get more ideas on your own initiative, following these leads. For example, training manuals and publications of the government agency which employs workers in your field can be useful, particularly for technical and professional positions. A letter or visit to the government department involved may result in more specific study suggestions, and certainly will provide you with a more definite idea of the exact nature of the position you are seeking.

III. KINDS OF TESTS

Tests are used for purposes other than measuring knowledge and ability to perform specified duties. For some positions, it is equally important to test ability to make adjustments to new situations or to profit from training. In others, basic mental abilities not dependent on information are essential. Questions which test these things may not appear as pertinent to the duties of the position as those which test for knowledge and information. Yet they are often highly important parts of a fair examination. For very general questions, it is almost impossible to help you direct your study efforts. What we can do is to point out some of the more common of these general abilities needed in public service positions and describe some typical questions.

1) General information

Broad, general information has been found useful for predicting job success in some kinds of work. This is tested in a variety of ways, from vocabulary lists to questions about current events. Basic background in some field of work, such as sociology or economics, may be sampled in a group of questions. Often these are principles which have become familiar to most persons through exposure rather than through formal training. It is difficult to advise you how to study for these questions; being alert to the world around you is our best suggestion.

2) Verbal ability

An example of an ability needed in many positions is verbal or language ability. Verbal ability is, in brief, the ability to use and understand words. Vocabulary and grammar tests are typical measures of this ability. Reading comprehension or paragraph interpretation questions are common in many kinds of civil service tests. You are given a paragraph of written material and asked to find its central meaning.

3) Numerical ability

Number skills can be tested by the familiar arithmetic problem, by checking paired lists of numbers to see which are alike and which are different, or by interpreting charts and graphs. In the latter test, a graph may be printed in the test booklet which you are asked to use as the basis for answering questions.

4) Observation

A popular test for law-enforcement positions is the observation test. A picture is shown to you for several minutes, then taken away. Questions about the picture test your ability to observe both details and larger elements.

5) Following directions

In many positions in the public service, the employee must be able to carry out written instructions dependably and accurately. You may be given a chart with several columns, each column listing a variety of information. The questions require you to carry out directions involving the information given in the chart.

6) Skills and aptitudes

Performance tests effectively measure some manual skills and aptitudes. When the skill is one in which you are trained, such as typing or shorthand, you can practice. These tests are often very much like those given in business school or high school courses. For many of the other skills and aptitudes, however, no short-time preparation can be made. Skills and abilities natural to you or that you have developed throughout your lifetime are being tested.

Many of the general questions just described provide all the data needed to answer the questions and ask you to use your reasoning ability to find the answers. Your best preparation for these tests, as well as for tests of facts and ideas, is to be at your physical and mental best. You, no doubt, have your own methods of getting into an exam-taking mood and keeping "in shape." The next section lists some ideas on this subject.

IV. KINDS OF QUESTIONS

Only rarely is the "essay" question, which you answer in narrative form, used in civil service tests. Civil service tests are usually of the short-answer type. Full instructions for answering these questions will be given to you at the examination. But in case this is your first experience with short-answer questions and separate answer sheets, here is what you need to know:

1) Multiple-choice Questions

Most popular of the short-answer questions is the "multiple choice" or "best answer" question. It can be used, for example, to test for factual knowledge, ability to solve problems or judgment in meeting situations found at work.

A multiple-choice question is normally one of three types—
- It can begin with an incomplete statement followed by several possible endings. You are to find the one ending which *best* completes the statement, although some of the others may not be entirely wrong.
- It can also be a complete statement in the form of a question which is answered by choosing one of the statements listed.

- It can be in the form of a problem – again you select the best answer.

Here is an example of a multiple-choice question with a discussion which should give you some clues as to the method for choosing the right answer:

When an employee has a complaint about his assignment, the action which will *best* help him overcome his difficulty is to
   A. discuss his difficulty with his coworkers
   B. take the problem to the head of the organization
   C. take the problem to the person who gave him the assignment
   D. say nothing to anyone about his complaint

In answering this question, you should study each of the choices to find which is best. Consider choice "A" – Certainly an employee may discuss his complaint with fellow employees, but no change or improvement can result, and the complaint remains unresolved. Choice "B" is a poor choice since the head of the organization probably does not know what assignment you have been given, and taking your problem to him is known as "going over the head" of the supervisor. The supervisor, or person who made the assignment, is the person who can clarify it or correct any injustice. Choice "C" is, therefore, correct. To say nothing, as in choice "D," is unwise. Supervisors have and interest in knowing the problems employees are facing, and the employee is seeking a solution to his problem.

2) True/False Questions

The "true/false" or "right/wrong" form of question is sometimes used. Here a complete statement is given. Your job is to decide whether the statement is right or wrong.

SAMPLE: A roaming cell-phone call to a nearby city costs less than a non-roaming call to a distant city.

This statement is wrong, or false, since roaming calls are more expensive.

This is not a complete list of all possible question forms, although most of the others are variations of these common types. You will always get complete directions for answering questions. Be sure you understand *how* to mark your answers – ask questions until you do.

V. RECORDING YOUR ANSWERS

Computer terminals are used more and more today for many different kinds of exams.

For an examination with very few applicants, you may be told to record your answers in the test booklet itself. Separate answer sheets are much more common. If this separate answer sheet is to be scored by machine – and this is often the case – it is highly important that you mark your answers correctly in order to get credit.

An electronic scoring machine is often used in civil service offices because of the speed with which papers can be scored. Machine-scored answer sheets must be marked with a pencil, which will be given to you. This pencil has a high graphite content which responds to the electronic scoring machine. As a matter of fact, stray dots may register as answers, so do not let your pencil rest on the answer sheet while you are pondering the correct answer. Also, if your pencil lead breaks or is otherwise defective, ask for another.

Since the answer sheet will be dropped in a slot in the scoring machine, be careful not to bend the corners or get the paper crumpled.

The answer sheet normally has five vertical columns of numbers, with 30 numbers to a column. These numbers correspond to the question numbers in your test booklet. After each number, going across the page are four or five pairs of dotted lines. These short dotted lines have small letters or numbers above them. The first two pairs may also have a "T" or "F" above the letters. This indicates that the first two pairs only are to be used if the questions are of the true-false type. If the questions are multiple choice, disregard the "T" and "F" and pay attention only to the small letters or numbers.

Answer your questions in the manner of the sample that follows:

32. The largest city in the United States is
    A. Washington, D.C.
    B. New York City
    C. Chicago
    D. Detroit
    E. San Francisco

1) Choose the answer you think is best. (New York City is the largest, so "B" is correct.)
2) Find the row of dotted lines numbered the same as the question you are answering. (Find row number 32)
3) Find the pair of dotted lines corresponding to the answer. (Find the pair of lines under the mark "B.")
4) Make a solid black mark between the dotted lines.

VI. BEFORE THE TEST

Common sense will help you find procedures to follow to get ready for an examination. Too many of us, however, overlook these sensible measures. Indeed, nervousness and fatigue have been found to be the most serious reasons why applicants fail to do their best on civil service tests. Here is a list of reminders:

- Begin your preparation early – Don't wait until the last minute to go scurrying around for books and materials or to find out what the position is all about.
- Prepare continuously – An hour a night for a week is better than an all-night cram session. This has been definitely established. What is more, a night a week for a month will return better dividends than crowding your study into a shorter period of time.
- Locate the place of the exam – You have been sent a notice telling you when and where to report for the examination. If the location is in a different town or otherwise unfamiliar to you, it would be well to inquire the best route and learn something about the building.
- Relax the night before the test – Allow your mind to rest. Do not study at all that night. Plan some mild recreation or diversion; then go to bed early and get a good night's sleep.
- Get up early enough to make a leisurely trip to the place for the test – This way unforeseen events, traffic snarls, unfamiliar buildings, etc. will not upset you.
- Dress comfortably – A written test is not a fashion show. You will be known by number and not by name, so wear something comfortable.

- Leave excess paraphernalia at home – Shopping bags and odd bundles will get in your way. You need bring only the items mentioned in the official notice you received; usually everything you need is provided. Do not bring reference books to the exam. They will only confuse those last minutes and be taken away from you when in the test room.
- Arrive somewhat ahead of time – If because of transportation schedules you must get there very early, bring a newspaper or magazine to take your mind off yourself while waiting.
- Locate the examination room – When you have found the proper room, you will be directed to the seat or part of the room where you will sit. Sometimes you are given a sheet of instructions to read while you are waiting. Do not fill out any forms until you are told to do so; just read them and be prepared.
- Relax and prepare to listen to the instructions
- If you have any physical problem that may keep you from doing your best, be sure to tell the test administrator. If you are sick or in poor health, you really cannot do your best on the exam. You can come back and take the test some other time.

VII. AT THE TEST

The day of the test is here and you have the test booklet in your hand. The temptation to get going is very strong. Caution! There is more to success than knowing the right answers. You must know how to identify your papers and understand variations in the type of short-answer question used in this particular examination. Follow these suggestions for maximum results from your efforts:

1) Cooperate with the monitor

The test administrator has a duty to create a situation in which you can be as much at ease as possible. He will give instructions, tell you when to begin, check to see that you are marking your answer sheet correctly, and so on. He is not there to guard you, although he will see that your competitors do not take unfair advantage. He wants to help you do your best.

2) Listen to all instructions

Don't jump the gun! Wait until you understand all directions. In most civil service tests you get more time than you need to answer the questions. So don't be in a hurry. Read each word of instructions until you clearly understand the meaning. Study the examples, listen to all announcements and follow directions. Ask questions if you do not understand what to do.

3) Identify your papers

Civil service exams are usually identified by number only. You will be assigned a number; you must not put your name on your test papers. Be sure to copy your number correctly. Since more than one exam may be given, copy your exact examination title.

4) Plan your time

Unless you are told that a test is a "speed" or "rate of work" test, speed itself is usually not important. Time enough to answer all the questions will be provided, but this does not mean that you have all day. An overall time limit has been set. Divide the total time (in minutes) by the number of questions to determine the approximate time you have for each question.

5) Do not linger over difficult questions

If you come across a difficult question, mark it with a paper clip (useful to have along) and come back to it when you have been through the booklet. One caution if you do this – be sure to skip a number on your answer sheet as well. Check often to be sure that you have not lost your place and that you are marking in the row numbered the same as the question you are answering.

6) Read the questions

Be sure you know what the question asks! Many capable people are unsuccessful because they failed to *read* the questions correctly.

7) Answer all questions

Unless you have been instructed that a penalty will be deducted for incorrect answers, it is better to guess than to omit a question.

8) Speed tests

It is often better NOT to guess on speed tests. It has been found that on timed tests people are tempted to spend the last few seconds before time is called in marking answers at random – without even reading them – in the hope of picking up a few extra points. To discourage this practice, the instructions may warn you that your score will be "corrected" for guessing. That is, a penalty will be applied. The incorrect answers will be deducted from the correct ones, or some other penalty formula will be used.

9) Review your answers

If you finish before time is called, go back to the questions you guessed or omitted to give them further thought. Review other answers if you have time.

10) Return your test materials

If you are ready to leave before others have finished or time is called, take ALL your materials to the monitor and leave quietly. Never take any test material with you. The monitor can discover whose papers are not complete, and taking a test booklet may be grounds for disqualification.

VIII. EXAMINATION TECHNIQUES

1) Read the general instructions carefully. These are usually printed on the first page of the exam booklet. As a rule, these instructions refer to the timing of the examination; the fact that you should not start work until the signal and must stop work at a signal, etc. If there are any *special* instructions, such as a choice of questions to be answered, make sure that you note this instruction carefully.

2) When you are ready to start work on the examination, that is as soon as the signal has been given, read the instructions to each question booklet, underline any key words or phrases, such as *least*, *best*, *outline*, *describe* and the like. In this way you will tend to answer as requested rather than discover on reviewing your paper that you *listed without describing*, that you selected the *worst* choice rather than the *best* choice, etc.

3) If the examination is of the objective or multiple-choice type – that is, each question will also give a series of possible answers: A, B, C or D, and you are called upon to select the best answer and write the letter next to that answer on your answer paper – it is advisable to start answering each question in turn. There may be anywhere from 50 to 100 such questions in the three or four hours allotted and you can see how much time would be taken if you read through all the questions before beginning to answer any. Furthermore, if you come across a question or group of questions which you know would be difficult to answer, it would undoubtedly affect your handling of all the other questions.

4) If the examination is of the essay type and contains but a few questions, it is a moot point as to whether you should read all the questions before starting to answer any one. Of course, if you are given a choice – say five out of seven and the like – then it is essential to read all the questions so you can eliminate the two that are most difficult. If, however, you are asked to answer all the questions, there may be danger in trying to answer the easiest one first because you may find that you will spend too much time on it. The best technique is to answer the first question, then proceed to the second, etc.

5) Time your answers. Before the exam begins, write down the time it started, then add the time allowed for the examination and write down the time it must be completed, then divide the time available somewhat as follows:
    - If 3-1/2 hours are allowed, that would be 210 minutes. If you have 80 objective-type questions, that would be an average of 2-1/2 minutes per question. Allow yourself no more than 2 minutes per question, or a total of 160 minutes, which will permit about 50 minutes to review.
    - If for the time allotment of 210 minutes there are 7 essay questions to answer, that would average about 30 minutes a question. Give yourself only 25 minutes per question so that you have about 35 minutes to review.

6) The most important instruction is to *read each question* and make sure you know what is wanted. The second most important instruction is to *time yourself properly* so that you answer every question. The third most important instruction is to *answer every question*. Guess if you have to but include something for each question. Remember that you will receive no credit for a blank and will probably receive some credit if you write something in answer to an essay question. If you guess a letter – say "B" for a multiple-choice question – you may have guessed right. If you leave a blank as an answer to a multiple-choice question, the examiners may respect your feelings but it will not add a point to your score. Some exams may penalize you for wrong answers, so in such cases *only*, you may not want to guess unless you have some basis for your answer.

7) Suggestions
    a. Objective-type questions
        1. Examine the question booklet for proper sequence of pages and questions
        2. Read all instructions carefully
        3. Skip any question which seems too difficult; return to it after all other questions have been answered
        4. Apportion your time properly; do not spend too much time on any single question or group of questions

5. Note and underline key words – *all, most, fewest, least, best, worst, same, opposite,* etc.
6. Pay particular attention to negatives
7. Note unusual option, e.g., unduly long, short, complex, different or similar in content to the body of the question
8. Observe the use of "hedging" words – *probably, may, most likely,* etc.
9. Make sure that your answer is put next to the same number as the question
10. Do not second-guess unless you have good reason to believe the second answer is definitely more correct
11. Cross out original answer if you decide another answer is more accurate; do not erase until you are ready to hand your paper in
12. Answer all questions; guess unless instructed otherwise
13. Leave time for review

b. Essay questions
1. Read each question carefully
2. Determine exactly what is wanted. Underline key words or phrases.
3. Decide on outline or paragraph answer
4. Include many different points and elements unless asked to develop any one or two points or elements
5. Show impartiality by giving pros and cons unless directed to select one side only
6. Make and write down any assumptions you find necessary to answer the questions
7. Watch your English, grammar, punctuation and choice of words
8. Time your answers; don't crowd material

8) Answering the essay question

Most essay questions can be answered by framing the specific response around several key words or ideas. Here are a few such key words or ideas:

M's: manpower, materials, methods, money, management
P's: purpose, program, policy, plan, procedure, practice, problems, pitfalls, personnel, public relations

a. Six basic steps in handling problems:
1. Preliminary plan and background development
2. Collect information, data and facts
3. Analyze and interpret information, data and facts
4. Analyze and develop solutions as well as make recommendations
5. Prepare report and sell recommendations
6. Install recommendations and follow up effectiveness

b. Pitfalls to avoid
1. *Taking things for granted* – A statement of the situation does not necessarily imply that each of the elements is necessarily true; for example, a complaint may be invalid and biased so that all that can be taken for granted is that a complaint has been registered

2. *Considering only one side of a situation* – Wherever possible, indicate several alternatives and then point out the reasons you selected the best one
3. *Failing to indicate follow up* – Whenever your answer indicates action on your part, make certain that you will take proper follow-up action to see how successful your recommendations, procedures or actions turn out to be
4. *Taking too long in answering any single question* – Remember to time your answers properly

IX. AFTER THE TEST

Scoring procedures differ in detail among civil service jurisdictions although the general principles are the same. Whether the papers are hand-scored or graded by machine we have described, they are nearly always graded by number. That is, the person who marks the paper knows only the number – never the name – of the applicant. Not until all the papers have been graded will they be matched with names. If other tests, such as training and experience or oral interview ratings have been given, scores will be combined. Different parts of the examination usually have different weights. For example, the written test might count 60 percent of the final grade, and a rating of training and experience 40 percent. In many jurisdictions, veterans will have a certain number of points added to their grades.

After the final grade has been determined, the names are placed in grade order and an eligible list is established. There are various methods for resolving ties between those who get the same final grade – probably the most common is to place first the name of the person whose application was received first. Job offers are made from the eligible list in the order the names appear on it. You will be notified of your grade and your rank as soon as all these computations have been made. This will be done as rapidly as possible.

People who are found to meet the requirements in the announcement are called "eligibles." Their names are put on a list of eligible candidates. An eligible's chances of getting a job depend on how high he stands on this list and how fast agencies are filling jobs from the list.

When a job is to be filled from a list of eligibles, the agency asks for the names of people on the list of eligibles for that job. When the civil service commission receives this request, it sends to the agency the names of the three people highest on this list. Or, if the job to be filled has specialized requirements, the office sends the agency the names of the top three persons who meet these requirements from the general list.

The appointing officer makes a choice from among the three people whose names were sent to him. If the selected person accepts the appointment, the names of the others are put back on the list to be considered for future openings.

That is the rule in hiring from all kinds of eligible lists, whether they are for typist, carpenter, chemist, or something else. For every vacancy, the appointing officer has his choice of any one of the top three eligibles on the list. This explains why the person whose name is on top of the list sometimes does not get an appointment when some of the persons lower on the list do. If the appointing officer chooses the second or third eligible, the No. 1 eligible does not get a job at once, but stays on the list until he is appointed or the list is terminated.

X. HOW TO PASS THE INTERVIEW TEST

The examination for which you applied requires an oral interview test. You have already taken the written test and you are now being called for the interview test – the final part of the formal examination.

You may think that it is not possible to prepare for an interview test and that there are no procedures to follow during an interview. Our purpose is to point out some things you can do in advance that will help you and some good rules to follow and pitfalls to avoid while you are being interviewed.

What is an interview supposed to test?

The written examination is designed to test the technical knowledge and competence of the candidate; the oral is designed to evaluate intangible qualities, not readily measured otherwise, and to establish a list showing the relative fitness of each candidate – as measured against his competitors – for the position sought. Scoring is not on the basis of "right" and "wrong," but on a sliding scale of values ranging from "not passable" to "outstanding." As a matter of fact, it is possible to achieve a relatively low score without a single "incorrect" answer because of evident weakness in the qualities being measured.

Occasionally, an examination may consist entirely of an oral test – either an individual or a group oral. In such cases, information is sought concerning the technical knowledges and abilities of the candidate, since there has been no written examination for this purpose. More commonly, however, an oral test is used to supplement a written examination.

Who conducts interviews?

The composition of oral boards varies among different jurisdictions. In nearly all, a representative of the personnel department serves as chairman. One of the members of the board may be a representative of the department in which the candidate would work. In some cases, "outside experts" are used, and, frequently, a businessman or some other representative of the general public is asked to serve. Labor and management or other special groups may be represented. The aim is to secure the services of experts in the appropriate field.

However the board is composed, it is a good idea (and not at all improper or unethical) to ascertain in advance of the interview who the members are and what groups they represent. When you are introduced to them, you will have some idea of their backgrounds and interests, and at least you will not stutter and stammer over their names.

What should be done before the interview?

While knowledge about the board members is useful and takes some of the surprise element out of the interview, there is other preparation which is more substantive. It *is* possible to prepare for an oral interview – in several ways:

1) Keep a copy of your application and review it carefully before the interview

This may be the only document before the oral board, and the starting point of the interview. Know what education and experience you have listed there, and the sequence and dates of all of it. Sometimes the board will ask you to review the highlights of your experience for them; you should not have to hem and haw doing it.

2) Study the class specification and the examination announcement

Usually, the oral board has one or both of these to guide them. The qualities, characteristics or knowledges required by the position sought are stated in these documents. They offer valuable clues as to the nature of the oral interview. For example, if the job involves supervisory responsibilities, the announcement will usually indicate that knowledge of modern supervisory methods and the qualifications of the candidate as a supervisor will be tested. If so, you can expect such questions, frequently in the form of a hypothetical situation which you are expected to solve. NEVER go into an oral without knowledge of the duties and responsibilities of the job you seek.

3) Think through each qualification required
Try to visualize the kind of questions you would ask if you were a board member. How well could you answer them? Try especially to appraise your own knowledge and background in each area, *measured against the job sought*, and identify any areas in which you are weak. Be critical and realistic – do not flatter yourself.

4) Do some general reading in areas in which you feel you may be weak
For example, if the job involves supervision and your past experience has NOT, some general reading in supervisory methods and practices, particularly in the field of human relations, might be useful. Do NOT study agency procedures or detailed manuals. The oral board will be testing your understanding and capacity, not your memory.

5) Get a good night's sleep and watch your general health and mental attitude
You will want a clear head at the interview. Take care of a cold or any other minor ailment, and of course, no hangovers.

What should be done on the day of the interview?
Now comes the day of the interview itself. Give yourself plenty of time to get there. Plan to arrive somewhat ahead of the scheduled time, particularly if your appointment is in the fore part of the day. If a previous candidate fails to appear, the board might be ready for you a bit early. By early afternoon an oral board is almost invariably behind schedule if there are many candidates, and you may have to wait. Take along a book or magazine to read, or your application to review, but leave any extraneous material in the waiting room when you go in for your interview. In any event, relax and compose yourself.

The matter of dress is important. The board is forming impressions about you – from your experience, your manners, your attitude, and your appearance. Give your personal appearance careful attention. Dress your best, but not your flashiest. Choose conservative, appropriate clothing, and be sure it is immaculate. This is a business interview, and your appearance should indicate that you regard it as such. Besides, being well groomed and properly dressed will help boost your confidence.

Sooner or later, someone will call your name and escort you into the interview room. *This is it.* From here on you are on your own. It is too late for any more preparation. But remember, you asked for this opportunity to prove your fitness, and you are here because your request was granted.

What happens when you go in?
The usual sequence of events will be as follows: The clerk (who is often the board stenographer) will introduce you to the chairman of the oral board, who will introduce you to the other members of the board. Acknowledge the introductions before you sit down. Do not be surprised if you find a microphone facing you or a stenotypist sitting by. Oral interviews are usually recorded in the event of an appeal or other review.

Usually the chairman of the board will open the interview by reviewing the highlights of your education and work experience from your application – primarily for the benefit of the other members of the board, as well as to get the material into the record. Do not interrupt or comment unless there is an error or significant misinterpretation; if that is the case, do not hesitate. But do not quibble about insignificant matters. Also, he will usually ask you some question about your education, experience or your present job – partly to get you to start talking and to establish the interviewing "rapport." He may start the actual questioning, or turn it over to one of the other members. Frequently, each member undertakes the questioning on a particular area, one in which he is perhaps most competent, so you can expect each member to participate in the examination. Because time is limited, you may also expect some rather abrupt switches in the direction the questioning takes, so do not be upset by it. Normally, a board member will not pursue a single line of questioning unless he discovers a particular strength or weakness.

After each member has participated, the chairman will usually ask whether any member has any further questions, then will ask you if you have anything you wish to add. Unless you are expecting this question, it may floor you. Worse, it may start you off on an extended, extemporaneous speech. The board is not usually seeking more information. The question is principally to offer you a last opportunity to present further qualifications or to indicate that you have nothing to add. So, if you feel that a significant qualification or characteristic has been overlooked, it is proper to point it out in a sentence or so. Do not compliment the board on the thoroughness of their examination – they have been sketchy, and you know it. If you wish, merely say, "No thank you, I have nothing further to add." This is a point where you can "talk yourself out" of a good impression or fail to present an important bit of information. Remember, *you close the interview yourself.*

The chairman will then say, "That is all, Mr. _____, thank you." Do not be startled; the interview is over, and quicker than you think. Thank him, gather your belongings and take your leave. Save your sigh of relief for the other side of the door.

How to put your best foot forward
Throughout this entire process, you may feel that the board individually and collectively is trying to pierce your defenses, seek out your hidden weaknesses and embarrass and confuse you. Actually, this is not true. They are obliged to make an appraisal of your qualifications for the job you are seeking, and they want to see you in your best light. Remember, they must interview all candidates and a non-cooperative candidate may become a failure in spite of their best efforts to bring out his qualifications. Here are 15 suggestions that will help you:

1) Be natural – Keep your attitude confident, not cocky
If you are not confident that you can do the job, do not expect the board to be. Do not apologize for your weaknesses, try to bring out your strong points. The board is interested in a positive, not negative, presentation. Cockiness will antagonize any board member and make him wonder if you are covering up a weakness by a false show of strength.

2) Get comfortable, but don't lounge or sprawl
Sit erectly but not stiffly. A careless posture may lead the board to conclude that you are careless in other things, or at least that you are not impressed by the importance of the occasion. Either conclusion is natural, even if incorrect. Do not fuss with your clothing, a pencil or an ashtray. Your hands may occasionally be useful to emphasize a point; do not let them become a point of distraction.

3) Do not wisecrack or make small talk
This is a serious situation, and your attitude should show that you consider it as such. Further, the time of the board is limited – they do not want to waste it, and neither should you.

4) Do not exaggerate your experience or abilities

In the first place, from information in the application or other interviews and sources, the board may know more about you than you think. Secondly, you probably will not get away with it. An experienced board is rather adept at spotting such a situation, so do not take the chance.

5) If you know a board member, do not make a point of it, yet do not hide it

Certainly you are not fooling him, and probably not the other members of the board. Do not try to take advantage of your acquaintanceship – it will probably do you little good.

6) Do not dominate the interview

Let the board do that. They will give you the clues – do not assume that you have to do all the talking. Realize that the board has a number of questions to ask you, and do not try to take up all the interview time by showing off your extensive knowledge of the answer to the first one.

7) Be attentive

You only have 20 minutes or so, and you should keep your attention at its sharpest throughout. When a member is addressing a problem or question to you, give him your undivided attention. Address your reply principally to him, but do not exclude the other board members.

8) Do not interrupt

A board member may be stating a problem for you to analyze. He will ask you a question when the time comes. Let him state the problem, and wait for the question.

9) Make sure you understand the question

Do not try to answer until you are sure what the question is. If it is not clear, restate it in your own words or ask the board member to clarify it for you. However, do not haggle about minor elements.

10) Reply promptly but not hastily

A common entry on oral board rating sheets is "candidate responded readily," or "candidate hesitated in replies." Respond as promptly and quickly as you can, but do not jump to a hasty, ill-considered answer.

11) Do not be peremptory in your answers

A brief answer is proper – but do not fire your answer back. That is a losing game from your point of view. The board member can probably ask questions much faster than you can answer them.

12) Do not try to create the answer you think the board member wants

He is interested in what kind of mind you have and how it works – not in playing games. Furthermore, he can usually spot this practice and will actually grade you down on it.

13) Do not switch sides in your reply merely to agree with a board member

Frequently, a member will take a contrary position merely to draw you out and to see if you are willing and able to defend your point of view. Do not start a debate, yet do not surrender a good position. If a position is worth taking, it is worth defending.

14) Do not be afraid to admit an error in judgment if you are shown to be wrong
   The board knows that you are forced to reply without any opportunity for careful consideration. Your answer may be demonstrably wrong. If so, admit it and get on with the interview.

15) Do not dwell at length on your present job
   The opening question may relate to your present assignment. Answer the question but do not go into an extended discussion. You are being examined for a *new* job, not your present one. As a matter of fact, try to phrase ALL your answers in terms of the job for which you are being examined.

Basis of Rating
   Probably you will forget most of these "do's" and "don'ts" when you walk into the oral interview room. Even remembering them all will not ensure you a passing grade. Perhaps you did not have the qualifications in the first place. But remembering them will help you to put your best foot forward, without treading on the toes of the board members.
   Rumor and popular opinion to the contrary notwithstanding, an oral board wants you to make the best appearance possible. They know you are under pressure – but they also want to see how you respond to it as a guide to what your reaction would be under the pressures of the job you seek. They will be influenced by the degree of poise you display, the personal traits you show and the manner in which you respond.

ABOUT THIS BOOK

   This book contains tests divided into Examination Sections. Go through each test, answering every question in the margin. We have also attached a sample answer sheet at the back of the book that can be removed and used. At the end of each test look at the answer key and check your answers. On the ones you got wrong, look at the right answer choice and learn. Do not fill in the answers first. Do not memorize the questions and answers, but understand the answer and principles involved. On your test, the questions will likely be different from the samples. Questions are changed and new ones added. If you understand these past questions you should have success with any changes that arise. Tests may consist of several types of questions. We have additional books on each subject should more study be advisable or necessary for you. Finally, the more you study, the better prepared you will be. This book is intended to be the last thing you study before you walk into the examination room. Prior study of relevant texts is also recommended. NLC publishes some of these in our Fundamental Series. Knowledge and good sense are important factors in passing your exam. Good luck also helps. So now study this Passbook, absorb the material contained within and take that knowledge into the examination. Then do your best to pass that exam.

EXAMINATION SECTION

EVALUATING CONCLUSIONS BASED ON FACTUAL INFORMATION

Test material will be presented in a multiple-choice question format.

Test Task: You will be given a set of statements and a conclusion based on the statements. You are to assume the statements are true. The conclusion is reached from these statements *only*- not on what you may happen to know about the subject discussed. Each question has three possible answers. You must then select the correct answer in the following manner:

Select A, if the statements prove that the conclusion is true.
Select B, if the statements prove that the conclusion is false.
Select C, if the statements are inadequate to prove the conclusion either true or false.

SAMPLE QUESTION #1:

STATEMENTS: All uniforms are cleaned by the Conroy Company. Blue uniforms are cleaned on Mondays or Fridays; green or brown uniforms are cleaned on Wednesdays. Alan and Jean have blue uniforms, Gary has green uniforms and Ryan has brown uniforms.

CONCLUSION: Jean's uniforms are cleaned on Wednesdays.
   A. statements prove the conclusion TRUE
   B. statements prove the conclusion FALSE
   C. statements are INADEQUATE to prove the conclusion

The correct answer to this sample question is Choice B.

Solution:

The last sentence of the statements says that jean has blue uniforms. the second sentence of the statements says that blue uniforms are cleaned on Monday or Friday.
the conclusion says jean's uniforms are cleaned on Wednesday. Wednesday is neither Monday or Friday. Therefore, the conclusion must be false (choice B).

SAMPLE QUESTION #2:

STATEMENTS: If Beth works overtime, the assignment will be completed. If the assignment is completed, then all unit employees will receive a bonus. Beth works overtime.

CONCLUSION: A bonus will be given to all employees in the unit.
  A. statement prove the conclusion TRUE
  B. statements prove the conclusion FALSE
  C. statements are INADEQUATE to prove the conclusion

The correct answer to this sample question is Choice A.

Solution:

The conclusion follows necessarily from the statements. Beth works overtime. The assignment is completed. Therefore, all unit employees will receive a bonus.

SAMPLE QUESTION #3:

STATEMENTS: Bill is older than Wanda. Edna is older than Bill. Sarah is twice as old as Wanda.

CONCLUSION: Sarah is older than Edna.

  A. statement prove the conclusion TRUE
  B. statements prove the conclusion FALSE
  C. statements are INADEQUATE to prove the conclusion

The correct answer to this sample question is Choice C.

Solution:

We know from the statements that both Sarah and Edna are older than Wanda. We do not have any other information about Sarah and Edna. Therefore, no conclusion about whether or not Sarah is older than Edna can be made.

EVALUATING CONCLUSIONS IN LIGHT OF KNOWN FACTS

EXAMINATION SECTION

TEST 1

DIRECTIONS: Each question or incomplete statement is followed by several suggested answers or completions. Select the one that BEST answers the question or completes the statement. *PRINT THE LETTER OF THE CORRECT ANSWER IN THE SPACE AT THE RIGHT.*

Questions 1-9.

DIRECTIONS: In Questions 1 through 9, you will read a set of facts and a conclusion drawn from them. The conclusion may be valid or invalid, based on the facts. It is your task to determine the validity of the conclusion.
For each question, select the letter before the statement that BEST expresses the relationship between the given facts and the conclusion that has been drawn from them. Your choices are:
    A. The facts prove the conclusion.
    B. The facts disprove the conclusion; or
    C. The facts neither prove nor disprove the conclusion.

1. FACTS: Lauren must use Highway 29 to get to work. Lauren has a meeting today at 9:00 A.M. If she misses the meeting, Lauren will probably lose a major account. Highway 29 is closed all day today for repairs.

    CONCLUSION: Lauren will not be able to get to work.

    A. The facts prove the conclusion.
    B. The facts disprove the conclusion.
    C. The facts neither prove nor disprove the conclusion.

    1.____

2. FACTS: The Tumbleweed Follies, a traveling burlesque show, is looking for a new line dancer. The position requires both singing and dancing skills. If the show cannot fill the position by Friday, it will begin to look for a magician to fill the time slot currently held by the line dancers. Willa, who wants to audition for the line dancing position, can sing, but cannot dance.

    CONCLUSION: Willa is qualified to audition for the part of line dancer.

    A. The facts prove the conclusion.
    B. The facts disprove the conclusion.
    C. The facts neither prove nor disprove the conclusion.

    2.____

2 (#1)

3. FACTS: Terry owns two dogs, Spike and Stan. One of the dogs is short-haired and has blue eyes. One dog as a pink nose. The blue-eyed dog never barks. One of the dogs has white fur on its paws. Sam has long hair.

   CONCLUSION: Spike never barks.

   A. The facts prove the conclusion.
   B. The facts disprove the conclusion.
   C. The facts neither prove nor disprove the conclusion.

   3.____

4. FACTS: No science teachers are members of the PTA. Some English teachers are members of the PTA. Some English teachers in the PTA also wear glasses. Every PTA member is required to sit on the dunking stool at the student carnival except for those who wear glasses, who will be exempt. Those who are exempt, however, will have to officiate the hamster races. All of the English teachers in the PTA who do not wear glasses are married.

   CONCLUSION: All the married English teachers in the PTA will set on the dunking stool at the student carnival.

   A. The facts prove the conclusion.
   B. The facts disprove the conclusion.
   C. The facts neither prove nor disprove the conclusion.

   4.____

5. FACTS: If the price of fuel is increased and sales remain constant, oil company profits will increase. The price of fuel was increased, and market experts project that sales levels are likely to be maintained.

   CONCLUSION: The price of fuel will increase.

   A. The facts prove the conclusion.
   B. The facts disprove the conclusion.
   C. The facts neither prove nor disprove the conclusion.

   5.____

6. FACTS: Some members of the gymnastics team are double-jointed, and some members of the gymnastics team ae also on the lacrosse team. Some double-jointed members of the gymnastics team are also coaches. All gymnastics team members perform floor exercises, except the coaches. All the double-jointed members of the gymnastics team who are not coaches are freshmen.

   CONCLUSION: Some double-jointed freshmen are coaches.

   A. The facts prove the conclusion.
   B. The facts disprove the conclusion.
   C. The facts neither prove nor disprove the conclusion.

   6.____

3 (#1)

7. FACTS: Each member of the International Society speaks at least one foreign language, but no member speaks more than four foreign languages. Five members speak Spanish; three speak Mandarin; four speak French; four speak German; and five speak a foreign language other than Spanish, Mandarin, French, or German.

   CONCLUSION: The lowest possible number of members in the International Society is eight.

   A. The facts prove the conclusion.
   B. The facts disprove the conclusion.
   C. The facts neither prove nor disprove the conclusion.

   7._____

8. FACTS: Mary keeps seven cats in her apartment. Only three of the cats will eat the same kind of food. Mary wants to keep at least one extra bag of each kind of food.

   CONCLUSION: The minimum number of bags Mary will need to keep as extra is 7.

   A. The facts prove the conclusion.
   B. The facts disprove the conclusion.
   C. The facts neither prove nor disprove the conclusion.

   8._____

9. FACTS: In Ed and Marie's exercise group, everyone likes the treadmill or the stationary bicycle, or both, but Ed does not like the stationary bicycle. Marie has not expressed a preference, but spends most of her time on the stationary bicycle.

   CONCLUSION: Everyone in the group who does not like the treadmill likes the stationary bicycle.

   A. The facts prove the conclusion.
   B. The facts disprove the conclusion.
   C. The facts neither prove nor disprove the conclusion.

   9._____

Questions 10-17.

DIRECTIONS: Questions 10 through 17 are based on the following reading passage. It is not your knowledge of the particular topic that is being tested, but your ability to reason based on what you have read. The passage is likely to detail several proposed courses of action and factors affecting these proposals. The reading passage is followed by a conclusion or outcome based on the facts in the passage, or a description of a decision taken regarding the situation. The conclusion is followed by a number of statements that have a possible connection to the conclusion. For each statement, you are to determine whether:

A. The statement proves the conclusion.
B. The statement supports the conclusion but does not prove it.
C. The statement disproves the conclusion.
D. The statement weakens the conclusion but does not disprove it.
E. The statement has no relevance to the conclusion.

Remember that the conclusion after the passage is to be accepted as the outcome of what actually happened, and that you are being asked to evaluate the impact each statement would have had on the conclusion.

PASSAGE

The Owyhee Mission School District's Board of Directors is hosting a public meeting to debate the merits of the proposed abolition of all bilingual education programs within the district. The group that has made the proposal believes the programs, which teach immigrant children academic subjects in their native language until they have learned English well enough to join mainstream classes, inhibit the ability of students to acquire English quickly and succeed in school and in the larger American society. Such programs, they argue, are also a wasteful drain on the district's already scant resources.

At the meeting, several teachers and parents stand to speak out against the proposal. The purpose of an education, they say, should be to build upon, rather than dismantle, a minority child's language and culture. By teaching children in academic subjects in their native tongues, while simultaneously offering English language instruction, schools can meet the goals of learning English and progressing through academic subjects along with their peers.

Hiram Nguyen, a representative of the parents whose children are currently enrolled in bilingual education, stands at the meeting to express the parents' wishes. The parents have been polled, he says, and are overwhelmingly of the opinion that while language and culture are important to them, they are not things that will disappear from the students' lives if they are no longer taught in the classroom. The most important issue for the parents is whether their children will succeed in school and be competitive in the larger American society. If bilingual education can be demonstrated to do that, then the parents are in favor of continuing it.

At the end of the meeting, a proponent of the plan, Oscar Ramos, stands to clarify some misconceptions about the proposal. It does not call for a "sink or swim" approach, he says, but allows for an interpreter to be present in mainstream classes to explain anything a student finds too complex or confusing.

The last word of the meeting is given to Delia Cruz, a bilingual teacher at one of the district's elementary schools. A student is bound to find anything complex or confusing, she says, if it is spoken in a language he has never heard before. It is more wasteful to place children in classrooms where they don't understand anything, she says, than it is to try to teach them something useful as they are learning the English language.

CONCLUSION: After the meeting, the Owyhee Mission School District's Board of Directors votes to terminate all the district's bilingual education programs at the end of the current academic year, but to maintain the current level of funding to each of the schools that have programs cut.

10. A poll conducted by the *Los Angeles Times* at approximately the same time as the Board's meeting indicated that 75% of the people were opposed to bilingual education; among Latinos, opposition was 84%.
    A. The statement proves the conclusion.
    B. The statement supports the conclusion but does not prove it.
    C. The statement disproves the conclusion.
    D. The statement weakens the conclusion but does not disprove it.
    E. The statement has no relevance to the conclusion.

10.____

11. Of all the studies connected on bilingual education programs, 64% indicate that students learned English grammar better in "sink or swim" classes without any special features than they did in bilingual education classes.
    A. The statement proves the conclusion.
    B. The statement supports the conclusion but does not prove it.
    C. The statement disproves the conclusion.
    D. The statement weakens the conclusion but does not disprove it.
    E. The statement has no relevance to the conclusion.

11.____

12. In the academic year that begins after the Board's vote, Montgomery Burns Elementary, an Owyhee Mission District school, launches a new bilingual program for the children of Somali immigrants.
    A. The statement proves the conclusion.
    B. The statement supports the conclusion but does not prove it.
    C. The statement disproves the conclusion.
    D. The statement weakens the conclusion but does not disprove it.
    E. The statement has no relevance to the conclusion.

12.____

13. In the previous academic year, under severe budget restraints, the Owyhee Mission District cut all physical education, music, and art classes, but its funding for bilingual education classes increased by 18%.
    A. The statement proves the conclusion.
    B. The statement supports the conclusion but does not prove it.
    C. The statement disproves the conclusion.
    D. The statement weakens the conclusion but does not disprove it.
    E. The statement has no relevance to the conclusion.

13.____

14. Before the Board votes, a polling consultant conducts randomly sampled assessments of immigrant students who enrolled in Owyhee District schools at a time when they did not speak any English at all. Ten years after graduating from high school, 44% of those who received bilingual education were professionals – doctors, lawyers, educators, engineers, etc. Of those who did not receive bilingual education, 38% were professionals.
    A. The statement proves the conclusion.
    B. The statement supports the conclusion but does not prove it.
    C. The statement disproves the conclusion.
    D. The statement weakens the conclusion but does not disprove it.
    E. The statement has no relevance to the conclusion.

14.____

15. Over the past several years, the scores of Owyhee District students have gradually declined, and enrollment numbers have followed as anxious parents transferred their children to other schools or applied for a state-funded voucher program.   15.____
    A. The statement proves the conclusion.
    B. The statement supports the conclusion but does not prove it.
    C. The statement disproves the conclusion.
    D. The statement weakens the conclusion but does not disprove it.
    E. The statement has no relevance to the conclusion.

16. California and Massachusetts, two of the most liberal states in the country, have each passed ballot measures banning bilingual education in public schools.   16.____
    A. The statement proves the conclusion.
    B. The statement supports the conclusion but does not prove it.
    C. The statement disproves the conclusion.
    D. The statement weakens the conclusion but does not disprove it.
    E. The statement has no relevance to the conclusion.

17. In the academic year that begins after the Board's vote, no Owyhee Mission Schools are conducting bilingual instruction.   17.____
    A. The statement proves the conclusion.
    B. The statement supports the conclusion but does not prove it.
    C. The statement disproves the conclusion.
    D. The statement weakens the conclusion but does not disprove it.
    E. The statement has no relevance to the conclusion.

Questions 18-25.

DIRECTIONS: Questions 18 through 25 each provide four factual statements and a conclusion based on these statements. After reading the entire question, you will decide whether:
A. The conclusion is proved by Statements 1-4;
B. The conclusion is disproved by Statements 1-4;
C. The facts are not sufficient to prove or disprove the conclusion.

18. FACTUAL STATEMENTS: 18.____
    1) Gear X rotates in a clockwise direction if Switch C is in the OFF position.
    2) Gear X will rotate in a counter-clockwise direction if Switch C is ON.
    3) If Gear X is rotating in a clockwise direction, then Gear Y will not be rotating at all.
    4) Switch C is OFF.

    CONCLUSION: Gear Y is rotating.

    A. The conclusion is proved by Statements 1-4;
    B. The conclusion is disproved by Statements 1-4;
    C. The facts are not sufficient to prove or disprove the conclusion.

7 (#1)

19. FACTUAL STATEMENTS:
    1) Mark is older than Jim but younger than Dan.
    2) Fern is older than Mark but younger than Silas.
    3) Dan is younger than Silas but older than Edward.
    4) Edward is older than Mark but younger than Fern.

    CONCLUSION: Dan is older than Fern.

    A. The conclusion is proved by Statements 1-4;
    B. The conclusion is disproved by Statements 1-4;
    C. The facts are not sufficient to prove or disprove the conclusion.

    19.____

20. FACTUAL STATEMENTS:
    1) Each of Fred's three sofa cushions lies on top of four lost coins.
    2) The cushion on the right covers two pennies and two dimes.
    3) The middle cushion covers two dimes and two quarters.
    4) The cushion on the left covers two nickels and two quarters.

    CONCLUSION: To be guaranteed of retrieving at least one coin of each denomination, and without looking at any of the coins, Frank must take three coins each from under the cushions on the right and the left.

    A. The conclusion is proved by Statements 1-4;
    B. The conclusion is disproved by Statements 1-4;
    C. The facts are not sufficient to prove or disprove the conclusion.

    20.____

21. FACTUAL STATEMENTS:
    1) The door to the hammer mill chamber is locked if light 6 is red.
    2) The door to the hammer mill chamber is locked only when the mill is operating.
    3) If the mill is not operating, light 6 is blue.
    4) The door to the hammer mill chamber is locked.

    CONCLUSION: The mill is in operation.

    A. The conclusion is proved by Statements 1-4;
    B. The conclusion is disproved by Statements 1-4;
    C. The facts are not sufficient to prove or disprove the conclusion.

    21.____

22. FACTUAL STATEMENTS:
    1) In a five-story office building, where each story is occupied by a single professional, Dr. Kane's office is above Dr. Assad's.
    2) Dr. Johnson's office is between Dr. Kane's and Dr. Conlon's.
    3) Dr. Steen's office is between Dr. Conlon's and Dr. Assad's.
    4) Dr. Johnson is on the fourth story.

    CONCLUSION: Dr. Steen occupies the second story.

    22.____

A. The conclusion is proved by Statements 1-4;
B. The conclusion is disproved by Statements 1-4;
C. The facts are not sufficient to prove or disprove the conclusion.

23. FACTUAL STATEMENTS: 23.____
   1) On Saturday, farmers Hank, Earl, Roy, and Cletus plowed a total of 520 acres.
   2) Hank plowed twice as many acres as Roy.
   3) Roy plowed half as much as the farmer who plowed the most.
   4) Cletus plowed 160 acres.

   CONCLUSION: Hank plowed 200 acres.
   A. The conclusion is proved by Statements 1-4;
   B. The conclusion is disproved by Statements 1-4;
   C. The facts are not sufficient to prove or disprove the conclusion.

24. FACTUAL STATEMENTS: 24.____
   1) Four travelers – Tina, Jodie, Alex, and Oscar – each traveled to a different island – Aruba, Jamaica, Nevis, and Barbados – but not necessarily respectively.
   2) Tina did not travel as far to Jamaica as Jodie traveled to her island.
   3) Oscar traveled twice as far as Alex, who traveled the same distance as the traveler who went to Aruba.
   4) Oscar went to Barbados.

   CONCLUSION: Oscar traveled the farthest.

   A. The conclusion is proved by Statements 1-4;
   B. The conclusion is disproved by Statements 1-4;
   C. The facts are not sufficient to prove or disprove the conclusion.

25. FACTUAL STATEMENT: 25.____
   1) In the natural history museum, every Native American display that contains pottery also contains beadwork.
   2) Some of the displays containing lodge replicas also contain beadwork.
   3) The display on the Choctaw, a Native American tribe, contains pottery.
   4) The display on the Modoc, a Native American tribe, contains only two of these items.

   CONCLUSION: If the Modoc display contains pottery, it does not contain lodge replicas.

   A. The conclusion is proved by Statements 1-4;
   B. The conclusion is disproved by Statements 1-4;
   C. The facts are not sufficient to prove or disprove the conclusion.

KEY (CORRECT ANSWERS)

1.	A		11.	B
2.	B		12.	C
3.	A		13.	B
4.	A		14.	D
5.	C		15.	E
6.	B		16.	E
7.	B		17.	A
8.	B		18.	B
9.	A		19.	C
10.	B		20.	A

21. A
22. A
23. C
24. A
25. A

TEST 2

DIRECTIONS: Each question or incomplete statement is followed by several suggested answers or completions. Select the one that BEST answers the question or completes the statement. *PRINT THE LETTER OF THE CORRECT ANSWER IN THE SPACE AT THE RIGHT.*

Questions 1-9.

DIRECTIONS: In Questions 1 through 9, you will read a set of facts and a conclusion drawn from them. The conclusion may be valid or invalid, based on the facts. It is your task to determine the validity of the conclusion.
For each question, select the letter before the statement that BEST expresses the relationship between the given facts and the conclusion that has been drawn from them. Your choices are:
- A. The facts prove the conclusion.
- B. The facts disprove the conclusion; or
- C. The facts neither prove nor disprove the conclusion.

1. FACTS: If the maximum allowable income for Medicaid recipients is increased, the number of Medicaid recipients will increase. If the number of Medicaid recipients increases, more funds must be allocated to the Medicaid program, which will require a tax increase. Taxes cannot be approved without the approval of the legislature. The legislature probably will not approve a tax increase.

    CONCLUSION: The maximum allowable income for Medicaid recipients will increase.

    A. The facts prove the conclusion.
    B. The facts disprove the conclusion; or
    C. The facts neither prove nor disprove the conclusion.

2. FACTS: All the dentists on the baseball team are short. Everyone in the dugout is a dentist, but not everyone in the dugout is short. The baseball team is not made up of people of any particular profession.

    CONCLUSION: Some people who are not dentists are in the dugout.

    A. The facts prove the conclusion.
    B. The facts disprove the conclusion; or
    C. The facts neither prove nor disprove the conclusion.

3. FACTS: A taxi company's fleet is divided into two fleets. Fleet One contains cabs A, B, C, and D. Fleet Two contains E, F, G, and H. Each cab is either yellow or green. Five of the cabs are yellow. Cabs A and E are not both yellow. Either Cab C or F, or both, are not yellow. Cabs B and H are either both yellow or both green.

    CONCLUSION: Cab H is green.

1.____

2.____

3.____

A. The facts prove the conclusion.
B. The facts disprove the conclusion; or
C. The facts neither prove nor disprove the conclusion.

4. FACTS: Most people in the skydiving club are not afraid of heights. Everyone in the skydiving club makes three parachute jumps a month.

   CONCLUSION: At least one person who is afraid of heights makes three parachute jumps a month.

   A. The facts prove the conclusion.
   B. The facts disprove the conclusion; or
   C. The facts neither prove nor disprove the conclusion.

4._____

5. FACTS: If the Board approves the new rule, the agency will move to a new location immediately. If the agency moves, five new supervisors will be immediately appointed. The Board has approved the new proposal.

   CONCLUSION: No new supervisors were appointed.

   A. The facts prove the conclusion.
   B. The facts disprove the conclusion; or
   C. The facts neither prove nor disprove the conclusion.

5._____

6. FACTS: All the workers at the supermarket chew gum when they sack groceries. Sometimes Lance, a supermarket worker, doesn't chew gum at all when he works. Another supermarket worker, Jenny, chews gum the whole time she is at work.

   CONCLUSION: Jenny always sacks groceries when she is at work.

6._____

7. FACTS: Lake Lottawatta is bigger than Lake Tacomi. Lake Tacomi and Lake Ottawa are exactly the same size. All lakes in Montana are bigger than Lake Ottawa.

   CONCLUSION: Lake Lottawatta is in Montana.

   A. The facts prove the conclusion.
   B. The facts disprove the conclusion; or
   C. The facts neither prove nor disprove the conclusion.

7._____

8. FACTS: Two men, Cox and Taylor, are playing poker at a table. Taylor has a pair of aces in his hand. One man is smoking a cigar. One of them has no pairs in his hand and is wearing an eye patch. The man wearing the eye patch is smoking a cigar. One man is bald.

   CONCLUSION: Cox is smoking a cigar.

8._____

A. The facts prove the conclusion.
B. The facts disprove the conclusion; or
C. The facts neither prove nor disprove the conclusion.

9.   FACTS: All Kwakiutls are Wakashan Indians. All Wakashan Indians originated on Vancouver Island. The Nootka also originated on Vancouver Island.

9._____'

CONCLUSION: Kwakiutls originated on Vancouver Island.

A. The facts prove the conclusion.
B. The facts disprove the conclusion; or
C. The facts neither prove nor disprove the conclusion.

Questions 10-17.

DIRECTIONS: Questions 10 through 17 are based on the following reading passage. It is not your knowledge of the particular topic that is being tested, but your ability to reason based on what you have read. The passage is likely to detail several proposed courses of action and factors affecting these proposals. The reading passage is followed by a conclusion or outcome based on the facts in the passage, or a description of a decision taken regarding the situation. The conclusion is followed by a number of statements that have a possible connection to the conclusion. For each statement, you are to determine whether:
A. The statement proves the conclusion.
B. The statement supports the conclusion but does not prove it.
C. The statement disproves the conclusion.
D. The statement weakens the conclusion but does not disprove it.
E. The statement has no relevance to the conclusion.

Remember that the conclusion after the passage is to be accepted as the outcome of what actually happened, and that you are being asked to evaluate the impact each statement would have had on the conclusion.

PASSAGE

The World Wide Web portal and search engine, HipBot, is considering becoming a subscription-only service, locking out nonsubscribers from the content on its web site. HipBot currently relies solely on advertising revenues.

HipBot's content director says that by taking in an annual fee from each customer, the company can both increase profits and provide premium content that no other portal can match.

The marketing director disagrees, saying that there is no guarantee that anyone who now visits the web site for free will agree to pay for the privilege of visiting it again. Most will probably simply use the other major portals. Also, HipBot's advertising clients will not be happy when they learn that the site will be viewed by a more limited number of people.

4 (#2)

CONCLUSION: In January of 2016, the CEO of HipBot decides to keep the portal open to all web users, with some limited "premium content" available to subscribers who don't mind paying a little extra to access it. The company will aim to maintain, or perhaps increase, its advertising revenue.

10. In an independent marketing survey, 62% of respondents said they "strongly agree" with the following statement: "I almost never pay attention to advertisements that appear on the World Wide Web."
    A. The statement proves the conclusion.
    B. The statement supports the conclusion but does not prove it.
    C. The statement disproves the conclusion.
    D. The statement weakens the conclusion but does not disprove it.
    E. The statement has no relevance to the conclusion.

10.____

11. When it learns about the subscription-only debate going on at HipBot, Wernham Hogg Entertainment, one of HipBot's most reliable clients, says it will withdraw its ads and place them on a free web portal if HipBot decides to limit its content to subscribers. Wernham Hogg pays HipBot about $6 million annually – about 12% of HipBot's gross revenues – to run its ads online.
    A. The statement proves the conclusion.
    B. The statement supports the conclusion but does not prove it.
    C. The statement disproves the conclusion.
    D. The statement weakens the conclusion but does not disprove it.
    E. The statement has no relevance to the conclusion.

11.____

12. At the end of the second quarter of FY 2016, after continued stagnant profits, the CEO of HipBot assembles a blue ribbon commission to gather and analyze data on the costs, benefits, and feasibility of adding a limited amount of "premium" content to the HipBot portal.
    A. The statement proves the conclusion.
    B. The statement supports the conclusion but does not prove it.
    C. The statement disproves the conclusion.
    D. The statement weakens the conclusion but does not disprove it.
    E. The statement has no relevance to the conclusion.

12.____

13. In the following fiscal year, Wernham Hogg Entertainment, satisfied with the "hit counts" on HipBot's free web site, spends another $1 million on advertisements that will appear on web pages that are available to HipBot's "premium subscribers.
    A. The statement proves the conclusion.
    B. The statement supports the conclusion but does not prove it.
    C. The statement disproves the conclusion.
    D. The statement weakens the conclusion but does not disprove it.
    E. The statement has no relevance to the conclusion.

13.____

14. HipBot's information technology director reports that the engineers in his department have come up with a feature that will search not only individual web pages, but tie into other web-based search engines, as well, and then comb through all these results to find those most relevant to the user's search.

14.____

A. The statement proves the conclusion.
B. The statement supports the conclusion but does not prove it.
C. The statement disproves the conclusion.
D. The statement weakens the conclusion but does not disprove it.
E. The statement has no relevance to the conclusion.

15. In an independent marketing survey, 79% of respondents said they "strongly agree" with the following statement: "Many web sites are so dominated by advertisements these days that it is increasingly frustrating to find the content I want to read or see."
    A. The statement proves the conclusion.
    B. The statement supports the conclusion but does not prove it.
    C. The statement disproves the conclusion.
    D. The statement weakens the conclusion but does not disprove it.
    E. The statement has no relevance to the conclusion.

15.____

16. After three years of studies at the federal level, the Department of Commerce releases a report suggesting that, in general, the only private "subscriber-only" web sites that do well financially are those with a very specialized user population.
    A. The statement proves the conclusion.
    B. The statement supports the conclusion but does not prove it.
    C. The statement disproves the conclusion.
    D. The statement weakens the conclusion but does not disprove it.
    E. The statement has no relevance to the conclusion.

16.____

17. HipBot's own marketing research indicates that the introduction of premium content has the potential to attract new users to the HipBot portal.
    A. The statement proves the conclusion.
    B. The statement supports the conclusion but does not prove it.
    C. The statement disproves the conclusion.
    D. The statement weakens the conclusion but does not disprove it.
    E. The statement has no relevance to the conclusion.

17.____

Questions 18-25.

DIRECTIONS: Questions 18 through 25 each provide four factual statements and a conclusion based on these statements. After reading the entire question, you will decide whether:
A. The conclusion is proved by Statements 1-4;
B. The conclusion is disproved by Statements 1-4;
C. The facts are not sufficient to prove or disprove the conclusion.

18. **FACTUAL STATEMENTS:**
    1) If the alarm goes off, Sam will wake up.
    2) If Tandy wakes up before 4:00, Linda will leave the bedroom and sleep on the couch.
    3) If Linda leaves the bedroom, she'll check the alarm to make sure it is working.
    4) The alarm goes off.

    CONCLUSION: Tandy woke up before 4:00.

    A. The conclusion is proved by Statements 1-4;
    B. The conclusion is disproved by Statements 1-4;
    C. The facts are not sufficient to prove or disprove the conclusion.

19. **FACTUAL STATEMENTS:**
    1) Four brothers are named Earl, John, Gary, and Pete.
    2) Earl and Pete are unmarried.
    3) John is shorter than the youngest of the four.
    4) The oldest brother is married, and is also the tallest.

    CONCLUSION: Pete is the youngest brother.

    A. The conclusion is proved by Statements 1-4;
    B. The conclusion is disproved by Statements 1-4;
    C. The facts are not sufficient to prove or disprove the conclusion.

20. **FACTUAL STATEMENTS:**
    1) Automobile engines are cooled either by air or by liquid.
    2) If the engine is small and simple enough, air from a belt-driven fan will cool it sufficiently.
    3) Most newer automobile engines are too complicated to be air-cooled.
    4) Air-cooled engines are cheaper and easier to build then liquid-cooled engines.

    CONCLUSION: Most newer automobile engines use liquid coolant.

    A. The conclusion is proved by Statements 1-4;
    B. The conclusion is disproved by Statements 1-4;
    C. The facts are not sufficient to prove or disprove the conclusion.

21. **FACTUAL STATEMENTS:**
    1) Erica will only file a lawsuit if she is injured while parasailing.
    2) If Rick orders Trip to run a rope test, Trip will check the rigging.
    3) If the rigging does not malfunction, Erica will not be injured.
    4) Rick orders Trip to run a rope test.

7 (#2)

CONCLUSION: Erica does not file a lawsuit.

- A. The conclusion is proved by Statements 1-4;
- B. The conclusion is disproved by Statements 1-4;
- C. The facts are not sufficient to prove or disprove the conclusion.

22. FACTUAL STATEMENTS: 22.____
    1) On Maple Street, which is four blocks long, Bill's shop is two blocks east of Ken's shop.
    2) Ken's shop is one block west of the only shop on Maple Street with an awning.
    3) Erma's shop is one block west of the easternmost block.
    4) Bill's shop is on the easternmost block.

    CONCLUSION: Bill's shop has an awning.

    - A. The conclusion is proved by Statements 1-4;
    - B. The conclusion is disproved by Statements 1-4;
    - C. The facts are not sufficient to prove or disprove the conclusion.

23. FACTUAL STATEMENTS: 23.____
    1) Gear X rotates in a clockwise direction if Switch C is in the OFF position.
    2) Gear X will rotate in a counter-clockwise direction if Switch C is ON.
    3) If Gear X is rotating in a clockwise direction, then Gear Y will not be rotating at all.
    4) Gear Y is rotating.

    CONCLUSION: Gear X is rotating in a counter-clockwise direction.

    - A. The conclusion is proved by Statements 1-4;
    - B. The conclusion is disproved by Statements 1-4;
    - C. The facts are not sufficient to prove or disprove the conclusion.

24. FACTUAL STATEMENTS: 24.____
    1) The Republic of Garbanzo's currency system has four basic denominations: the pastor, the noble, the donner, and the rojo.
    2) A pastor is worth 2 nobles.
    3) 2 donners can be exchanged for a rojo.
    4) 3 pastors are equal in value to 2 donners.

    CONCLUSION: The rojo is most valuable.

    - A. The conclusion is proved by Statements 1-4;
    - B. The conclusion is disproved by Statements 1-4;
    - C. The facts are not sufficient to prove or disprove the conclusion.

8 (#2)

25. **FACTUAL STATEMENTS:** 25.____
    1) At Prickett's Nursery, the only citrus trees left are either Meyer lemons or Valencia oranges, and every citrus tree left is either a dwarf or a semidwarf.
    2) Half of the semidwarf trees are Meyer lemons.
    3) There are more semidwarf trees left than dwarf trees.
    4) A quarter of the dward trees are Valencia oranges.

    CONCLUSION: There are more Valencia oranges left at Prickett's Nursery than Meyer lemons.

    A. The conclusion is proved by Statements 1-4;
    B. The conclusion is disproved by Statements 1-4;
    C. The facts are not sufficient to prove or disprove the conclusion.

KEY (CORRECT ANSWERS)

1.	C		11.	B
2.	B		12.	C
3.	B		13.	A
4.	A		14.	E
5.	B		15.	D
6.	C		16.	B
7.	C		17.	B
8.	A		18.	C
9.	A		19.	C
10.	E		20.	A

21. C
22. B
23. C
24. A
25. B

LOGICAL REASONING
EVALUATING CONCLUSIONS IN LIGHT OF KNOWN FACTS

EXAMINATION SECTION
TEST 1

COMMENTARY

This section is designed to provide practice questions in evaluating conclusions when you are given specific data to work with.

We suggest you do the questions three at a time, consulting the answer key and then the solution section for any questions you may have missed. It's a good idea to try the questions again a week before the exam.

In the validity of conclusion type of question, you are first given a reading passage which describes a particular situation. The passage may be on any topic, as it is not your knowledge of the topic that is being tested, but your reasoning abilities. The passage is likely to detail several proposed courses of action and factors affecting these proposals. The reading passage is followed by a conclusion based on the facts in the passage, or a description of a decision taken regarding the situation. The conclusion is followed by a number of statements which have a possible connection to the conclusion. For each statement, you are to determine whether:

    A. The statement proves the conclusion.
    B. The statement supports the conclusion but does not prove it.
    C. The statement disproves the conclusion.
    D. The statement weakens the conclusion but does not disprove it.
    E. The statement has no relevance to the conclusion.

Remember that the conclusion after the passage is to be accepted as the outcome of what actually happened, and that you are being asked to evaluate the impact each statement would have had on the conclusion.

Questions 1-8 are based on the following paragraph.

In May of 1993, Mr. Bryan inherited a clothing store on Main Street in a small New England town. The store has specialized in selling quality men's and women's clothing since 1885. Business has been stable throughout the years, neither increasing nor decreasing. He has an opportunity to buy two adjacent stores which would enable him to add a wider range and style of clothing. In order to do this, he would have to borrow a substantial amount of money. He also risks losing the goodwill of his present clientele.

CONCLUSION: On November 7, 1993, Mr. Bryan tells the owner of the two adjacent stores that he has decided not to purchase them. He feels that it would be best to simply maintain his present marketing position, as there would not be enough new business to support an expansion.

    A. The statement proves the conclusion.
    B. The statement supports the conclusion but does not prove it.
    C. The statement disproves the conclusion.
    D. The statement weakens the conclusion.
    E. The statement is irrelevant to the conclusion.

1. A large new branch of the county's community college holds its first classes in September of 1993.   1.__

2. The town's largest factory shuts down with no indication that it will reopen.   2.__

3. The 1990 United States Census showed that the number of children per household dropped from 2.4 to 2.1 since the 1980 census.   3.__

4. Mr. Bryan's brother tells him of a new clothing boutique specializing in casual women's clothing which is opening soon.   4.__

5. Mr. Bryan's sister buys her baby several items for Christmas at Mr. Bryan's store.   5.__

6. Mrs. McIntyre, the President of the Town Council, brings Mr. Bryan a home-baked pumpkin pie in honor of his store's 100th anniversary. They discuss the changes that have taken place in the town, and she comments on how his store has maintained the same look and feel over the years.   6.__

7. In October of 1993, Mr. Bryan's aunt lends him $50,000.   7.__

8. The Town Council has just announced that the town is eligible for funding from a federal project designed to encourage the location of new businesses in the central districts of cities and towns.   8.__

Questions 9-18 are based on the following paragraph.

A proposal has been put before the legislative body of a small European country to require air bags in all automobiles manufactured for domestic use in that country after 1999. The air bag, made of nylon or plastic, is designed to inflate automatically within a car at the impact of a collision, thus protecting front-seat occupants from being thrown forward. There has been much support of the measure from consumer groups, the insurance industry, key legislators, and the general public. The country's automobile manufacturers, who contend the new crash equipment would add up to $1,000 to car prices and provide no more protection than existing seat belts, are against the proposed legislation.

CONCLUSION: On April 21, 1994, the legislature passed legislation requiring air bags in all automobiles manufactured for domestic use in that country after 1999.

    A. The statement proves the conclusion.
    B. The statement supports the conclusion but does not prove it.
    C. The statement disproves the conclusion.
    D. The statement weakens the conclusion.
    E. The statement is irrelevant to the conclusion.

9. A study has shown that 59% of car occupants do not use seat belts.   9.__

10. The country's Department of Transportation has estimated that the crash protection equipment would save up to 5,900 lives each year.   10.__

11. On April 27, 1993, Augusta Raneoni was named head of an advisory committee to gather and analyze data on the costs, benefits, and feasibility of the proposed legislation on air bags in automobiles.   11.__

12. Consumer groups and the insurance industry accuse the legislature of rejecting passage of the regulation for political reasons.   12.____

13. A study by the Committee on Imports and Exports projected that the sales of imported cars would rise dramatically in 1999 because imported cars do not have to include air bags, and can be sold more cheaply.   13.____

14. Research has shown that air bags, if produced on a large scale, would cost about $200 apiece, and would provide more reliable protection than any other type of seat belt.   14.____

15. Auto sales in 1991 have increased 3% over the previous year.   15.____

16. A Department of Transportation report in July of 2000 credits a drop in automobile deaths of 4,100 to the use of air bags.   16.____

17. In June of 1994, the lobbyist of the largest insurance company receives a bonus for her work on the passage of the air bag legislation.   17.____

18. In 2000, the stock in crash protection equipment has risen three-fold over the previous year.   18.____

Questions 19-25 are based on the following paragraph.

On a national television talk show, Joan Rivera, a famous comedienne, has recently insulted the physical appearances of a famous actress and the dead wife of an ex-President. There has been a flurry of controversy over her comments, and much discussion of the incident has appeared in the press. Most of the comments have been negative. It appears that this time she might have gone too far. There have been cancellations of two of her five scheduled performances in the two weeks since the show was televised, and Joan's been receiving a lot of negative mail. Because of the controversy, she has an interview with a national news magazine at the end of the week, and her press agent is strongly urging her to apologize publicly. She feels strongly that her comments were no worse than any other she has ever made, and that the whole incident will *blow over* soon. She respects her press agent's judgment, however, as his assessment of public sentiment tends to be very accurate.

CONCLUSION: Joan does not apologize publicly, and during the interview she challenges the actress to a weight-losing contest. For every pound the actress loses, Joan says she will donate $1 to the Cellulite Prevention League.

    A. The statement proves the conclusion.
    B. The statement supports the conclusion but does not prove it.
    C. The statement disproves the conclusion.
    D. The statement weakens the conclusion.
    E. The statement is irrelevant to the conclusion.

19. Joan's mother, who she is very fond of, is very upset about Joan's comments.   19.____

20. Six months after the interview, Joan's income has doubled.   20.____

21. Joan's agent is pleased with the way Joan handles the interview.

22. Joan's sister has been appointed Treasurer of the Cellulite Prevention League. In her report, she states that Joan's $12 contribution is the only amount that has been donated to the League in its first six months.

23. The magazine receives many letters commending Joan for the courage it took for her to apologize publicly in the interview.

24. Immediately after the interview appears, another one of Joan's performances is cancelled.

25. Due to a printers strike, the article was not published until the following week.

Questions 26-30 are based on the following paragraph.

The law-making body of Country X must decide what to do about the issue of videotaping television shows for home use. There is currently no law against taping shows directly from the TV as long as the videotapes are not used for commercial purposes. The increasing popularity of pay TV and satellite systems, combined with the increasing number of homes that own video-cassette recorders, has caused a great deal of concern in some segments of the entertainment industry. Companies that own the rights to films, popular television shows, and sporting events feel that their copyright privileges are being violated, and they are seeking compensation or the banning of TV home videotaping. Legislation has been introduced to make it illegal to videotape television programs for home use. Separate proposed legislation is also pending that would continue to allow videotaping of TV shows for home use, but would place a tax of 10% on each videocassette that is purchased for home use. The income from that tax would then be proportionately distributed as royalties to those owning the rights to programs being aired. A weighted point system coupled with the averaging of several national viewing rating systems would be used to determine the royalties. There is a great deal of lobbying being done for both bills, as the manufacturers of videocassette recorders and videocassettes are against the passage of the bills.

CONCLUSION: The legislature of Country X rejects both bills by a wide margin.

- A. The statement proves the conclusion.
- B. The statement supports the conclusion but does not prove it.
- C. The statement disproves the conclusion.
- D. The statement weakens the conclusion.
- E. The statement is irrelevant to the conclusion.

26. Country X's Department of Taxation hires 500 new employees to handle the increased paperwork created by the new tax on videocassettes.

27. A study conducted by the country's most prestigious accounting firm shows that the cost of implementing the proposed new videocassette tax would be greater than the income expected from it.

28. It is estimated that 80% of all those working in the entertainment industry, excluding per- 28.____
formers, own video-cassette recorders.

29. The head of Country X's law enforcement agency states that legislation banning the 29.____
home taping of TV shows would be unenforceable.

30. Financial experts predict that unless a tax is placed on videocassettes, several large 30.____
companies in the entertainment industry will have to file for bankruptcy.

Questions 31-38.

DIRECTIONS: The following questions 31 through 38 are variations on the type of question you just had. It is important that you read the question very carefully to determine exactly what is required.

31. In this question, select the choice that is most relevant to the conclusion. 31.____

   1. The Buffalo Bills football team is in second place in its division.
   2. The New England Patriots are in first place in the same division.
   3. There are two games left to play in the season, and the Bills will not play the Patriots again.
   4. The New England Patriots won ten games and lost four games, and the Buffalo Bills have won eight games and lost six games.

   CONCLUSION: The Buffalo Bills win their division.

   A. The conclusion is proved by sentences 1-4.
   B. The conclusion is disproved by sentences 1-4.
   C. The facts are not sufficient to prove or disprove the conclusion.

32. In this question, select the choice that is most relevant to the conclusion. 32.____

   1. On the planet of Zeinon there are only two different eye colors and only two different hair colors.
   2. Half of those beings with purple hair have golden eyes.
   3. There are more inhabitants with purple hair than there are inhabitants with silver hair.
   4. One-third of those with silver hair have green eyes.

   CONCLUSION: There are more golden-eyed beings on Zeinon than green-eyed ones.

   A. The conclusion is proved by sentences 1-4.
   B. The conclusion is disproved by sentences 1-4.
   C. The facts are not sufficient to prove or disprove the conclusion.

33. In this question, select the choice that is most relevant to the conclusion. 33.____
John and Kevin are leaving Amaranth to go to school in Bethany. They've decided to rent a small truck to move their possessions. Joe's Truck Rental charges $100 plus 30¢ a mile. National Movers charges $50 more but gives free mileage for the first 100 miles. After the first 100 miles, they charge 25¢ a mile.

CONCLUSION: John and Kevin rent their truck from National Movers because it is cheaper.

   A. The conclusion is proved by the facts in the above paragraph.
   B. The conclusion is disproved by the facts in the above paragraph.
   C. The facts are not sufficient to prove or disprove the conclusion.

34. For this question, select the choice that supports the information given in the passage.
Municipalities in Country X are divided into villages, towns, and cities. A village has a population of 5,000 or less. The population of a town ranges from 5,001 to 15,000. In order to be incorporated as a city, the municipality must have a population over 15,000. If, after a village becomes a town, or a town becomes a city, the population drops below the minimum required (for example, the population of a city goes below 15,000), and stays below the minimum for more than ten years, it loses its current status, and drops to the next category. As soon as a municipality rises in population to the next category (village to town, for example), however, it is immediately reclassified to the next category.

In the 1970 census, Plainfield had a population of 12,000. Between 1970 and 1980, Plainfield grew 10%, and between 1980 and 1990 Plainfield grew another 20%. The population of Springdale doubled from 1970 to 1980, and increased 25% from 1980 to 1990. The city of Smallville's population, 20,283, has not changed significantly in recent years. Granton had a population of 25,000 people in 1960, and has decreased 25% in each ten year period since then. Ellenville had a population of 4,283 in 1960, and grew 5% in each ten year period since 1960.

In 1990,

   A. Plainfield, Smallville, and Granton are cities
   B. Smallville is a city, Granton is a town, and Ellenville is a village
   C. Springdale, Granton, and Ellenville are towns
   D. Plainfield and Smallville are cities, and Ellenville is a town

35. For this question, select the choice that is most relevant to the conclusion.
A study was done for a major food distributing firm to determine if there is any difference in the kind of caffeine containing products used by people of different ages. A sample of one thousand people between the ages of twenty and fifty were drawn from selected areas in the country. They were divided equally into three groups.
Those individuals who were 20-29 were designated Group A, those 30-39 were Group B, and those 40-50 were placed in Group C.
It was found that on the average, Group A drank 1.8 cups of coffee, Group B 3.1, and Group C 2.5 cups of coffee daily. Group A drank 2.1 cups of tea, Group B drank 1.2, and Group C drank 2.6 cups of tea daily. Group A drank 3.1 8-ounce glasses of cola, Group B drank 1.9, and Group C drank 1.5 glasses of cola daily.

CONCLUSION: According to the study, the average person in the 20-29 age group drinks less tea daily than the average person in the 40-50 age group, but drinks more coffee daily than the average person in the 30-39 age group drinks cola.

   A. The conclusion is proved by the facts in the above paragraph.
   B. The conclusion is disproved by the facts in the above paragraph.
   C. The facts are not sufficient to prove or disprove the conclusion.

36. C
37. A
38. B

KEY (CORRECT ANSWERS)

1.	D	11.	C	21.	D	31.	C
2.	B	12.	C	22.	A	32.	A
3.	E	13.	D	23.	C	33.	C
4.	B	14.	B	24.	B	34.	B
5.	C	15.	E	25.	E	35.	B
6.	D	16.	B	26.	C	36.	C
7.	B	17.	A	27.	B	37.	A
8.	A	18.	B	28.	E	38.	B
9.	B	19.	D	29.	B		
10.	B	20.	E	30.	D		

SOLUTIONS TO QUESTIONS

1. The answer is D. This statement weakens the conclusion, but does not disprove it. If a new branch of the community college opened in September, it could possibly bring in new business for Mr. Bryant. Since it states in the conclusion that Mr. Bryant felt there would not be enough new business to support the additional stores, this would tend to disprove the conclusion. Choice C would not be correct because it's possible that he felt that the students would not have enough additional money to support his new venture, or would not be interested in his clothing styles. It's also possible that the majority of the students already live in the area, so that they wouldn't really be a new customer population. This type of question is tricky, and can initially be very confusing, so don't feel badly if you missed it. Most people need to practice with a few of these types of questions before they feel comfortable recognizing exactly what they're being asked to do.

2. The answer is B. It supports the conclusion because the closing of the factory would probably take money and customers out of the town, causing Mr. Bryant to lose some of his present business. It doesn't prove the conclusion, however, because we don't know how large the factory was. It's possible that only a small percentage of the population was employed there, or that they found other jobs.

3. The answer is E. The fact that the number of children per household dropped slightly nationwide from 1970 to 1980 is irrelevant. Statistics showing a drop nationwide doesn't mean that there was a drop in the number of children per household in Mr. Bryant's hometown. This is a tricky question, as choice B, supporting the conclusion but not proving it, may seem reasonable. If the number of children per household declined nationwide, then it may not seem unreasonable to feel that this would support Mr. Bryant's decision not to expand his business. However, we're preparing you for promotional exams, not "real life." One of the difficult things about taking exams is that sometimes you're forced to make a choice between two statements that both seem like they could be the possible answer. What you need to do in that case is choose the best choice. Becoming annoyed or frustrated with the question won't really help much. If there's a review of the exam, you can certainly appeal the question. There have been many cases where, after an appeal, two possible choices have been allowed as correct answers. We've included this question, however, to help you see what to do should you get a question like this. It's most important not to get rattled, and to select the best choice. In this case, the connection between the statistical information and Mr. Bryant's decision is pretty remote. If the question had said that the number of children in Mr. Bryant's town had decreased, then choice B would have been a more reasonable choice. It could also help in this situation to visualize the situation. Picture Mr. Bryant in his armchair reading that, nationwide, the average number of children per household has declined slightly. How likely would this be to influence his decision, especially since he sells men's and women's clothing? It would take a while for this decline in population to show up, and we're not even sure if it applies to Mr. Bryant's hometown. Don't feel badly if you missed this, it was tricky. The more of these you do, the more comfortable you'll feel.

4. The answer is B. If a new clothing boutique specializing in casual women's clothing were to open soon, this would lend support to Mr. Bryant's decision not to expand, but would not prove that he had actually made the decision not to expand. A new women's clothing boutique would most likely be in competition with his existing business, thus making any possible expansion a riskier venture. We can't be sure from this, however, that he didn't go ahead and expand his business despite the increased competition. Choice A, proves the conclusion, would only be the answer if we could be absolutely sure from the statement that Mr. Bryant had actually not expanded his business.

5. The answer is C. This statement disproves the conclusion. In order for his sister to buy several items for her baby at Mr. Bryant's store, he would have to have changed his business to include children's clothing.

6. The answer is A. It definitely proves the conclusion. The passage states that Mr. Bryant's store had been in business since 1885. A pie baked in honor of his store's 100th anniversary would have to be presented sometime in 1985. The conclusion states that he made his decision not to expand on November 7, 1983. If, more than a year later Mrs. MacIntyre comments that his store has maintained the same look and feel over the years, it could not have been expanded, or otherwise significantly changed.

7. The answer is D. If Mr. Bryant's aunt lent him $50,000 in October, this would tend to weaken the conclusion, which took place in November. Because it was stated that Mr. Bryant would need to borrow money in order to expand his business, it would be logical to assume that if he borrowed money he had decided to expand his business, weakening the conclusion. The reason C, disproves the conclusion, is not the correct answer is because we can't be sure Mr. Bryant didn't borrow the money for another reason.

8. The answer is B. If Mr. Bryant's town is eligible for federal funds to encourage the location of new businesses in the central district, this would tend to support his decision not to expand his business. Funds to encourage new business would increase the likelihood of there being additional competition for Mr. Bryant's store to contend with. Since we can't say for sure that there would be direct competition from a new business, however, choice A would be incorrect. Note that this is also a tricky question. You might have thought that the new funds weakened the conclusion because it would mean that Mr. Bryant could easily get the money he needed. Mr. Bryant is expanding his present business, not creating a new business. Therefore he is not eligible for the funding.

9. The answer is B. This is a very tricky question. It's stated that 59% of car occupants don't use seat belts. The legislature is considering the use of air bags because of safety issues. The advantage of air bags over seat belts is that they inflate upon impact, and don't require car occupants to do anything with them ahead of time. Since the population has strongly resisted using seat belts, the air bags could become even more important in saving lives. Since saving lives is the purpose of the proposed legislation, the information that a small percentage of people use seat belts could be helpful to the passage of the legislation. We can't be sure that this is reason enough for the legislature to vote for the legislation, however, so choice A is incorrect.

10. The answer is B, as the information that 5,900 lives could be saved would tend to support the conclusion. Saving that many lives through the use of air bags could be a very persuasive reason to vote for the legislation. Since we don't know for sure that it's enough of a compelling reason for the legislature to vote for the legislation, however, choice A could not be the answer.

11. The answer is C, disproves the conclusion. If the legislation had been passed as stated in the conclusion, there would be no reason to appoint someone head of an advisory committee six days later to analyze the "feasibility of the proposed legislation." The key word here is "proposed." If it has been proposed, it means it hasn't been passed. This contradicts the conclusion and therefore disproves it.

12. The answer is C, disproves the conclusion. If the legislation had passed, there would be no reason for supporters of the legislation to accuse the legislature of rejecting the legislation for political reasons. This question may have seemed so obvious that you might have thought there was a trick to it. Exams usually have a few obvious questions, which will trip you up if you begin reading too much into them.

13. The answer is D, as this would tend to disprove the conclusion. A projected dramatic rise in imported cars could be very harmful to the country's economy and could be a very good reason for some legislators to vote against the proposed legislation. It would be assuming too much to choose C, however, because we don't know if they actually did vote against it.

14. The answer is B. This information would tend to support the passage of the legislation. The estimate of the cost of the air bags is $800 less than the cost estimated by opponents, and it's stated that the protection would be more reliable than any other type of seat belt. Both of these would be good arguments in favor of passing the legislation. Since we don't know for sure, however, how persuasive they actually were, choice A would not be the correct choice.

15. The answer is E, as this is irrelevant information. It really doesn't matter whether auto sales in 1981 have increased slightly over the previous year. If the air bag legislation were to go into effect in 1984, that might make the information somehow more relevant. But the air bag legislation would not take effect until 1989, so the information is irrelevant, since it tells us nothing about the state of the auto industry then.

16. The answer is B, supports the conclusion. This is a tricky question. While at first it might seem to prove the conclusion, we can't be sure that the air bag legislation is responsible for the drop in automobile deaths. It's possible air bags came into popular use without the legislation, or with different legislation. There's no way we can be sure that it was the proposed legislation mandating the use of air bags that was responsible.

17. The answer is A. If, in June of 1984, the lobbyist received a bonus "for her work on the air bag legislation," we can be sure that the legislation passed. This proves the conclusion.

18. The answer is B. This is another tricky question. A three fold stock increase would strongly suggest that the legislation had been passed, but it's possible that factors other than the air bag legislation caused the increase. Note that the stock is in "crash protection equipment." Nowhere in the statement does it say air bags. Seat belts, motorcycle helmets, and collapsible bumpers are all crash protection equipment and could have contributed to the increase. This is just another reminder to read carefully because the questions are often designed to mislead you.

19. The answer is D. This would tend to weaken the conclusion because Marsha is very fond of her mother and she would not want to upset her unnecessarily. It does not prove it, however, because if Marsha strongly feels she is right, she probably wouldn't let her mother's opinion sway her. Choice E would also not be correct, because we cannot assume that Marsha's mother's opinion is of so little importance to her as to be considered irrelevant.

20. The answer is E. The statement is irrelevant. We are told that Marsha's income has doubled but we are not told why. The phrase "six months after the interview" can be misleading in that it leads us to assume that the increase and the interview are related. Her income could have doubled because she regained her popularity but it could also have come from stocks or some other business venture. Because we are not given any reason for her income doubling, it would be impossible to say whether or not this statement proves or disproves the conclusion. Choice E is the best choice of the five possible choices. One of the problems with promotional exams is that sometimes you need to select a choice you're not crazy about. In this case, "not having enough information to make a determination" would be the best choice. However, that's not an option, so you're forced to work with what you've got. On these exams it's sometimes like voting for President, you have to pick the "lesser of the two evils" or the least awful choice. In this case, the information is more irrelevant to the conclusion than it is anything else.

21. The answer is D, weakens the conclusion. We've been told that Marsha's agent feels that she should apologize. If he is pleased with her interview, then it would tend to weaken the conclusion but not disprove it. We can't be sure that he hasn't had a change of heart, or that there weren't other parts of the interview he liked so much that they outweighed her unwillingness to apologize.

22. The answer is A. The conclusion states that Marsha will donate $1 to the Cellulite Prevention League for every pound the actress loses. Marsha's sister's financial report on the League's activities directly supports and proves the conclusion.

23. The answer is C, disproves the conclusion. If the magazine receives many letters commending Marsha for her courage in apologizing, this directly contradicts the conclusion, which states that Marsha didn't apologize.

24. The answer is B. It was stated in the passage that two of Marsha's performances were cancelled after the controversy first occurred. The cancellation of another performance immediately after her interview was published would tend to support the conclusion that she refused to apologize. Because we can't be sure, however, that her performance wasn't cancelled for another reason, choice A would be incorrect.

25. The answer is E, as this information is irrelevant. Postponing the article an extra week does not affect Marsha's decision or the public's reaction to it.

26. The answer is C. If 500 new employees are hired to handle the "increased paperwork created by the new tax on videocassettes", this would directly contradict the conclusion, which states that the legislature defeated both bills. (They should all be this easy.)

27. The answer is B. The results of the study would support the conclusion. If implementing the legislation was going to be so costly, it is likely that the legislature would vote against it. Choice A is not the answer, however, because we can't be sure that the legislature didn't pass it anyway.

28. The answer is E. It's irrelevant to the conclusion that 80% of all those working in the entertainment industry own videocassette recorders. Sometimes if you're not sure about these, it can help a lot to try and visualize the situation. Why would someone voting on this legislation care about this fact? It doesn't seem to be the kind of information that would make any difference or impact upon the conclusion.

29. The answer is B. The head of the law enforcement agency's statement that the legislation would be unenforceable would support the conclusion. It's possible that many legislators would question why they should bother to pass legislation that would be impossible to enforce. Choice A would be incorrect however, because we can't be sure that the legislation wasn't passed in spite of his statement.

30. The answer is D. This would tend to weaken the conclusion because the prospect of several large companies going bankrupt would seem to be a good argument in favor of the legislation. The possible loss of jobs and businesses would be a good reason for some people to vote for the legislation. We can't be sure, however, that this would be a compelling enough reason to ensure passage of the legislation so choice C is incorrect.

This concludes our section on the "Validity of Conclusion" type of questions.

We hope these weren't too horrible for you. It's important to keep in mind <u>exactly</u> what you've been given and <u>exactly</u> what they want you to do with it. It's also necessary to remember that you may have to choose between two possible answers. In that case you must choose the one that seems the best. Sometimes you may think there is no good answer. You will probably be right but you can't let that upset you. Just choose the one you dislike the least.

We want to repeat that it is unlikely that this exact format will appear on the exam. The skills required to answer these questions, however, are the same as those you'll need for the exam so we suggest that you review this section before taking the actual exam.

31. The answer is C. This next set of questions requires you to "switch gears" slightly, and get used to different formats. In this type of question, you have to decide whether the conclusion is proved by the facts given, disproved by the facts given, or neither because not enough information has been provided. Fortunately, unlike the previous questions, you don't have to decide whether particular facts support or don't support the conclusion. This type of question is more straight forward, but the reasoning behind it is the same. We are told that the Bills have won two games less than the Patriots, and that the Patriots are in first place and the Bills are in second place. We are also told that there are two games left to play, and that they won't play each other again. The conclusion states that the Bills won the division. Is there anything in the four statements that would prove this? We have no idea what the outcome of the last two games of the season was. The

Bills and Patriots could have ended up tied at the end of the season, or the Bills could have lost both or one of their last games while the Patriots did the same. There might even be another team tied for first or second place with the Bills or Patriots. Since we don't know for sure, Choice A is incorrect. Choice B is trickier. It might seem at first glance that the best the Bills could do would be to tie the Patriots if the Patriots lost their last two games and the Bills won their last two games. But it would be too much to assume that there is no procedure for a tiebreaker that wouldn't give the Bills the division championship. Since we don't know what the rules are in the event of a tie (for example, what if a tie was decided on the results of what happened when the two teams had played each other, or on the best record in the division, or on most points scored?), we can't say for sure that it would be impossible for the Bills to win their division. For this reason, choice C is the answer, as we don't have enough information to prove or disprove the conclusion. This question looked more difficult than it actually was. It's important to disregard any factors outside of the actual question, and to focus only on what you've been given. In this case, as on all of these types of questions, what you know or don't know about a subject is actually irrelevant. It's best to concentrate only on the actual facts given.

32. The answer is A. The conclusion is proved by the facts given.

In this type of problem it is usually best to pull as many facts as possible from the sentences and then put them into a simpler form. The phrasing and the order of exam questions are designed to be confusing so you need to restate things as clearly as possible by eliminating the extras.

Sentence 1 tells us that there are only two possible colors for eyes and two for hair. Looking at the other sentences we learn that eyes are either green or gold and that hair is either silver or purple. If half the beings with purple hair have golden eyes then the other half must have green eyes since it is the only other eye color. Likewise, if one-third of those with silver hair have green eyes the other two-thirds must have golden eyes.

This information makes it clear that there are more golden-eyed beings on Zeinon than green-eyed ones. It doesn't matter that we don't know exactly how many are actually living on the planet. The number of those with gold eyes (1/2 plus 2/3) will always be greater than the number of those with green eyes (1/2 plus 1/3), no matter what the actual figures might be. Sentence 3 is totally irrelevant because even if there were more silver-haired inhabitants it would not affect the conclusion.

33. The answer is C. The conclusion is neither proved nor disproved by the facts because we don't know how many miles Bethany is from Amoranth.

With this type of question, if you're not sure how to approach it you can always substitute in a range of "real numbers" to see what the result would be. If they were 200 miles apart Joe's Truck Rental would be cheaper because they would charge a total of $160 while National Movers would charge $175.

Joe's - $100 plus .30 x 200 (or $60) = $160
National - $150 plus .25 x 100 (or $25) = $175

If the towns were 600 miles apart, however, National Movers would be cheaper. The cost of renting from National would be $275 compared to the $280 charged by Joe's Trucking.

   Joe's - $100 plus .30 x 600 (or $180) = $280
   National - $150 plus .25 x 500 (or $125) = $275

34. The answer is B. We've varied the format once more, but the reasoning is similar. This is a tedious question that is more like a math question, but we wanted to give you some practice with this type, just in case. You won't be able to do this question if you've forgotten how to do percents. Many exams require this knowledge, so if you feel you need a review we suggest you read Booklets 1, 2 or 3 in this series.

The only way to attack this problem is to go through each choice until you find the one that is correct. Choice A states that Plainfield, Smallville and Granton are cities. Let's begin with Plainfield. The passage states that in 1960 Plainfield had a population of 12,000, and that it grew 10% between 1960 and 1970, and another 20% between 1970 and 1980. Ten percent of 12,000 is 1200 (12,000 x .10 = 1200). Therefore, the population grew from 12,000 in 1960 to 12,000 + 1200 between 1960 and 1970. At the time of the 1970 Census, Plainfield's population was 13,200. It then grew another 20% between 1970 and 1980, so, 13,200 x .20 = 2640. 13,200 plus the additional increase of 2640 would make the population of Plainfield 15,840. This would qualify it as a city, since its population is over 15,000. Since a change upward in the population of a municipality is re-classified immediately, Plainfield would have become a city right away. So far, statement A is true. The passage states that Smallville's population has not changed significantly in the last twenty years. Since Smallville's population was 20,283, Smallville would still be a city. Granton had a population of 25,000 (what a coincidence that so many of these places have such nice, even numbers) in 1950. The population has decreased 25% in each ten year period since that time. So from 1950 to 1960 the population decreased 25%. 25,000 x .25 = 6,250. 25,000 minus 6,250 = 18,750. So the population of Granton in 1960 would have been 18,750. (Or you could have saved a step and multiplied 25,000 by .75 to get 18,750.) The population from 1960 to 1970 decreased an additional 25%. So: 18,750 x .25 = 4687.50. 18,750 minus 4687.50 = 14,062.50. Or: 18,750 x .75 = 14,062.50. (Don't let the fact that a half of a person is involved confuse you, these are exam questions, not real life.) From 1970 to 1980 the population decreased an additional 25%. This would mean that Granton's population was below 15,000 for more than ten years, so it's status as a city would have changed to that of a town, which would make choice A incorrect, since it states that Granton is a city.

Choice B states that Smallville is a city and Granton is a town which we know to be true from the information above. Choice B is correct so far. We next need to determine if Ellenville is a village. Ellenville had a population of 4,283 in 1950, and increased 5% in each ten year period since 1950. 4,283 x .05 = 214.15. 4,283 plus 214.15 = 4,497.15, so Ellenville's population from 1950 to 1960 increased to 4,497.15. (Or: 4,283 x 1.05 - 4,497.15.) From 1960 to 1970 Ellenville's population increased another 5%: 4,497.15 x .05 = 224.86. 4,497.15 plus 224.86 = 4,772.01 (or: 4,497.15 x 1.05 = 4,722.01.) From 1970 to 1980, Ellenville's population increased another 5%: 4,722.01 x .05 = 236.1. 4722.01 plus 236.10 = 4958.11. (Or: 4,722.01 x 1.05 = 4958.11.).

Ellenville's population is still under 5,000 in 1980 so it would continue to be classified as a village. Since all three statements in choice B are true, Choice B must be the answer. However, we'll go through the other choices. Choice C states that Springdale is a town. The passage tells us that the population of Springdale doubled from 1960 to 1970, and increased

25% from 1970 to 1980. It doesn't give us any actual population figures, however, so it's impossible to know what the population of Springdale is, making Choice C incorrect. Choice C also states that Granton is a town, which is true, and that Ellenville is a town, which is false (from Choice B we know it's a village). Choice D states that Plainfield and Smallville are cities, which is information we already know is true, and that Ellenville is a town. Since Ellenville is a village, Choice D is also incorrect.

This was a lot of work for just one question and we doubt you'll get one like this on this section of the exam, but we included it just in case. On an exam, you can always put a check mark next to a question like this and come back to it later, if you feel you're pressed for time and could spend your time more productively on other, less time consuming problems.

35. The answer is B. This question requires very careful reading. It's best to break the conclusion down into smaller parts in order to solve the problem. The first half of the conclusion states that the average person in the 20-29 age group (Group A) drinks less tea daily than the average person in the 40-50 age group (Group C). The average person in Group A drinks 2.1 cups of tea daily, while the average person in Group C drinks 2.6 cups of tea daily. Since 2.1 is less than 2.6, the conclusion is correct so far. The second half of the conclusion states that the average person in Group A drinks more coffee daily than the average person in the 30-39 age group (Group B) drinks cola. The average person in Group A drinks 1.8 cups of coffee daily while the average person in Group B drinks 1.9 glasses of cola. This disproves the conclusion, which states that the average person in Group A drinks more coffee daily than the average person in Group B drinks cola.

36. The answer is C. The easiest way to approach a problem that deals with the relationship between a number of different people or things is to set up a diagram. This type of problem is usually too confusing to do in your head. For this particular problem the "diagram" could be a line, one end of which would be labelled tall and the other end labelled short. Then, taking one sentence at a time, place the people on the line to see where they fall in relation to one another.

The diagram of the first sentence would look like this:

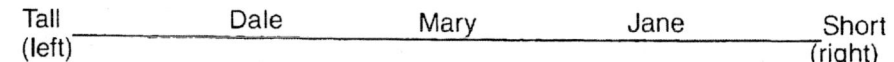

```
Tall         Dale         Mary         Jane         Short
(left)                                              (right)
```

Mary is taller than Jane but shorter than Dale so she would fall somewhere between the two of them. We have placed tall on the left and labelled it left just to make the explanation easier. You could just as easily have reversed the position.

The second sentence places Fred somewhere to the left of Mary because he is taller than she is. Steven would be to the left of Fred for the same reason. At this point we don't know whether Steven and Fred are taller or shorter than Dale. The new diagram would look like this:

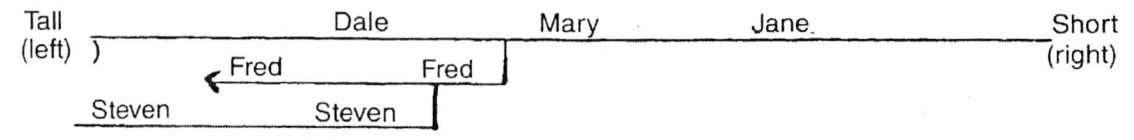

```
Tall                 Dale         Mary         Jane         Short
(left)  )                                                   (right)
           ← Fred         Fred
        Steven         Steven
```

The third stentence introduces Elizabeth, presenting a new problem. Elizabeth can be anywhere to the right of Dale. Don't make the mistake of assuming she falls between Dale and Mary. At this point we don't know where she fits in relation to Mary, Jane, or even Fred.

We do get information about Steven, however. He is taller than Dale so he would be to the left of Dale. Since he is also taller than Fred (see sentence two) we know that Steven is the tallest person thus far. The diagram would now look like this:

Tall (left)		Dale		Mary	Jane	Short (right)
	Fred		Fred			
Steven		Steven				

Fred's height is somewhere between Steven and Mary, Elizabeth's anywhere between Dale and the end of the line.

The fourth sentence tells us where Elizabeth stands, in relation to Fred and the others in the problem. The fact that she is taller than Mary means she is also taller than Jane. The final diagram would look like this:

Tall (left)	Steven	Dale	Elizabeth	Mary	Jane	Short (right)
		Fred				

We still don't know whether Dale or Fred is taller, however. Therefore, the conclusion that Dale is taller than Fred can't be proved. It also can't be disproved because we don't know for sure that he isn't. The answer has to be Choice C, as the conclusion can't be proved or disproved.

37. The answer is A. This is another problem that is easiest for most people if they make a diagram. Sentence 1 states that Main Street is between Spring Street and Glenn Blvd. At this point we don't know if they are next to each other or if they are separated by a number of streets. Therefore, you should leave space between streets as you plot your first diagram.

    The order of the streets could go either:

            Spring St.   or   Glenn Blvd.
            Main St.   Main St.
            Glenn Blvd.   Spring St.

    Sentence 2 states that Hawley Street is one block south of Spring Street and 3 blocks north of Main Street. Because most people think in terms of north as above and south as below and because it was stated that Hawley is one block south of Spring Street and three blocks north of Main Street, the next diagram could look like this:

    Spring
    Hawley

    ———

    ———
    Main
    Glenn

    The third sentence states that Glenn Street is five blocks south of Elm and four blocks south of Main. It could look like this:

Spring
Hawley
_____
Elm
Main
_____
_____
_____
Glenn

The conclusion states that Elm Street is between Hawley Avenue and Glenn Blvd. From the above diagram we can see that this is the case.

38. The answer is B. For most people the best way to do this problem is to draw a diagram, plotting the course of both trains. Sentence 1 states that train A leaves Hampshire at 5:50 a.m. and reaches New London at 6:42. Your first diagram might look like this:

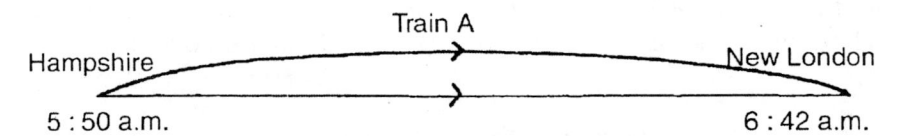

Train A
Hampshire → New London
5:50 a.m.   6:42 a.m.

Sentence 2 states that the train leaves New London at 7:00 a.m. and arrives in Kellogsville at 8:42 a.m. The diagram might now look like this:

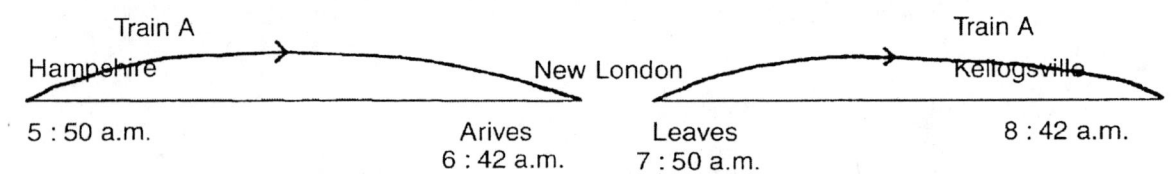

Train A   Train A
Hampshire → New London → Kellogsville
5:50 a.m.   Arives   Leaves   8:42 a.m.
              6:42 a.m.   7:50 a.m.

Sentence 3 gives us the rest of the information that must be included in the diagram. It introduces Train B, which moves in the opposite direction, leaving Kellogsville at 8:00 a.m. and arriving at Hampshire at 10:42 a.m. The final diagram might look like this:

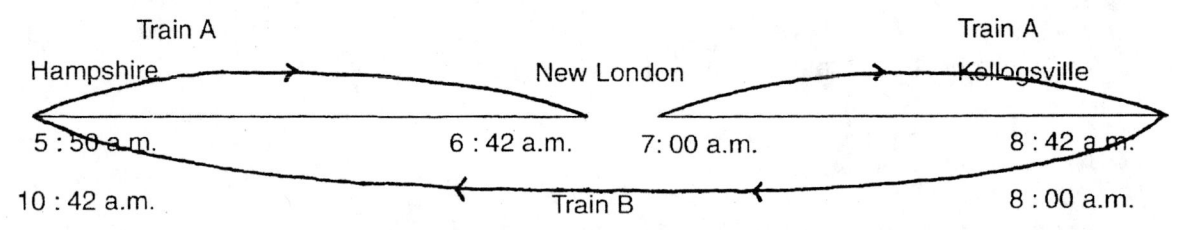

Train A   Train A
Hampshire → New London → Kellogsville
5:50 a.m.   6:42 a.m.   7:00 a.m.   8:42 a.m.
10:42 a.m.   ← Train B ←   8:00 a.m.

As you can see from the diagram, the routes of the two trains will overlap somewhere between Kellogsville and New London. If you read sentence 4 quickly and assumed that that was the section with only one track, you probably would have assumed that there would have had to be a collision. Sentence 4 states, however, that there is only one railroad track between New London and Hampshire. That is the only section, then, where the two trains could collide. By the time Train B gets to that section, however, Train A will have passed it. The two trains will pass each other somewhere between New London and Kellogsville, not New London and Hampshire.

EXAMINATION SECTION
TEST 1

DIRECTIONS: Each question or incomplete statement is followed by several suggested answers or completions. Select the one that BEST answers the question or completes the statement. *PRINT THE LETTER OF THE CORRECT ANSWER IN THE SPACE AT THE RIGHT.*

1. The PRIMARY purpose of program analysis as it is used in government is to

   A. replace political judgments with rational programs and policies
   B. help decision-makers to sharpen their judgments about program choices
   C. analyze the impact of past programs on the quality of public services
   D. reduce costs by eliminating waste in public programs and services

   1.____

2. While there is no complete method for program analysis that is agreed to by all the experts and is relevant to all types of problems, the MOST important element in program analysis involves the

   A. development of alternatives and the definition of objectives or criteria
   B. collection of information and the construction of a mathematical model
   C. design of experiments and procedures to validate results
   D. collection of expert opinion and the combination of their views

   2.____

3. Electronic data processing is a particularly valuable tool of analysis in situations where the analyst has a processing problem involving

   A. *small* input, *few* operations, and *small* output
   B. *large* input, *many* operations, and *small* output
   C. *large* input, *few* operations, and *large* output
   D. *small* input, *many* operations, and *small* output

   3.____

4. In order for an analyst to use electronic data processing to solve an analytic problem, the problem must be clearly defined.
   The BEST way to prepare material for such definition in electronic data processing is to

   A. discuss the problem with computer programmers in a meeting
   B. prepare a flow diagram outlining the steps in the analysis
   C. write a memorandum with a list of the relevant program issues
   D. write a computer program using FORTRAN, BASIC, or another language

   4.____

5. The "growth rate" referred to in current political and economic discussion refers to change from year to year in a country's

   A. investments   B. population
   C. gross national product   D. sale of goods

   5.____

6. Interactive or conversational programming is important to the program analyst ESPECIALLY for

   A. preparing analyses leading to management information systems
   B. communicating among analysts in different places

   6.____

C. using canned programs in statistical analysis
D. testing trial solutions in rapid sequence

7. Program analysis often calls for recommendation of a choice between competing program possibilities that differ in the timing of major costs.
Analysts using the present value technique by setting an interest or discount rate are in effect arguing that, other things being equal,

A. it is inadvisable to defer the start of projects because of rising costs
B. projects should be completed within a short time period to save money
C. expenditures should be made out of tax revenues to avoid payment of interest
D. postponing expenditures is advantageous at some measurable rate

8. Of the following, the formula which is MOST appropriately used to estimate the net need for a given type of service is that net need equals

A. current clients - anticipated losses + anticipated gains
B. $\dfrac{\text{current supply} + \text{current clients}}{\text{Standard}}$
C. (client population x standard) - current supply
D. current supply - anticipated losses + anticipated gains

9. The purpose of feasibility analysis is to protect the analyst from naive alternatives and, MOST generally, to

A. identify and quantify technological constraints
B. carry out a preliminary stage of analysis
C. anticipate potential blocks to implementation
D. line up the support of political leadership

Questions 10-11.

DIRECTIONS: Answer Questions 10 and 11 on the basis of the following chart. In a hypothetical problem involving four criteria and four alternatives, the following data have been assembled.

	Cost Criterion	Effectiveness Criterion	Timing Criterion	Feasibility Criterion
Alternative A	$500,000	50 units	3 months	probably feasible
Alternative B	$300,000	100 units	6 months	probably feasible
Alternative C	$400,000	50 units	12 months	probably infeasible
Alternative D	$200,000	75 units	3 months	probably infeasible

10. On the basis of the above data, it appears that the one alternative which is dominated by another alternative is Alternative

A. A   B. B   C. C   D. D

11. If the feasibility constraint is absolute and fixed, then the critical trade-off is between   11.____

    A. lower cost on the one hand and faster timing and higher effectiveness on the other
    B. lower cost and higher effectiveness on one hand and faster timing on the other
    C. lower cost and faster timing on the one hand and higher effectiveness on the other
    D. lower cost on the one hand and higher effectiveness on the other

12. A classification of an agency's activities in a program structure is MOST useful if it highlights   12.____

    A. trade-offs that might not otherwise be considered
    B. ways to improve the efficiency of each activity
    C. the true organizational structure of an agency
    D. bases for insuring that expenditures stay within limits

13. CPM, like PERT, is a useful tool for scheduling large-scale, complex processes.   13.____
    In CPM, the critical path is the

    A. path composed of important links
    B. path composed of uncertain links
    C. longest path through the network
    D. shortest path through the network

14. Classical evaluative research calls for the use of control groups. However, there are practical difficulties in collecting data on individuals to be used as "controls" in program evaluations.   14.____
    Researchers may attempt to overcome these difficulties by

    A. using control groups that have no choice such as prison inmates or inmates of other public institutions or facilities
    B. developing better measures of the inputs, processes, and outputs relevant to public programs and services
    C. using experimental demonstration projects with participants in the different projects serving as comparison groups for one another
    D. abandoning attempts at formal evaluation in favor of more qualitative approaches employing a journalistic style of analysis

15. During the course of an analysis of the remaining "life" of a certain city's landfill for refuse disposal, there was a great deal of debate about the impact of changing rates of garbage generation on the amount of landfill needed and about what rates of garbage generation to expect over the next decade.   15.____
    Faced with the need to attempt to resolve this debate, an analyst would construct a simple model of the refuse disposal system and

    A. project landfill needs without considering refuse generation in the future
    B. conduct a detailed household survey in order to estimate future garbage generation rates
    C. ask the experts to continue to debate the issue until the argument is won by one view
    D. do a sensitivity analysis to test the impact of alternative assumptions about refuse generation

16. The limitations of traditional surveys have fostered the development and use of panels. A panel is a

   A. group of respondents that serves as a continuous source of survey information
   B. group of advisors expert in the design and implementation of surveys
   C. representative sample of respondents at a single point in time
   D. post-survey discussion group composed of former respondents

17. The difference between sensitivity analysis and risk analysis is that risk analysis

   A. is applicable only to profit and loss situations where the concept of risk is operable
   B. includes an estimate of probabilities of different values of input factors
   C. is applicable to physical problems while sensitivity analysis is applicable to social ones
   D. requires a computer simulation while sensitivity analysis does not

18. A decision tree, although initially applied to business problems, is a graphic device which is useful to public analysts in

   A. scheduling complex processes
   B. doing long-range forecasting
   C. formulating the structure of alternatives
   D. solving production-inventory problems

19. The purpose of a management information system in an agency is to

   A. structure data relevant to managerial decision-making
   B. put all of an agency's data in machine-processing form
   C. simplify the record-keeping operations in an agency
   D. keep an ongoing record of management's activities

20. Assume that an analyst is presented with the following chart for a fire department and supplied also with information indicating a stable size firefighting staff over this time period.

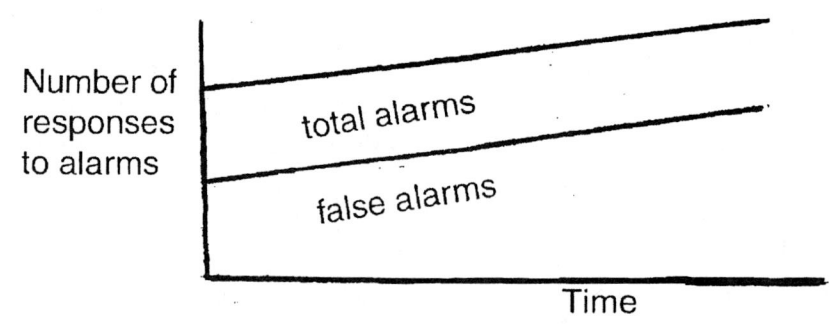

   The analyst could REASONABLY conclude regarding productivity that
   A. productivity over this time period was essentially stable for this firefighting force because the number of responses to real fires during this period was stable, as was the work force
   B. productivity was essentially increasing for this force because the number of total responses was increasing relative to a stable force
   C. productivity was declining because a greater proportion of the total work effort was wasted effort in responding to false alarms
   D. it is impossible to make a judgment about the productivity of the firefighting staff without a judgment about the value of a response to a false alarm

21. In the design of a productivity program for the sanitation department, the BEST measure of productivity would be

    A. tons of refuse collected annually
    B. number of collections made per week
    C. tons of refuse collected per truck shift
    D. number of trucks used per shift

22. The cohort-survival method for estimating future population has been widely employed. In this method,

    A. migration is assumed to be constant over time
    B. net migration within cohorts is assumed to be zero
    C. migration is included as a multiplier factor
    D. net migration within cohorts is assumed to be constant

23. Cost-effectiveness and cost-benefit analysis represent a systematic approach to balancing potential losses against potential gains as a prelude to public action.
    In addition to limitations based on difficulties of measurement and inadequacies in data that are typical of systematic program analysis, cost-benefit analysis suffers from a serious conceptual flaw in that

    A. the definition of benefit or cost does not typically distinguish to whom benefits or costs accrue
    B. a full-scale cost benefit analysis takes too long to do, is too expensive, and needs too much data
    C. it has been shown that such analyses are more suitable for defense or water resources problems
    D. such analyses are not useful in any problem involving capital and operating costs or benefits

24. If you were asked to develop a total cost estimate for one year for a program involving both a capital improvement and operating costs, the BEST way to estimate the capital cost component would be to

    A. divide the estimated cost of the capital improvement by the projected operating costs over the life of the improvement
    B. multiply the annual operating cost by the projected life of the capital improvement
    C. divide the amortized cost of the capital improvement by the projected life of the improvement
    D. multiply the portion of the capital improvement to be completed within the year by the cost of the improvement

25. In comparing the costs of two or more alternative programs, it is important to consider all relevant costs.
    The MOST important principle in defining "relevant cost" is that

    A. only marginal or incremental cost should be considered in the estimate
    B. only recurring costs should be considered for each alternative
    C. estimates should include the sunk costs for each alternative
    D. cost estimates need to be as precise as in budget preparation

26. Different techniques for projecting future costs may be suitable in different situations. Assume that it is necessary to estimate the future costs of maintaining garbage collection vehicles.
    Under which of the following conditions would it be advisable to develop a cost-estimating equation rather than to use unadjusted current data?

    A. When it is expected that more complex equipment will replace simpler equipment
    B. Whether or not it is expected that the nature of future garbage collection will change
    C. When the current unadjusted data still has to be verified
    D. When the nature of future garbage collection equipment is unknown

27. The following data has been collected on the costs of two pilot programs, each representing a different approach to the same problem.

	Total cost	Fixed cost	Variable cost	Average unit cost	Number of users
Program A	$45,000	$20,000	$50 per user	$90 per user	500
Program B	$42,000	$7,000	$100 per user	$120 per user	350

    Assume that the pilot programs are extended city-wide and other factors are constant. Using the above data, what would a cost analyst conclude about the relative costs of the two programs? Program

    A. B would be less costly with fewer than 300 users and Program A would be less costly with more than 300 users
    B. B would be less costly with fewer than 260 users and Program A would be less costly with more than 260 users
    C. A would be less costly without regard to the size of the program
    D. B would be less costly without regard to the size of the program

Questions 28-30.

DIRECTIONS: Answer Questions 28 through 30 on the basis of the following data assembled for a cost-benefit analysis.

	Cost	Benefit
No program	0	0
Alternative W	$3,000	$6,000
Alternative X	$10,000	$17,000
Alternative Y	$17,000	$25,000
Alternative Z	$30,000	$32,000

28. From the point of view of pushing public expenditure to the point where marginal benefit equals or exceeds marginal cost, the BEST alternative is Alternative

    A. W   B. X   C. Y   D. Z

29. From the point of view of selecting the alternative with the best cost-benefit ratio, the BEST alternative is Alternative.

    A. W   B. X   C. Y   D. Z

30. From the point of view of selecting the alternative with the best measure of net benefit, the BEST alternative is Alternative

    A. W   B. X   C. Y   D. Z

Questions 31-35.

DIRECTIONS: The set of answers listed below applies to Questions 31 through 35. Each answer is a type of statistical test.
A. Analysis of variance
B. Pearson Product-Moment Correlation (r)
C. t-test
D. x^2 test (Chi-squared)

Pick the test which is MOST appropriate to the situation described. An answer may be used more than once.

31. A comparison between two correlated means obtained from a small sample.
The CORRECT answer is:

A.   B.   C.   D.

32. A comparison of three or more means.
The CORRECT answer is:

A.   B.   C.   D.

33. A comparison of the divergence of observed frequencies with those expected on the hypothesis of equal probability of occurrence.
The CORRECT answer is:

A.   B.   C.   D.

34. A comparison of the divergence of observed frequencies with those expected on the hypothesis of a normal distribution.
The CORRECT answer is:

A.   B.   C.   D.

35. A comparison between two uncorrelated means obtained from small samples.
The CORRECT answer is:

A.   B.   C.   D.

36. There are many different models for evaluative research.
A time-series design is an example of a _____ experimental design.

A. field   B. true   C. quasi-   D. pre-

37. In policy research, as in all kinds of research, it is important to develop research hypotheses early.
The MAIN purpose of a research hypothesis is to

A. include the kind of statistical procedures to be used in the research
B. provide a ready answer in case data is not available for doing research
C. serve as a guide to the kind of data that must be collected in order to answer the research question
D. clarify what is known and what is not known in the research problem

38. While descriptive and causal research are not completely separable, there has been a distinct effort to move in the direction of causal research.
Such an effort is epitomized by the use of

   A. predictive models and measures of deviation from predictions
   B. option and attitudinal surveys in local neighborhoods
   C. community studies and area profiles of localities
   D. individual case histories and group case studies

39. The one of the following which BEST describes a periodic report is that it

   A. provides a record of accomplishments for a given time span and a comparison with similar time spans in the past
   B. covers the progress made in a project that has been postponed
   C. integrates, summarizes, and perhaps interprets published data on technical or scientific material
   D. describes a decision, advocates a policy or action, and presents facts in support of the writer's position

40. The PRIMARY purpose of including pictorial illustrations in a formal report is usually to

   A. amplify information which has been adequately treated verbally
   B. present details that are difficult to describe verbally
   C. provide the reader with a pleasant, momentary distraction
   D. present supplementary information incidental to the main ideas developed in the report.

KEY (CORRECT ANSWERS)

1.	B	11.	B	21.	C	31.	C
2.	A	12.	A	22.	B	32.	A
3.	B	13.	C	23.	A	33.	D
4.	B	14.	C	24.	C	34.	D
5.	C	15.	D	25.	A	35.	C
6.	D	16.	A	26.	A	36.	C
7.	D	17.	B	27.	B	37.	C
8.	C	18.	C	28.	C	38.	A
9.	C	19.	A	29.	A	39.	A
10.	C	20.	D	30.	C	40.	B

TEST 2

DIRECTIONS: Each question or incomplete statement is followed by several suggested answers or completions. Select the one that BEST answers the question or completes the statement. *PRINT THE LETTER OF THE CORRECT ANSWER IN THE SPACE AT THE RIGHT.*

1. A measurement procedure is considered to be RELIABLE to the extent that   1.____

   A. independent applications under similar conditions yield consistent results
   B. independent applications under different conditions yield similar results
   C. scores reflect true differences among individuals or situations
   D. scores reflect true differences in the same individual over time

2. Different scales of measurement are distinguished by the feasibility of various empirical operations.   2.____
   An ordinal scale of measurement

   A. is not as useful as a ratio or interval scale
   B. is useful in rank-ordering or priority setting
   C. provides the data for addition or subtraction
   D. provides the data for computation of means

3. A widely used approach to sampling is systematic sampling, i.e., selecting every Kth element in a listing.   3.____
   Even with a random start, a DISADVANTAGE in this approach is that

   A. the listing used may contain a cyclical pattern
   B. it is too similar to a simple random sample
   C. the system does not insure a probability sample
   D. it yields an unpredictable sample size

4. A rule of thumb sometimes used in sample size selection is to set sample size equal to five percent of the population size. Other things being equal, this rule   4.____

   A. tends to oversample small populations
   B. tends to oversample large populations
   C. provides an accurate rule for sampling
   D. is a relatively inexpensive basis for sampling

5. With regard to a stratified random sample, it may be APPROPRIATE to sample the various strata in different proportions in order to   5.____

   A. approximate the characteristics of a true random sample
   B. establish classes that are internally heterogenous in each case
   C. avoid the necessity of subdividing the cases within each stratum
   D. adequately cover important strata that have small numbers of cases

6. One possible response to the "unknown" or "no answer" category in a tabulation of survey information is to "allocate" the unknown responses, i.e., to estimate the missing data on the basis of other known information about the respondents.   6.____
   This technique is APPROPRIATE when the unknown category

A. is very small and is randomly distributed within all subgroups of respondents
B. is very large and is randomly distributed within all subgroups of respondents
C. reflects an interviewing failure and a subgroup in the sample tends to produce more unknowns
D. is a legitimate category and a subgroup in the sample tends to produce more unknowns

7. In presenting cross-tabulated data showing the relation ship between two variables, it is MOST meaningful to compute percentages

   A. in both directions in all instances
   B. of each cell in relation to the grand total
   C. in the direction of the smaller number of cells
   D. in the direction of the causal factor

8. In portraying data based on a sampling operation, it is MOST meaningful and comprehensible to the reader to present

   A. percentages for the sample and the universe
   B. percentages by themselves
   C. percentages and the base figures
   D. numbers by themselves

9. A new bridge spanning a river is expected to carry 60,000 cars a day on a rainy day and 80,000 cars a day on other kinds of days.
   If there is a $5 toll and one chance in four of a rainy day, the expected value of a day's revenue is

   A. $175,000   B. $375,000   C. $475,000   D. $700,000

10. The analyst who is asked to estimate the probability of a relatively rare event occurring cannot use the classical frequency measures of probability but rather should

    A. use a random-numbers table to pick a probability
    B. project historical data into the future
    C. indicate that no probabilistic judgment is possible
    D. make the best possible judgment as to the subjective probability

11. A useful source of census data for computing annual indicators is the

    A. Public Use Sample   B. Continuing Population Survey
    C. Census of Population   D. Census of Governments

12. An analyst presented with a set of household records showing age, ethnicity, income, and family status and wishing to study the inter-relationship of all of these variables simultaneously will probably request

    A. one four-way cross-tabulation
    B. four three-way cross-tabulations
    C. six two-way cross-tabulations
    D. four single tabulations

13. Downward communication, from high management to lower levels in an organization, will often not be fully accepted at the lowest levels of an organization unless high-level management   13.____

    A. communicates through several levels of mid-level management, where the message can be properly modified and interpreted
    B. communicates directly with the level of the organization it wishes to reach, bypassing any intermediate levels
    C. first establishes an atmosphere in which upward communication is encouraged and listened to
    D. establishes penalties for non-compliance with its communications

14. A top-level manager sometimes has an inaccurate view of the actual lower-level operations of his agency, particularly of those operations which are not running well.
    Of the following, the MOST frequent cause of this is the   14.____

    A. general unconcern of top-level management with the way an agency actually operates
    B. tendency of the people at the lowest level in an agency to lie about their actual performance
    C. unwillingness of top-level management to deal with unfavorable information when it is presented
    D. tendency of mid-level management to edit bad news and unpleasant information from reports directed to top management

15. In the conduct of productivity analyses, work measurement is a USEFUL technique for   15.____

    A. substantiating executive decisions
    B. designing a research study
    C. developing performance yardsticks
    D. preparing a manual of procedure

16. Issue analysis is closely identified with the "fire-fighting" function of management. As such, issue analysis is a(n)   16.____

    A. systematic assessment over time of an agency's strategic options
    B. annual review of the issues that have come up during the past year
    C. basis for a set of procedures to be followed in an emergency
    D. analysis of a specific policy question often performed in a crisis environment

17. The transportation agency in a large city wishes to study the impact of fare increases on ridership in buses. Rider-ship data for peak hours has been assembled for the same time period for three geographic subareas (A, B and C) with approximately the same socio-economic characteristics, residential density, and distance from the central business district (CBD). Subarea A had experienced a moderate fare increase on its bus line; Subarea B had had no fare increase; and Subarea C had experienced a major fare increase during the time period.
    In the design of this study, the analysis should be framed :   17.____

    A. Ridership = f (fare level)
    B. Ridership = f (fare level, distance from CBD)
    C. Fare level = f (ridership)
    D. Ridership = f (fare level, socio-economic characteristics, residential density)

18. What organizational concept is illustrated when a group is organized on an *ad hoc* basis to accomplish a specific goal?

    A. Functional Teamwork
    B. Line/staff
    C. Task Force
    D. Command

19. The concept of "demand" provides an appropriate theoretical basis for estimating the needs for public services or programs where the service will be on a

    A. fee basis and involves life-sustaining necessities
    B. free basis and involves life-sustaining necessities
    C. free basis and does not involve life-sustaining necessities
    D. fee basis and does not involve life-sustaining necessities

20. Analysts should be wary of relying exclusively on traditional service standards (e.g., one acre of playground per 1,000 population).
Such standards are often DEFICIENT because they tend to overstate

    A. the consumer view and understate behavior and values of producers
    B. the producer view and understate behavior and values of users or consumers
    C. local conditions and understate national conditions
    D. behavioral factors and understate practical effects

21. The BEST measure of the performance of a manpower program would be the

    A. percentage reduction in unemployment by impacted population groups
    B. number of trainees placed in jobs at the beginning of the training program
    C. percentage of students completing a training program
    D. cost per student of the training program and the job placement effort

22. Indices are single figures that measure multi-dimensional concepts.
The critical judgment in the construction of an index involves

    A. the trade-off between accuracy and simplicity
    B. determination of enough data to do the measurement
    C. avoidance of all possible error
    D. developing a theoretical basis for it

23. Evaluation of public programs is complicated by the reality that programs tend to reflect negotiated compromises among conflicting objectives.
The absence of clear, unitary objectives PARTICULARLY complicates the

    A. assessment of program input or effort
    B. development of effectiveness criteria
    C. design of new programs to replace the old
    D. diagnosis of a program's processes

24. The basic purpose of the "Super-Agencies" is to

    A. reduce the number of departments and agencies in the city government
    B. reduce the number of high-level administrators
    C. coordinate agencies reporting to the mayor and supervise agencies in related fields
    D. supervise departments and agencies in unrelated fields

25. In most municipal budgeting systems involving capital and operating budgets, the leasing or renting of facilities is usually shown in   25.____

    A. the operating budget
    B. the capital budget
    C. a separate schedule
    D. either budget

26. New York City's budgeting procedure is unusual in that budget appropriations are considered in two parts, as follows: 26.____

    A. Capital budget and income budget
    B. Expense budget and income budget
    C. Revenue budget and expense budget
    D. Expense budget and capital budget

27. The "growth rate" referred to in current political and economic discussion refers to change from year to year in a country's   27.____

    A. gross national product
    B. population
    C. available labor force
    D. capital goods investment

Questions 28-29.

DIRECTIONS: Questions 28 and 29 are based on the following illustration. Assume that the figures in the chart are cubes.

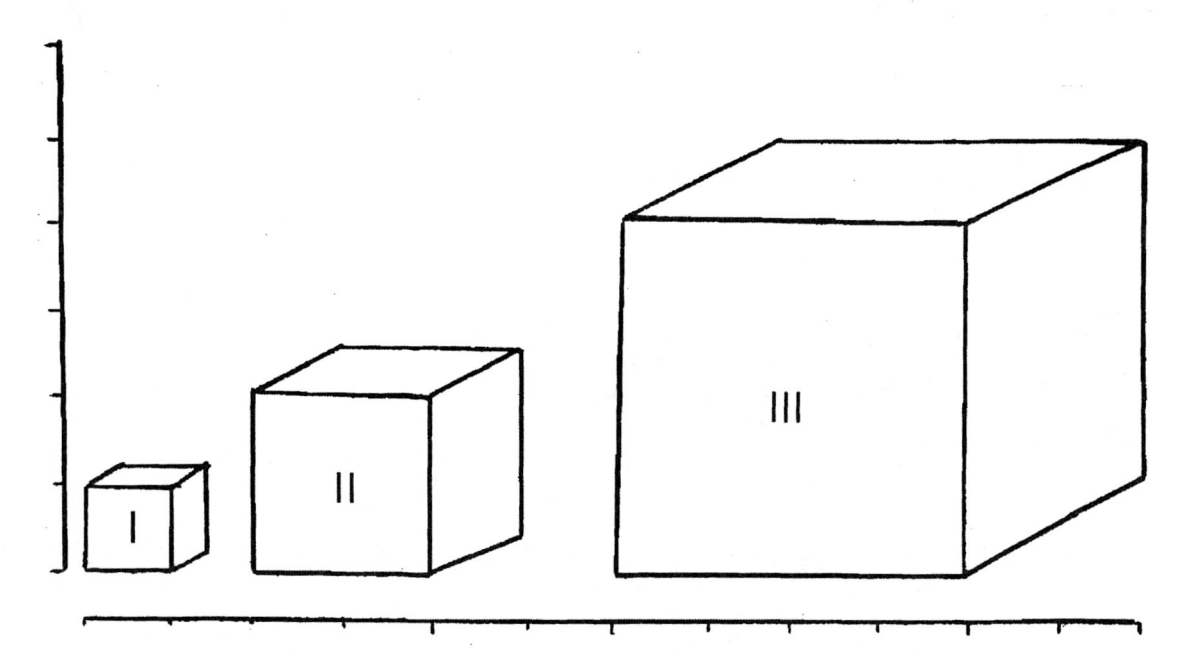

28. In the illustration above, how many times GREATER is the quantity represented by Figure III than the quantity represented by Figure II?   28.____

    A. 2   B. 4   C. 8   D. 16

29. The illustration above illustrates a progression in quantity BEST described as   29.____

    A. arithmetic   B. geometric   C. discrete   D. linear

Questions 30-35.

DIRECTIONS: Answer Questions 30 through 35 on the basis of the following chart.

In a national study of poverty trends, the following data have been assembled for interpretation.

Persons Below Poverty Level, By Residence

	Number (millions)		Percent	
Item	U.S.	Metropolitan Areas	U.S.	Metropolitan Areas
2005				
Total	38.8	17.0	22.0	15.3
Under 25 years	20.0	8.8	25.3	18.1
65 years & over	5.5	2.5	35.2	26.9
Black	9.9	5.0	55.1	42.8
Other	28.3	11.8	18.1	12.0
2015				
Total	24.3	12.3	12.2	9.5
Under 25 years	12.2	6.4	13.2	10.4
65 years & over	4.8	2.3	25.3	20.2
Black	7.2	3.9	32.3	24.4
Other	16.7	8.2	9.5	7.3

30. If no other source of data were available, which of the following groups would you expect to have the HIGHEST rate of poverty?

    A. Others over 65
    B. Others under 65
    C. Blacks over 65
    D. Blacks under 65

31. Between 2005 and 2015, the percentage of poor in the United States who were black

    A. increased from 25.5% to 29.6%
    B. decreased from 55.1% to 32.3%
    C. decreased from 9.9% to 7.2%
    D. stayed the same

32. The data in the second column of the table indicate that, in the metropolitan areas, the number of poor declined by 4.7 million or 36.2% between 2005 and 2015. Yet, the fourth column shows a corresponding decline from 15.3% to 9.5%, or only 5.8%
This apparent discrepancy reflects the fact that the

    A. metropolitan areas are growing while the number of poor is contracting
    B. two columns in question are based on different sources of information
    C. difference between two percentages is not the same as the percent change in total numbers
    D. tables have inherent errors and must be carefully checked

33. The percentages in each of the last two columns of the table for 1969 and 1979 don't add up to 100%. This is for the reason that

   A. rounding off each entry to the nearest decimal place caused an error in the total such that the total is not equal to 100%
   B. these columns show the percentage of Blacks, aged, etc. who are poor rather than the percentage of poor who are Black, aged, etc.
   C. there was an error in the construction of the table which was not noticed until the table was already in print
   D. there is double counting in the entries in the table; some people are counted more than once

34. Data such as that presented in the table on persons below poverty level are shown to a single decimal place because

   A. data in every table should always be shown to a single decimal place
   B. it is the minimal number of decimal places needed to distinguish among table entries
   C. there was no room for more decimal places in the table without crowding
   D. the more accurately a figure is shown the better it is for the user

35. In comparing the poverty of the young (under 25 years) with that of the older population (65 years and over) in 2005 and 2015, one could REASONABLY conclude that

   A. more young people than old people were poor but older people had a higher rate of poverty
   B. more older people than young people were poor but young people had a higher rate of poverty
   C. there is a greater degree of poverty among the younger population than among the older people
   D. young people and old people have the same rate of poverty

Questions 36-37.

DIRECTIONS: Answer Questions 36 and 37 ONLY on the basis of information given in the passage below.

Two approaches are available in developing criteria for the evaluation of plans. One approach, designated Approach A, is a review and analysis of characteristics that differentiate successful plans from unsuccessful plans. These criteria are descriptive in nature and serve as a checklist against which the plan under consideration may be judged. These characteristics have been observed by many different students of planning, and there is considerable agreement concerning the characteristics necessary for a plan to be successful.

A second approach to the development of criteria for judging plans, designated Approach B, is the determination of the degree to which the plan under consideration is economic. The word "economic" is used here in its broadest sense; i.e., effective in its utilization of resources. In order to determine the economic worth of a plan, it is necessary to use a technique that permits the description of any plan in economic terms and to utilize this technique to the extent that it becomes a "way of thinking" about plans.

36. According to *Approach B*, the MOST successful plan is generally one which 36.___

    A. costs least to implement
    B. gives most value for resources expended
    C. uses the least expensive resources
    D. utilizes the greatest number of resources

37. According to *Approach A*, a successful plan is one which is 37.___

    A. descriptive in nature
    B. lowest in cost
    C. similar to other successful plans
    D. agreed upon by many students of planning

Questions 38-40.

DIRECTIONS: Answer Questions 38 through 40 ONLY on the basis of information provided in the passage below.

The primary purpose of control reports is to supply information intended to serve as the basis for corrective action if needed. At the same time, the significance of control reports must be kept in proper perspective. Control reports are only a part of the planning-management information system. Control, information includes non-financial as well as financial data that measure performance and isolate variances from standard. Control information also provides feedback so that planning information may be updated and corrected. Whenever possible, control reports should be designed so that they provide feedback for the planning process as well as provide information of immediate value to the control process.

Since the culmination of the control process is the taking of necessary corrective action to bring performance in line with standards, it follows that control information must be directed to the person who is organizationally responsible for taking the required action. Usually the same information, though in a somewhat abbreviated form, is given to the responsible manager's superior. A district sales manager needs a complete daily record of the performance of each of his salesmen; yet, the report forwarded to the regional sales manager summarizes only the performance of each sales district in his region. In preparing reports for higher echelons of management, summary statements and recommendations for action should appear on the first page; substantiating data, usually the information presented to the person directly responsible for the operation, may be included if needed.

38. A control report serves its primary purpose as part of the process which leads DIRECTLY to 38.___

    A. better planning for future action
    B. increasing the performance of district salesmen
    C. the establishment of proper performance standards
    D. taking corrective action when performance is poor

39. The one of the following which would be the BEST description of a control report is that a control report is a form of 39.___

    A. planning   B. communication
    C. direction   D. organization

40. If control reports are to be effective, the one of the following which is LEAST essential to the effectiveness of control reporting is a system of

    A. communication   B. standards
    C. authority   D. work simplification

40. ____

KEY (CORRECT ANSWERS)

1.	A	11.	B	21.	A	31.	B
2.	B	12.	A	22.	A	32.	C
3.	A	13.	C	23.	B	33.	B
4.	B	14.	D	24.	C	34.	D
5.	D	15.	C	25.	A	35.	A
6.	C	16.	D	26.	D	36.	B
7.	D	17.	A	27.	A	37.	C
8.	C	18.	C	28.	C	38.	D
9.	B	19.	D	29.	B	39.	B
10.	D	20.	B	30.	C	40.	D

EXAMINATION SECTION
TEST 1

DIRECTIONS: Each question or incomplete statement is followed by several suggested answers or completions. Select the one that *BEST* answers the question or completes the statement. *PRINT THE LETTER OF THE CORRECT ANSWER IN THE SPACE AT THE RIGHT.*

1. An analyst is writing a report dealing with the distribution of deaths caused by various types of cardiovascular diseases. He decides to facilitate the reader's grasp of the information presented by including in the report a device that permits comparison of parts to each other, and to the whole at the same time.
Of the following, the *MOST* appropriate and efficient device he should use for this purpose is the

   A. graph
   B. pie diagram
   C. flow sheet
   D. line chart with one series

1.____

2. In carrying out a cost-effectiveness analysis, the analyst should follow certain guidelines. The *MOST* important of these guidelines involves the

   A. utilization of both the fixed utility approach and the fixed budget approach
   B. proper structuring of the problem and design of the analysis
   C. necessity of building a model that is highly formal and mathematical
   D. provision for implicit treatment of uncertainty

2.____

3. In a decision which involves fairness -- such as assigning new office equipment to workers when the agency does not receive enough new office equipment for the entire group -- the *PRIMARY* determinant of the decision's effectiveness will be the

   A. systematic or traditional approach which is emphasized in reaching the decision
   B. random nature of the assignment
   C. feedback a decisionmaker receives concerning the decision
   D. acceptance of the decision by the persons who have to execute it

3.____

4. In order to give line personnel some insight into staff problems and vice versa it has been suggested that line and staff assignments within a particular city agency be rotated. Which of the following criticisms would be *MOST* valid for opposing such a proposal?

   A. Generally speaking, line and staff personnel have different perspectives on organizational structures which makes rotation in assignments extremely difficult.
   B. Since their educational backgrounds are often quite diverse, staff personnel are often at a disadvantage when serving in line assignments.
   C. Line personnel frequently resent having to perform the more difficult tasks that staff assignments entail.
   D. Serving in a rotating assignment may not necessarily provide the personnel with any significant degree of insight as anticipated.

4.____

5. Which one of the following approaches to criticism of a subordinate or associate is *generally* the *MOST* appropriate and effective?
Criticize

   A. by making a comparison with a more exemplary employee

5.____

B. the act, not the person
C. in a humorous vein
D. in general rather than specific terms

6. Assume that two policy units have been formed to study the impact of Federal programs in the city. The two units operate in an essentially similar manner, except for their communications procedures. In unit A any member may communicate and exchange information with any other member of the unit; in unit B a member may only communicate information with the unit supervisor.
In evaluating the effect that these communications procedures have on the level of productivity, it will *generally* be found that

   A. unit A's level of productivity will be greater than unit B's level of productivity for simple problems
   B. unit B's level of productivity will be greater than unit A's level of productivity for simple problems
   C. initial levels of profuctivity are higher in unit A than unit B for complex problems
   D. initial levels of productivity are higher in unit B than in unit A for complex problems

7. In the process of communicating an idea, the following five distinct steps are generally involved:
   I. Selection of a media and transmission of the message
   II. Decoding of a message, i.e., meaning is extracted from the message
   III. Message is received
   IV. Idea is organized into a series of symbols designed to give meaning
   V. Action is taken and/or feedback is given

   In what logical, sequential order should these steps be arranged for effective two-way communications to take place?

   A. V, I, II, III, IV
   B. II, I, III, IV, V
   C. IV, I, III, II, V
   D. I, III, IV, II, V

8. Informal employee groups that share certain norms and strive for member satisfaction through the achievement of group goals are known as work groups.
Which of the following statements can *generally* be considered as being *FALSE* in describing work groups in a moderate size organization?

   A. Formation of work groups is ubiquitous and inevitable.
   B. Work groups strongly influence the overall behavior and performance of their members.
   C. An organization can reap positive and negative consequences as a result of work groups.
   D. Elimination of work groups can be easily achieved by management pressure.

9. Under the management approach known as *management by objectives* which of the following criteria is *generally* used to determine whether the manager has been successful?

   A. Activities performed
   B. Results achieved
   C. Production schedules completed
   D. Financial savings accomplished

10. Of the following, the MOST accurate statement relative to job attitudes is that they

    A. cannot be influenced by only one person
    B. are always the result of work groups
    C. have no relationship to productivity
    D. are strongly influenced by work situation

11. Assume that measures to overcome a budget deficit, including attrition and a hiring freeze, have significantly decreased the work-output of a city agency. The agency administrator desires to develop a plan to restore production to its former level by increasing the work-load and responsibility of the agency's employees.
    In order to obtain *maximum* employee cooperation and *minimize* employee resistance, it would be MOST advisable for the

    A. administrator of the agency to personally describe to the employees the new work changes that they are to follow
    B. employees to decide what the optimal changes in the work load should be
    C. management representatives to consult with employee representatives on these matters
    D. immediate supervisor of the employees to decide on the work changes to be implemented

12. Eliciting the support and cooperation of others often requires a great deal of persuasion. Which one of the following persuasive techniques or practices is generally the LEAST desirable for you, an analyst, to use?

    A. Establish your expertness and authority
    B. Present your arguments without emotion
    C. In presenting your arguments, express yourself in the manner to which you are accustomed
    D. Try to find a face-saving way for your opponent to change his/her mind

13. The following illustration depicts the structure of a municipal agency.

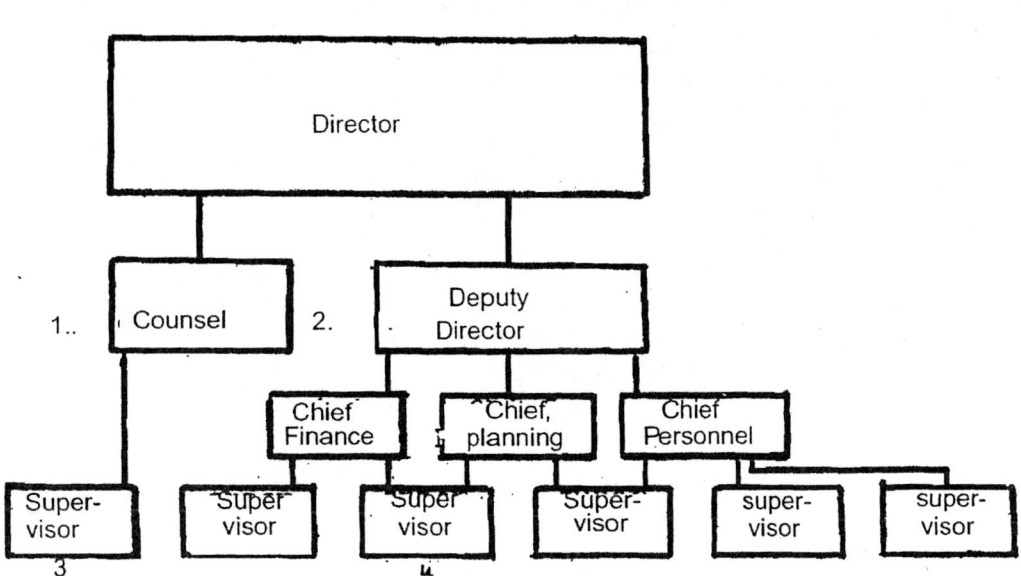

    In the above illustration, which individual would generally be expected to encounter the MOST difficulty in carrying out his organizational functions?

    A. 1   B. 2   C. 3   D. 4

14. An agency in which a free flow of communication exists is an agency in which no barriers or structures are erected to control or bar the flow of information and messages between and among management and staff, horizontally or vertically.
Of the following, the GREATEST disadvantage that would be most likely to occur in an agency in which such a free flow of communication exists, is that

    A. it would be difficult to determine which information is important and which is irrelevant
    B. there would be a lesser degree of staff-employee participation and cooperation in communicating
    C. more restrictive controls would be placed on managerial employees
    D. important communications would tend to be eliminated, and and trivial communications over-emphasized

15. Feedback is generally considered an essential factor in oral communication MAINLY because

    A. it enables the speaker to know whether he is understood
    B. the speed of communication is accelerated
    C. it eliminates the necessity of the speaker to use gestures and facial expressions when speaking
    D. the listener is unable to immediately respond to the speaker until the latter is finished

16. Assume that two employees are working on a joint project and they have a difference of opinion on the methodology to be used. Each employee not only listens to the other's opinion on methodology but projects him-self into the other's position.
This type of listening is *usually* considered

    A. *ineffective*, mainly because it will be impossible for the employees to reach a satisfactory agreement
    B. *effective*, mainly because each employee will then be more critical of the other's argument
    C. *ineffective*, mainly because each worker will unconsciously and unintentionally accept the other's viewpoint
    D. *effective*, mainly because each speaker can understand the other's viewpoint and can then respond intelligently to his remarks

17. The arithmetic mean is commonly used in describing data. Which one of the following statements is NOT true about the arithmetic mean?

    A. It is a measure of dispersion.
    B. The sum of the deviations around it is zero.
    C. It is easy to compute, understand and recognize.
    D. It may be treated alegebraically.

Questions 18 - 20.

DIRECTIONS: Answer Questions 18 through 20 on the basis of the following data. Assume that you are using these data in assessing the impact of Federal and State income taxes on New York City residents, and comparing it to the effect of Federal and State taxes in other areas.

EFFECT OF DEDUCTIBILITY (i.e., deductibility of taxes levied by other jurisdictions in calculating the net base of the tax in the taxing jurisdiction.)

Net income before personal exemption	Effective rate of tax				
	Federal (assuming no state tax)	State		Combined Federal and State	
		New York*	Minnesota (assuming no federal tax)	New York	Minnesota
	(1)	(2)	(3)	(4)	(5)
$20,000	25.0	4.1	6.9	27.6	27.9
50,000	42.2	5.4	9.1	44.0	43.9
100,000	56.0	5.9	9.8	57.5	57.1
200,000	69.2	6.1	10.1	69.9	69.5
1,500,000	88.0	6.3	10.5	89.3	88.9

*New York has no deductibility; the Federal government has deductibility.

18. In which of the following columns is the tax rate shown to be the LEAST progressive?   18._____

   A. 1   B. 2   C. 4   D. 5

19. Which of the following statements is TRUE about the reasons why Columns 1 and 2 do not equal Column 4 for each salary level?   19._____

   A. Personal deductions are taken into account in Column 4 but not in Columns 1 and 2.
   B. Federal deducibility of state taxes only is taken into account in Column 4 but not in Columns 1 and 2.
   C. Reciprocal deductibility is taken into account in Column 4 but not in Columns 1 and 2.
   D. State deductibility of federal taxes only is taken into account in Column 4 but not in Columns 1 and 2.

20. The EFFECT of the State's introducing deductibility, given that the Federal government maintains deductibility, is to   20._____

   A. increase Federal and State income
   B. decrease Federal and State income
   C. decrease Federal income and increase State income
   D. increase Federal income and decrease State income

21. Assume that you have been made project coordinator for a study concerning the implementation of casino gambling in the city. You have assigned each of the professional staff members simple tasks in specialized areas for the duration of the project. For you to make such job assignments would *generally* be

    A. *desirable;* the performance of simple tasks will motivate individuals to work diligently
    B. *desirable;* specialized tasks induce a sense of accomplishment to individuals
    C. *undesirable;* specialized tasks are more difficult to learn
    D. *undesirable;* specialized tasks may lead to a loss of feeling of accomplishment

22. Assume that you have been asked to submit a proposal for the reorganization of a unit that is charged with performing difficult nonroutine work. Frequently decisions must be made quickly and concurrence obtained from high-level agency heads.
    Given the above conditions, of the following it would be MOST logical to structure the organization

    A. on the basis of a relatively wide span of control
    B. on the basis of a relatively narrow span of control
    C. with many organizational levels with a wide span of control
    D. with more emphasis on line than staff units

23. Assume that a study has indicated that a recently created city *superagency* has had formal communication difficulties among various component agencies. It appears that jurisdictional overlapping among those agencies has caused frequent rerouting and unnecessary duplication of communications within the organization. Which one of the following proposals would MOST effectively deal with the communications problem encountered by this *superagency?*

    A. Create a central communications office to handle all communications for this *superagency.*
    B. Duplicate and distribute all communications to each component within this *superagency.*
    C. Reduce the overlapping areas of jurisdiction among the component agencies
    D. Decentralize the *superagency* on a *borough* basis to expedite mail delivery

24. The utilization of input-output concepts in connection with the application of the systems concept to government raises the problem of the quantification of objectives and performance (the value of the public benefit). The one of the following which is MOST easily *quantifiable* is

    A. education
    B. police service
    C. subway car maintenance
    D. the effectiveness of a welfare administrator

25. When an analyst tries to conceive of a city management problem as a *systems* problem, he is, first of all, confronted with establishing the boundaries of the system. Of the following, the city problem which can *most likely* be conceived of within a system whose boundaries are roughly equivalent to those of the city is

 A. taxation
 B. welfare
 C. fire protection
 D. transportation

25.____

KEY (CORRECT ANSWERS)

1. B
2. B
3. D
4. D
5. B

6. C
7. C
8. D
9. B
10. D

11. C
12. B
13. D
14. A
15. A

16. D
17. A
18. B
19. B
20. D

21. D
22. B
23. C
24. C
25. C

TEST 2

DIRECTIONS: Each question or incomplete statement is followed by several suggested answers or completions. Select the one that *BEST* answers the question or completes the statement. *PRINT THE LETTER OF THE CORRECT ANSWER IN THE SPACE AT THE RIGHT.*

1. When installing a new *system,* an analyst may choose among several types of installation plans - the *all-at-once type,* the *piecemeal type,* or the *parallel type* each suited to a particular problem or degree of complexity in the system.
   The one of the following situations in which the *parallel type* would be *MOST* appropriate is a situation

   A. in which a minimum installation cost is required
   B. involving a small volume of transactions
   C. in which the change is not radical or does not involve new machines
   D. involving large installation projects and intricate processing

   1.___

2. Many decision situations involve a great deal of uncertainty about the future, which is difficult to take into account in the analysis of alternatives. One technique developed for treating such uncertainty is designed to measure the possible effects on alternatives under analysis resulting from variations in uncertain elements. The analyst uses several *expected values* for uncertain parameters in an attempt to ascertain how the results vary (i.e., the relative ranking of the alternatives under consideration) in light of variations in the uncertain parameters. The analyst attempts to determine the alternative (or feasible combination of alternatives) likely to achieve a specified objective, gain or utility at the lowest cost. The one of the following which *BEST* describes the above technique is:

   A. Contingency analysis employing the fixed-budget approach
   B. Contingency analysis employing the fixed-benefits approach
   C. Sensitivity analysis employing the fixed-budget approach
   D. Sensitivity analysis employing the fixed-benefits approach

   2.___

3. In general, the analytical techniques of management science are of the *LEAST* value when

   A. the effects of a small number of controlled variables must be considered
   B. the number of relevant uncontrolled variables is small
   C. relevant causes and effects are factual in nature and can be stated and measured numerically or symbolically
   D. There are reasons to believe that past relationships will continue to hold in the future

   3.___

4. During the installation period of a new system, tight controls must be maintained over every phase of the operation. To do this, an analyst may set up a *warning system* within the system which forecasts potential bottle-necks and affords sufficient clues for correcting any problems, errors or fall-downs.
   The one of the following control devices or techniques which would be *most likely* to involve extra effort during the installation, and slow down the processing time is

   4.___

A. paper flow controls - log sheets, numerical controls, etc. (a system of logging input and output)
B. timing controls - to inform the analyst about the proper time interval between certain activities with-in the systems
C. program check points - a periodic review of processing to date at each check point
D. accounting control totals, to accumulate invoice numbers as the first and last steps in the system and compare the totals

5. Which of the following types of work measurement techniques would be MOST appropriate for obtaining details of a particular job for cost analysis purposes, such as the operating costs of various types of duplicating machines?

   A. Work sampling
   B. Predetermined time standards
   C. The time study (stop-watch timing)
   D. Historical

5.____

6. It is anticipated that a certain cancer detection program will be capable of detecting many cases at an early stage and that society will be thus enabled to cure twice as many cases as it cures currently. The benefits to society include the reduction in cost of hospitalization, etc., that would have been incurred otherwise.
Benefits such as a reduction in the cost of hospitalization are *most usually* called

   A. direct benefits   B. secondary benefits
   C. intergenerational benefits   D. external benefits

6.____

7. The results of departmental and agency programs can be measured in terms of EFFECTIVENESS or BENEFITS. Thus, careful budget preparation will permit the calculation of costs which can then be compared, or equated, to these results. Which one of the following statements pertaining to cost-effectiveness measurements is MOST valid?

   A. In cost-effectiveness measurements, a dollar value is assigned to the output.
   B. The measurement is expressed in terms of quality of output for a given cost.
   C. Cost effectiveness ratios express the relationship between the costs of programs
   D. A cost-effectiveness measurement will show the number of outputs which can be achieved for the expenditure of a given amount of money.

7.____

8. Assume that you have been asked to evaluate personnel programs in four city agencies The statistical test that would be MOST appropriate for testing the significance of the differences in the mean number of days absent (normality may be assumed) during the year 2004 in four different agencies is the

   A. one-way analysis of variance
   B. standard deviation
   C. regression analysis
   D. Chi-square test (x^2-test)

8.____

9. Assume that you have been asked to evaluate differences in the children just enrolled in two youth programs. In reviewing the relevant published material you find that in one particular study involving two groups, N = 9 and N = 13, there is a significant difference in the mean scores of the two groups on a characteristic which you believe to be normally distributed.
The statistical test *most likely* used in this study to determine the significance of the difference in the means of the two groups on this characteristic is the

   A. Chi-square test (x2-test)
   B. Pearson Product-Moment correlation (r)
   C. t-test
   D. two-way analysis of variance

10. In statistics, three common measures of central tendency are the mean, median and mode.
For which of the following conditions would the median generally be the *BEST* choice to use? When the

   A. distribution of scores is skewed
   B. scores are distributed symmetrically around a central point
   C. standard deviation must also be calculated
   D. most frequently occurring value is required

11. Nonparametric statistical tests are *usually* employed when

   A. large samples are used
   B. a very powerful or exact test is needed
   C. data cannot be expressed in ranks
   D. a normally distributed population cannot be assumed

12. Assume that in a report presented to you by an employee under your supervision, a coefficient of correlation of +1.73 is reported between the age at which one first smokes cigarettes and the age at which one first smokes marijuana.
You should *most reasonably* interpret this figure to mean there is a

   A. strong positive correlation
   B. weak positive correlation
   C. weak negative correlation
   D. typographical error

13. One of the major research techniques most often used in studies of organizational behavior problems is the survey. An analyst who utilizes the survey technique should be aware that its *MAJOR* drawback is

   A. the lack of depth obtained from the two major data-collection tolls used in surveys: the mailed question-naire and the personal interview
   B. its impracticality in assessing or estimating the present state of affairs with regard to a variable that changes over time for a large group of subjects
   C. the restriction of this technique to a single, or very few, units of analysis
   D. its absence of dependence upon the collection of empirical data

14. In order for an analyst to understand and interpret statistical data he/she must understand which types of data tend to approximate the normal probability curve, i.e., are normally distributed.
Which of the following types of data falls into this category?
Frequency of

   A. educational test scores for students of a given age, plotted against test score
   B. filing of income tax returns for citizens of a given age, plotted against date of filing
   C. deaths due to childhood disease plotted against age
   D. deaths due to degenerative diseases, plotted against age

14.____

15. Which of the following terms describes a line or curve formed by plotting employees salaries that increase yearly by a fixed percentage over the previous year? (In answering the question, assume that time is on the horizontal axis (abscissa) and salary is on the vertical axis (ordinate) - both axes are marked linearly.)

   A. Linear (increasing at a constant rate)
   B. Positively accelerating (increasing at an increasing rate)
   C. Negatively accelerating (increasing at a decreasing rate)
   D. Negatively decelerating (decreasing at a decreasing rate)

15.____

Questions 16 - 17

DIRECTIONS: Answer Questions 16 and 17 on the basis of the following groups, both of which depict the same information in different ways.

The x and y axes in graphs A and B are not necessarily drawn in the same scale. The points along the curves on both graphs represent corresponding points, and are the upper limits of class intervals.

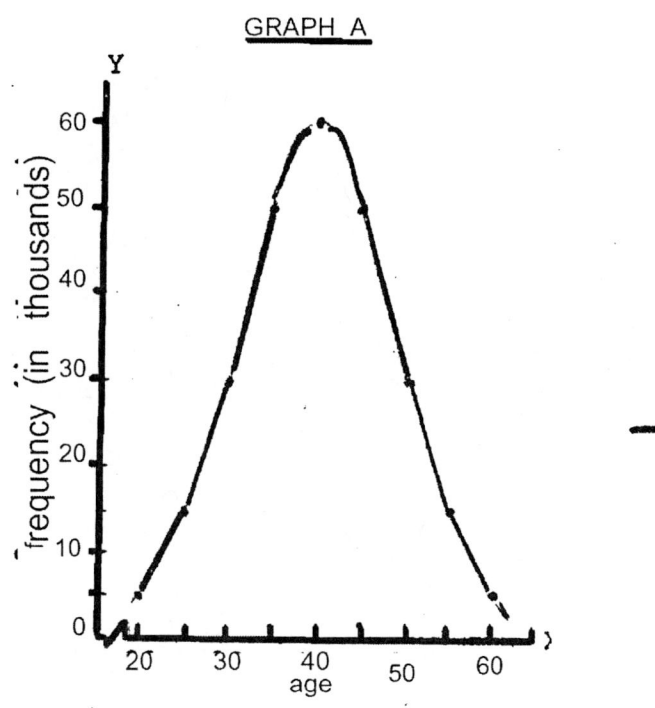

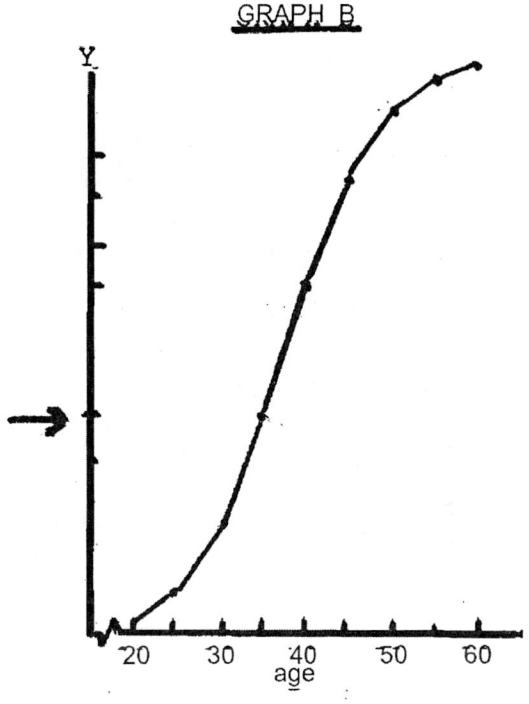

16. The ordinate (y-axis) in graph B is

   A. frequency
   B. cumulative frequency
   C. average frequency
   D. log frequency

17. The arrow on the y-axis in graph B indicates a particular number. That number is, *most nearly*

   A. 100
   B. 50,000
   C. 100,000
   D. 150,000

Questions 18 - 19

   DIRECTIONS: Answer Questions 18 and 19 on the basis of the graphs that appear on the following page.

18. In Graph I, the vertical distance between lines E and T within the crosshatched area represents the

   A. savings to the city if work of less than 50 miles is performed by the city
   B. loss to the city if work of less than 50 miles is performed by the city
   C. savings to the city if work of more than 50 miles is performed by the city
   D. loss to the city if work of more than 50 miles is performed by the city

19. Graph II is identical to Graph I except that contractor costs have been eliminated. Total costs (line E) are the sum of fixed costs (line F) and variable costs. Variable costs are represented by line

   A. A
   B. B
   C. C
   D. D

ROAD REPAIR COSTS IF PERFORMED BY
CITY STAFF OR AN OUTSIDE CONTRACTOR

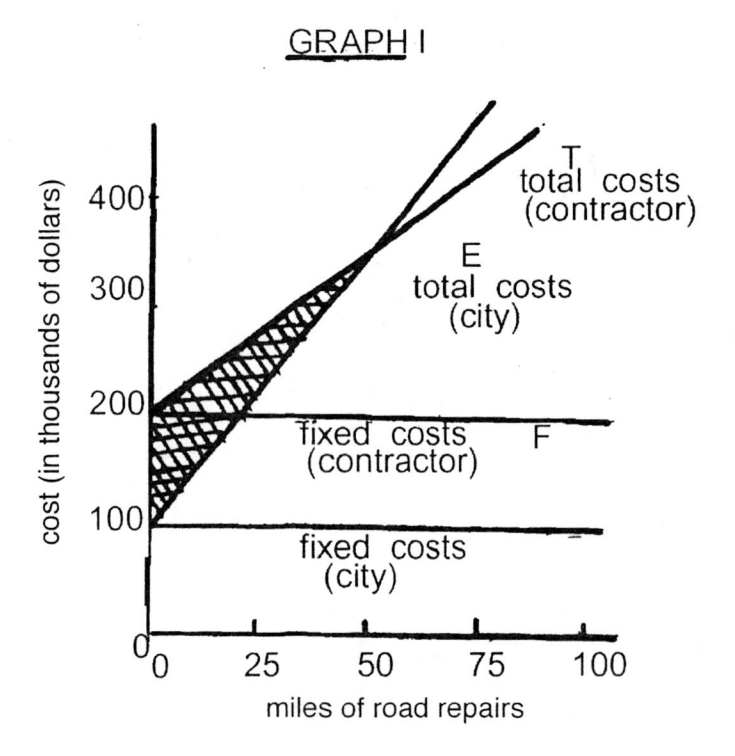

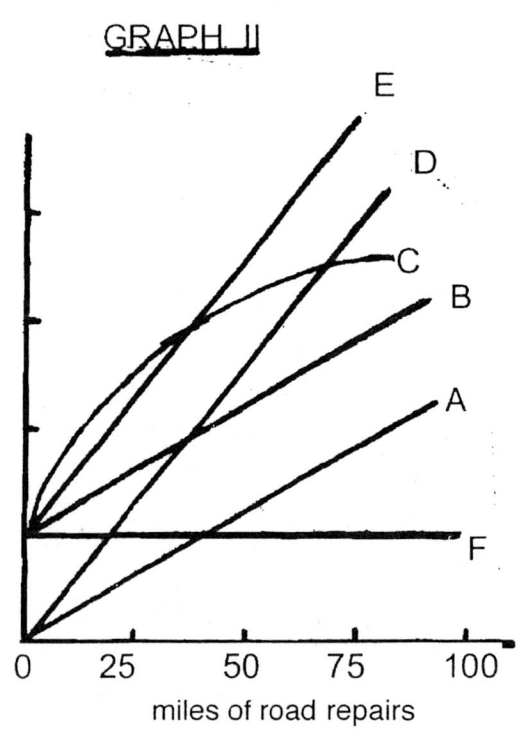

20. Fiscal experts in municipal affairs have contended that the most acute problem facing the city today seems to be the growth of the city's short-term debt.
    Of the following, the LEAST likely reason for the city to engage in short-term borrowing is that the city

    A. expects money from long-term borrowing that it plans to undertake
    B. needs to be tided over until funds due from the Federal or State government arrive
    C. needs money to finance big construction outlays
    D. anticipates money from future tax collections

21. A MAJOR criticism of the *superagency* has been the

    A. additional layers of control and additional lines of command
    B. merger of departmental functions
    C. political manipulation
    D. professional incompetence in administration

22. The management of a large urban city is different in many ways from the management of other systems, particularly large business organizations.
    The one of the following which does NOT exemplify these differences is:

    A. A mayor, in contrast to a manager of a large business, is often held responsible for services, etc., over which he has little authority.
    B. Top management of a large urban city must deal with a greater number of different pressures from diverse interest groups.
    C. The city government, in contrast to a large business organization, often lacks adequate management controls, and goals are often ill-defined.
    D. The multiplicity of alternatives available to city government as opposed to large businesses, are substantially greater, making decision-making haphazard.

23. The function called internal control applies to those measures taken by a government agency to protect its assets. Internal control has a role to play as an enforcer of administrative edicts as well as for purposes of asset protection.
    Of the following statements relating to internal control, as described above, select the *one* usually considered to be LEAST valid.

    A. Internal control makes auditing by an external agency more difficult.
    B. The function of internal control often involves the auditing process.
    C. That people cannot be trusted to act wisely and honestly seems to be implicit in all the principles of internal control.
    D. Internal control is simply a form of self-audit by the agency itself.

24. In addition to the new effect on workers who are unskilled and undereducated, the severe effect of the high unemployment rate in the city has recently become MOST apparent among

    A. skilled craftsmen in the building trades
    B. clerical employees
    C. middle management personnel
    D. architects and engineers

25. The fact that the city has the second highest jobless rate of any major U.S. city except Detroit is considered particularly significant because, compared to Detroit, unemployment in the city

    A. is caused by city government fiscal measures rather than private business conditions
    B. exists in more than one industry
    C. results in an increase in welfare expenditures to a greater extent
    D. more seriously affects the world-wide economy

KEY (CORRECT ANSWERS)

1.	D	11.	D
2.	D	12.	D
3.	A	13.	A
4.	A	14.	A
5.	C	15.	B
6.	A	16.	B
7.	D	17.	C
8.	A	18.	A
9.	C	19.	D
10.	A	20.	C
21.	A		
22.	D		
23.	A		
24.	A		
25.	B		

EXAMINATION SECTION
TEST 1

DIRECTIONS: Each question or incomplete statement is followed by several suggested answers or completions. Select the one that BEST answers the question or completes the statement. *PRINT THE LETTER OF THE CORRECT ANSWER IN THE SPACE AT THE RIGHT.*

1. Constitutional limitations on borrowing by local governments are less relevant today than 20 to 30 years ago PRIMARILY because of the

   A. continually rising rate of interest on mortgages
   B. growing importance of local non-property taxes
   C. growth in federal aid
   D. more rapid growth of the suburbs relative to central cities

   1.____

2. Assume that the manager of an office or administrative activity has been cautioned to control the cost of peak load fluctuations and unforeseen emergencies in preparing his budget estimates.
   In conforming to these instructions, the manager should NOT budget for

   A. a reserve of trained employees
   B. *floating* or traveling trouble-shooting employees
   C. overtime work
   D. part-time help

   2.____

3. A mail section consisted of incoming and outgoing units. By applying an hourly work count, a supervisor found that the peak load of the incoming unit occurred in the morning and almost equalled the peak load of the outgoing unit in the afternoon. As a result, the two units were combined. The former condition is BEST described as an example of

   A. decentralization   B. overspecialization
   C. overstaffing   D. reorganization

   3.____

4. Of the following, the one whose yield would be MOST difficult to predict in preparing a budget is the _____ tax.

   A. commercial rent or occupancy   B. general corporation
   C. sales   D. transportation corporation

   4.____

5. Of the following, the MOST useful data to use in predicting the yield of the sales tax normally are

   A. corporate profits
   B. personal incomes
   C. the deflated gross national product
   D. unemployment rates

   5.____

6. Of the following, the criterion that is LEAST desirable for the selection of an output indicator for use in multi-year program analysis is

   A. cost effectiveness   B. data availability
   C. relevance   D. simplicity

   6.____

7. The MOST valid generalization regarding the <u>attribute</u> as a form of data is that it is

   A. a source of contamination in the analysis of the basic problem
   B. distinguishable from other forms of data in varying amounts
   C. relatively impervious to scientific treatment because of its subjectivity
   D. a quality, trait, or function that is present or absent

8. The one of the following management techniques that would generally be LEAST useful in the work of a budget examiner is a _____ system.

   A. management information
   B. network type planning and scheduling
   C. paperwork simplification
   D. work measurement

9. A supervisor thought it necessary to maintain a double check for accuracy on the review of cases. A work count showed him that Reviewer A found a percentage of errors of 12 percent, whereas Reviewer B, spending the same amount of time, turned up an additional 0.1 percent of errors. Of the following, it would be MOST advisable for the supervisor to

   A. commend the first reviewer and discipline the second reviewer
   B. divide the percentage of errors equally between the two
   C. eliminate a second review in the future
   D. reclassify the first reviewer

10. Of the following, the one that BEST describes a well-defined economic criterion for assigning priorities to feasible projects is

    A. unit pricing theory
    B. diminishing marginal utility
    C. discounted cash flow rate of return
    D. economies of scale

11. The technical research term *stanine* refers to a(n)

    A. economical approximation for validity
    B. regressed form of the true score
    C. reliable measure of physical fitness
    D. special form of the standard score

12. A score NOT based upon the standard deviation is the

    A. scaled score
    B. T-score
    C. z-score
    D. percentile rank

13. PPBS is MOST difficult to apply to problems of

    A. fire
    B. health
    C. public works
    D. welfare

14. Which of the following types of problems would be LEAST likely to lend itself to *operations research*?

    A. Determining program priorities
    B. Developing a controlled backlog
    C. Distribution of resources and jobs
    D. Sequence of work

15. The MOST valid of the following statements regarding measurement of government activities is: 15.____

    A. A viable program cannot be planned without work measurement
    B. Most government activities cannot be measured
    C. Some aspects of every activity can be measured
    D. Work measurement takes more time and effort than it is worth

16. In correlating results on reading and intelligence tests for a given set of population, the BEST data to utilize are 16.____

    A. intelligence quotient and reading quotient
    B. mental age and reading age
    C. mental age and reading grade
    D. raw scores on both tests

17. For the purpose of conducting a school survey, the practice of selecting a typical county on the basis of considerable known information about all of the counties in the United States is an example of _____ sampling. 17.____

    A. purposive   B. representative
    C. nested   D. cluster

18. Which one of the following problems is generally NOT encountered in cost analysis of multi-year plans for an ongoing program? 18.____

    A. Form in which costs should be summarized for decision-making
    B. Magnitude of uncertainty in cost estimates
    C. The obtaining of historical costs
    D. The question of price level changes

19. Select the statement which is MOST valid: 19.____

    A. Accounting object classes should be the categories of a program structure
    B. Each program should be related to the operations of a single agency
    C. The costs for each program should form the basis of the accounting system
    D. The costs for each program should include the costs of all relevant object classes

20. Assume that the number of buses (U_t) required for a given line-haul system serving the Central Business District depends upon roundtrip time (t), capacity of bus (c), and the total number of people to be moved in a peak hour (P) in the major direction, i.e., in the morning and out in the evening. 20.____
    The formula for the number of buses required is: $U_t =$

    A. Ptc   B. $\frac{tp}{c}$ C. $\frac{cp}{t}$ D. $\frac{ct}{p}$

21. The area, in blocks, that can be served by a single stop for any maximum walking distance is given by the following formula: $a = 2w^2$. In this formula, a = the area served by a stop, and w = maximum walking distance. 21.____
    If people will tolerate a walk of up to three blocks, how many stops would be needed to service an area of 288 square blocks?

    A. 9   B. 16   C. 18   D. 27

22. Among the following, the MOST appropriate technique for ascertaining the content of educational achievement is

    A. the analysis of textbooks and courses of study
    B. the reliance on the judgment of experts
    C. differential achievement by varied grades
    D. statistical correlations with class marks

23. Which of the following is a network chart? _____ chart.

    A. Critical path method   B. Gantt
    C. Multi-column process   D. Single-column process

24. Such measures as cost of square foot per road are MOST useful for

    A. evaluating goal attainment
    B. evaluation of current operations
    C. manning tables
    D. output plans

Questions 25-28.

DIRECTIONS: Questions 25 through 28 are to be answered on the basis of the following paragraph.

Under institutional training program 1, two-thirds of the recipients are poor, 40 percent are under 21 years of age, and the average net earnings gained by the participants are almost three times the per trainee cost. A competing program 2 increases the average earnings by only 120 percent of the per trainee cost but all participants are poor and under 21.

25. If the sole objective of the governmental agency is the greatest return to national income per dollar invested, the PREFERABLE alternative is

    A. 1   B. either 1 or 2
    C. 2   D. a combination of 1 and 2

26. If the basic objective is to assist youth, the PREFERABLE alternative is

    A. 1   B. either 1 or 2
    C. 2   D. a combination of 1 and 2

27. If the basic objective is to assist the poor, the PREFERABLE alternative is

    A. 1   B. either 1 or 2
    C. 2   D. a combination of 1 and 2

28. If the objectives are multiple: assist youth, assist the poor, and the greatest return to national income per dollar invested, the choice of the PREFERABLE program

    A. cannot be made
    B. is 1
    C. is 2
    D. depends on an appropriate weighting of objectives

29. ACIR refers to Advisory Commission on

   A. Industrial Resources
   B. Intergovernmental Relations
   C. Internal Revenue
   D. Institutional Research

30. The Constitution of the United States

   A. does not mention the budget process
   B. provides for an executive budget
   C. mandates a national budget, but does not specify procedure
   D. specifies the basic steps of budget preparation and authorization

31. The following four steps represent an analysis of an experimental procedure:
   I. Collection of evidence
   II. Appraisal of the tentative generalization
   III. Adoption of the operational hypotheses
   IV. Definition of problem

   The steps should be taken in the following order:

   A. III, IV, I, II
   B. I, II, III, IV
   C. IV, III, I, II
   D. II, I, IV, III

Questions 32-34.

DIRECTIONS: Questions 32 through 34 are to be answered on the basis of the following data.

A series of cost-benefit studies of various alternative health programs yields the following results:

Program	Benefit	Cost
K	30	15
L	60	60
M	300	150
N	600	500

In answering Questions 32 through 34, assume that all programs can be increased or decreased in scale without affecting their individual benefit-to-cost ratios.

32. The benefit-to-cost ratio of Program M is

   A. 10:1   B. 5:1   C. 2:1   D. 1:2

33. The budget ceiling for one or more of the programs included in the study is set at 75 units.
   It may MOST logically be concluded that

   A. Programs K and L should be chosen to fit within the budget ceiling
   B. Program K would be the most desirable one that could be afforded
   C. Program M should be chosen rather than Program K
   D. the choice should be between Program M and K

34. If no assumptions can be made regarding the effects of change of scale, the MOST logical conclusion, on the basis of the data available, is that

   A. more data are needed for a budget choice of program
   B. Program K is the most preferable because of its low cost and good benefit-to-cost ratio
   C. Program M is the most preferable because of its high benefits and good benefit-to-cost ratio
   D. there is no difference between Programs K and M, and either can be chosen for any purpose

35. The PRIMARY obstacle to the interpretation of educational experiments in which two or more groups of students have been matched on chronological age or intelligence is:

   A. Significance tests are not adequate to handle the data
   B. The matching process frequently inflates group differences
   C. Chronological age and intelligence are usually the wrong variables on which to equate students
   D. Populations of matched students do not exist to which to generalize

36. The LARGEST item of expenditure in the typical office or administrative organization is usually for

   A. charges for office machine usage
   B. office supplies, forms, and other materials
   C. rent of space occupied
   D. salaries and wages

37. Of the following, the MOST appropriate indicator of quality of service in a health program is usually

   A. average daily in-patient load in a general hospital
   B. number of children served in a disease-screening clinic
   C. number of patients treated in an alcoholic clinic
   D. number of therapy hours of care provided in a mental hospital

Questions 38-47.

DIRECTIONS: Questions 38 through 47 consists of a quotation which contains one word that is incorrectly used because it is not in keeping with the meaning that the quotation is evidently intended to convey. Determine which word is INCORRECTLY used. Then, select from the words lettered A, B, C, or D the word which, when substituted for the incorrectly used word, would BEST help to convey the meaning of the quotation.

38. A measure must be developed of all direct and indirect benefits, recognizing the non-quantifiable nature of many of the latter, yet guarding against the tendency to use the quantifiable as a justification for any difference between costs and benefits.

   A. cannot
   B. non-quantifiable
   C. effects
   D. ability

39. A persistent problem in the rationalization of public expenditures in the natural resources field stems from the varied objectives of different interests. A primary reason for this is that the cost and gains of contemplated actions are perceived clearly.

    A. differently   B. minor
    C. potential   D. programs

40. It is not imperative that the agency's table of organization follow the program structure rigidly, but a general parallelism is helpful, both in placing legislative responsibility for goal attainment and in program evaluation.

    A. executive   B. harmful
    C. ineffective   D. initiative

41. Some of the impediments to developing appropriate data systems stem from the fact that organization lines and program structures do not expand. The requirement for accounting on a program basis is superimposed across organizational requirements.

    A. coincide   B. conflict
    C. inducements   D. planning

42. Examples of a public good may be found also in domestic programs, although national income is probably the purest and most extreme example of a public good.

    A. international   B. least
    C. private   D. security

43. To avoid distortions in cost-benefit calculations, an appropriate discount interest rate should be calculated on the basis of the marginal cost principle.

    A. analysis   B. estimated
    C. opportunity   D. time horizon

44. Where budget deficits are developed at the agency level for use by operating bureaus, they must be harmonious with the directives that have come from the central budget office.

    A. assumptions   B. consistent
    C. departmental   D. large

45. A possible source of budgetary waste could be eliminated if estimates were prepared in no greater detail than was justified by their magnitude.

    A. accuracy   B. budgets
    C. complexity   D. mechanical

46. A capital budget may provide information useful in estimating national income. This is a very different type of consideration from budgetary and policy-formulation purposes.

    A. contain   B. economic   C. program   D. wealth

47. In some governments, the failure to bring budgeting and policy-making together at the operating level is often unfortunately attributable to the presence of a strong budget office attached to the chief executive, which is too concerned with threats to its authority.

    A. departmental   B. effectiveness
    C. involved   D. planning

48. The MOST important function served by a line-item budget is to 48.___

   A. control appropriations and expenditures in detail
   B. give the Budget Bureau information on each operating agency's financial plans
   C. measure cost-effectiveness
   D. provide a basis for management analysis

49. Assume that work to be distributed varies in difficulty and complexity. The workers are at 49.___
junior and senior levels and differ in competence within each level.
Of the following, the BEST policy for the supervisor to follow in this case when distributing work is usually to

   A. divide the work among workers based on the individual speed and competence of each worker, regardless of worker level
   B. give the more difficult work to the seniors, and base the number of work units given to each level on the estimated time needed to complete each different work unit
   C. give the more difficult work to the seniors and the less difficult to the juniors, but give more units of work to the juniors
   D. give the work which will require the longest time to complete to the seniors

50. Generally, authority and responsibility for an activity should NOT be delegated until 50.___

   A. all authorized positions have been filled
   B. an organization is mature
   C. personnel have been trained in the staff functions
   D. policies can be spelled out so as to insure uniform administration

KEY (CORRECT ANSWERS)

1. B	11. D	21. B	31. C	41. A
2. A	12. D	22. A	32. C	42. D
3. B	13. D	23. A	33. D	43. C
4. B	14. A	24. B	34. A	44. A
5. B	15. C	25. A	35. D	45. A
6. A	16. D	26. C	36. D	46. D
7. D	17. A	27. C	37. D	47. A
8. C	18. C	28. D	38. B	48. A
9. C	19. D	29. B	39. A	49. B
10. C	20. B	30. A	40. A	50. D

TEST 2

DIRECTIONS: Each question or incomplete statement is followed by several suggested answers or completions. Select the one that BEST answers the question or completes the statement. *PRINT THE LETTER OF THE CORRECT ANSWER IN THE SPACE AT THE RIGHT.*

Questions 1-7.

DIRECTIONS: Questions 1 through 7 are to be answered on the basis of the following paragraphs. Indicate the correct answer for these questions as follows: If the paragraphs indicate it is true, mark answer A. If the paragraphs indicate it is probably true, mark answer B. If the paragraphs indicate it is probably false, mark answer C. If the paragraphs indicate it is false, mark answer D.

The fallacy underlying what some might call the eighteenth and nineteenth century misconceptions of the nature of scientific investigations seems to lie in a mistaken analogy. Those who said they were investigating the structure of the universe imagined themselves as the equivalent of the early explorers and mapmakers. The explorers of the fifteenth and sixteenth centuries had opened up new worlds with the aid of imperfect maps; in their accounts of distant lands, there had been some false and many ambiguous statements. But by the time everyone came to believe the world was round, the maps of distant continents were beginning to assume a fairly consistent pattern. By the seventeenth century, methods of measuring space and time had laid the foundations for an accurate geography.

On this basic issue, there is far from complete agreement among philosophers of science today. You can, each of you, choose your side and find highly distinguished advocates for the point of view you have selected. However, in view of the revolution in physics, anyone who now asserts that science is an exploration of the universe must be prepared to shoulder a heavy burden of proof. To my mind, the analogy between the mapmaker and the scientist is false. A scientific theory is not even the first approximation to a map; it is not a need; it is a policy -- an economical and fruitful guide to action, by scientific investigators.

1. The author thinks that 18th and 19th century science followed the same technique as the 15th century geographers.   1._____

2. The author disagrees with the philosophers who are labelled realists.   2._____

3. The author believes there is a permanent structure to the universe.   3._____

4. A scientific theory is an economical guide to exploring what cannot be known absolutely.   4._____

5. Philosophers of science accept the relativity implications of recent research in physics.   5._____

6. It is a matter of time and effort before modern scientists will be as successful as the geographers.   6._____

7. The author believes in an indeterminate universe.   7._____

8. Total government expenditures, Federal, State, and local, are APPROXIMATELY the following proportion of Gross National Product: 8._____

    A. 1/10   B. 1/5   C. 1/3   D. 1/2

Questions 9-12.

DIRECTIONS: Questions 9 through 12 are to be answered on the basis of the following.

The income elasticity of demand for selected items of consumer demand in the United States are:

Item	Elasticity
Airline travel	5.66
Alcohol	.62
Dentist fees	1.00
Electric utilities	3.00
Gasoline	1.29
Intercity bus	1.89
Local bus	1.41
Restaurant meals	.75

9. The demand for the item listed below that would be MOST adversely affected by a decrease in income is

   A. alcohol
   B. electric utilities
   C. gasoline
   D. restaurant meals

10. The item whose relative change in demand would be the same as the relative change in income would be

    A. dentist fees
    B. gasoline
    C. restaurant meals
    D. none of the above

11. If income increases by 12 percent, the demand for restaurant meals may be expected to increase by

    A. 9 percent
    B. 12 percent
    C. 16 percent
    D. none of the above

12. On the basis of the above information, the item whose demand would be MOST adversely affected by an increase in the sales tax from 7 percent to 8 percent to be passed on to the consumer in the form of higher prices

    A. would be airline travel
    B. would be alcohol
    C. would be gasoline
    D. cannot be determined

13. The PRIMARY purpose of randomization principles in the design of experiments is to

    A. exclude a number of alternative interpretations
    B. objectify the experimental evidence
    C. validate the tests of significance
    D. equate the number of degrees of freedom in the cells

14. Of the following, the GREATEST advantage of state collection as against local collection of local sales taxes in the state is:

A. Payments by retailers to the tax agency may be made at less frequent intervals
B. The burden of the tax is decreased
C. The net yield of the tax is increased
D. The tax rate is uniform throughout the state

15. A criticism of a *pay-as-you-go* policy in financing capital outlay is that it

    A. is more costly
    B. is more difficult to administer
    C. may be difficult to determine priorities among projects
    D. may lead to the postponement of needed projects

16. Which of the following tends to be the LEAST constraint encountered in the preparation of a municipal budget?

    A. Legislative   B. Political
    C. Revenue   D. Personnel

17. In the last two decades, the ability of the legislature to review the budget has been improved in many governments PRINCIPALLY by providing

    A. a long-range planning system
    B. for public hearings on the budget
    C. more details in the executive budget
    D. professional staff for the legislature

18. Recent research shows that some lower-level professional employees feel that they accomplish little in their work that is worthwhile.
    Management experts usually say that the one of the following which BEST explains such feelings is

    A. dissatisfaction among employees provoked by the activities of labor unions
    B. frequent salary increases unmatched by any significant increases in productivity
    C. the almost total indifference of employees to the vital issues of the times
    D. the failure to properly develop in these employees an understanding of the significance of their work

19. One way to get maximum effort from employees is for management to give employees the maximum possible personal freedom in accomplishing agency objectives.
    This encourages a feeling of self-management which is MOST basic to

    A. an impartial approach to work
    B. tightly coordinated team effort
    C. high levels of motivation
    D. uniformity of action

20. Interactions among public programs are often complex. The situation that is NOT an example of such interactions is:

    A. A solid waste disposal program may increase air pollution
    B. Changes in transportation may improve or reduce retail trade
    C. Paving of more highway mileage may enlarge traffic congestion
    D. Traffic control systems may reduce or enlarge motor vehicle accidents

21. The following are given as the objectives of a department's mission:
    I. Economic efficiency
    II. Optimal use of environmental resources
    III. Safety
    IV. Support of other national interests
    Which one of the departments listed below is MOST likely to have all four of the above objectives?

    A. Correction
    B. Education
    C. Health
    D. Transportation

22. An agency is considering the hiring of a consultant for a given project.
    Of the following, the GREATEST danger of reliance on outside experts is:

    A. It delays the work program because of the necessity of processing bids
    B. It does not contribute to internal staff capacity
    C. It involves greater project costs
    D. The resulting work, though excellent, may not be assimilated in the governmental process

23. Of the following, the MOST pertinent argument given against *revenue-sharing* is:

    A. Local governments are incapable of planning expenditures properly
    B. The expenditure needs of state and local governments have not grown as rapidly as the needs of the federal government
    C. The federal government has the more lucrative sources of revenue at its disposal
    D. There would be no flow-through to cities

24. In fixing beneficiary charges, governments generally do NOT consider

    A. the cost of the service
    B. the rate of return
    C. the value of the service
    D. what the market will bear

25. The MAXIMUM amount of the real property tax levy does NOT usually depend upon the

    A. assessed valuation
    B. equalization rate
    C. size of the budget
    D. value of tax-exempt property

26. An argument against the use of a task force for budget analysis is:
    It could

    A. facilitate participation of the agencies concerned
    B. not help clarify problems of coordination
    C. not result in in-depth considerations
    D. overemphasize subject matter areas singled out for intensive effort

27. A standard cost system produces 27.____

    A. a ratio of cost of goods sold to net sales
    B. a ratio of current assets to current liabilities
    C. original actual costs which may be compared to inflated costs
    D. predetermined costs which can be compared with actual costs

28. Which of the following is NOT a desirable characteristic of a capital budget? 28.____

    A. A long-range capital improvements plan (6 years)
    B. A master plan for physical development of the city (10-25 years)
    C. Financial analysis of present and anticipated municipal revenue
    D. Omission of operating expenses and other recurrent costs

29. The earmarking of revenues is often defended since it 29.____

    A. improves tax administration
    B. is a non-political device
    C. provides a direct link between the cost and benefit of a service
    D. simplifies the budgetary process

30. Of the following, the BEST measure of relative taxable capacity among states is 30.____

    A. per capita personal income
    B. per capita yield of a stock transfer tax
    C. personal income
    D. the yield of a sales tax

31. In identifying fundamental government objectives under PPBS, the LEAST important of the following questions is 31.____

    A. By whom is it to be done?
    B. For whom is it to be done?
    C. What is to be done?
    D. Why is each activity currently performed being done?

32. Which one of the following measures is of LEAST use as an output measure for a PPBS system? 32.____

    A. Gallons of water per housing unit
    B. Number of days of hospital care per capita
    C. Number of traffic accidents by 1,000 vehicle miles
    D. Number of traffic tickets per officer

33. Estimates of costs can be MOST *rough* for which of the following purposes? 33.____

    A. Budget
    B. One-year program and financial plan
    C. Program analyses
    D. Quarterly allotment system

34. A city built a golf course on land that it owns. In this situation, 34.____

    A. no additional costs are involved
    B. the cost is the initial cost of the land

C. the cost is related to possible alternate uses of the land
D. the cost is the initial cost adjusted for price changes

35. Two ten-year programs are estimated to have the same cost. Alternative 1 involves high costs in the early years and lower costs later. Alternative 2 incurs lowest costs initially and higher costs later.
In this case,

   A. Alternative 1 has the higher present discounted cost
   B. Alternative 2 has the higher present discounted cost
   C. the alternative with the higher present discounted cost cannot be determined from the information given
   D. both alternatives have exactly the same present discounted cost

36. Governmental accounting should serve as a tool of management.
This statement refers to the design of an accounting system to do which one of the following?

   A. Maintain accounts that permit an independent audit extending to all records, funds, securities, and property.
   B. Make possible a determination of the adequacy of custodianship of government assets by responsible officials.
   C. Make possible the measurements of activities at the administrative unit level.
   D. Show compliance with legal provisions.

37. Budgetary reform in the United States during the first quarter of the twentieth century emphasized control over the administrative agencies and _____ budgeting.

   A. accrual   B. executive
   C. legislative   D. program

38. The one basis of budgetary appropriation that is almost universally used is

   A. capital   B. economic character
   C. performance unit   D. organizational unit

39. The LEAST useful of the following bases of budgetary classification for a municipality would generally be by

   A. economic character   B. object-item of expetur
   C. organizational unit   D. program or activity

40. A functional classification of municipal budgetary expenditures is USUALLY prepared because it

   A. helps remove the budget from the political arena
   B. is required by local law
   C. keeps the public informed about the nature of governmental operations
   D. minimizes unnecessary budgetary appropriations

41. The following equation is used to estimate operating expenditures of a city: $Y = 90.2 + 6.2X$, where Y = operating expenditures in millions of dollars and where X = years.
Origin: Fiscal year 1989-90.
The equation indicates that operating expenditures may be expected to

A. level off at $96.4 million
B. increase at a rate of 6.2 percent per year
C. increase by $6.2 million per year
D. increase by $90.2 million per year

42. Of the following concepts associated with PPBS, the one that MOST distinguishes it from the basic characteristics of all prior forms of budgeting is

   A. input
   B. output
   C. systems analysis
   D. time span of budget appropriation

42.____

43. Of the following categories, the one which ivould receive the GREATEST percentage of total funds in a city executive capital budget would MOST LIKELY be for

   A. education
   C. health services
   B. environmental protection
   D. public safety

43.____

44. Among the sub-programs of a Physical and Mental Well-Being Program, a sub-program, Unassignable Items, is indicated. Unassignable items MOST likely would include

   A. Drug Addiction Treatment
   B. Mental Illness Prevention
   C. Physical Health
   D. Research and Planning

44.____

45. Under a PPBS system, it is BEST to account for employee benefit costs

   A. by applying them to individual programs
   B. by omitting them from relevant costs
   C. in a separate category
   D. in a special overhead account

45.____

46. In preparing the budget of expenses for any office or administrative unit, some expenses originate in and are chargeable directly to the office or administrative unit. Others must be allocated on some basis.
Of the following, the expense that is LEAST typical of a direct expense, and therefore should be charged on an allocated basis, is

   A. depreciation of machines and equipment
   B. employee fringe benefits and salaries
   C. printing expense
   D. rent

46.____

47. Justification materials generally found in conventional budgets have failings as analysis documents because they

   A. do not contain comparisons with prior year budgets
   B. seldom discuss alternatives sufficiently
   C. very rarely contain work-load data
   D. very rarely provide information

47.____

48. Post-completion audits of capital expense projects are made for a variety of purposes. Of the following, the LEAST appropriate purpose for such an audit is to

   A. aid in assessing future capital expenditures proposals
   B. assess the abilities and competence of the analyst who submitted the original project proposal
   C. reveal reasons for project failures
   D. verify the resulting savings

49. The one of the following kinds of problems for which administrative measuring techniques tend to be LEAST applicable is

   A. administrative planning
   B. decisions in the realm of human relations
   C. determining relative effectiveness of alternative procedures and methods
   D. work programming

50. The one of the following which is an example of transfer payments by government is

   A. intergovernmental aid
   B. late payments of encumbered balances
   C. social security payments
   D. transportation payments for government employees

KEY (CORRECT ANSWERS)

1.	D	11.	A	21.	D	31.	A	41.	C
2.	B	12.	D	22.	D	32.	D	42.	C
3.	D	13.	C	23.	A	33.	C	43.	A
4.	A	14.	C	24.	B	34.	C	44.	D
5.	D	15.	D	25.	C	35.	A	45.	A
6.	D	16.	D	26.	D	36.	C	46.	D
7.	B	17.	D	27.	D	37.	B	47.	B
8.	C	18.	D	28.	C	38.	D	48.	B
9.	B	19.	C	29.	C	39.	A	49.	B
10.	A	20.	B	30.	A	40.	C	50.	C

EXAMINATION SECTION
TEST 1

DIRECTIONS: Each question or incomplete statement is followed by several suggested answers or completions. Select the one that BEST answers the question or completes the statement. *PRINT THE LETTER OF THE CORRECT ANSWER IN THE SPACE AT THE RIGHT.*

1. The budget which shows the money to be spent to build and equip a new hospital is known as the _____ budget.

    A. capital   B. expense   C. planned   D. program

2. A significant characteristic of the program budget is that it lends itself to review and analysis.
   Why?

    A. The budget has a built-in accounting system that makes close control possible.
    B. The budget includes measurable objectives.
    C. It is possible to review performance based on units of service.
    D. All of the above

3. The advantages of program budgeting over line item and performance budgeting is:
    I. Tight, administrative control
    II. Forces the administrator to think through his total operation
    III. Measurable objectives
    IV. Simplicity of development
    V. Closer estimates of future costs

    The CORRECT answer is:

    A. I, II   B. II, III, IV
    C. II, III, V   D. III, IV, V

4. Of the following considerations, the one which is LEAST important in preparing a department budget request is the

    A. amounts in previous budget requests
    B. cost of material
    C. cost of personnel
    D. goals of the agency

5. The type of budget which provides the MOST flexibility in the use of appropriate funds is the _____ budget.

    A. accrual   B. item   C. line   D. program

6. A WEAKNESS of many budgetary systems today is that they

    A. are subjectively determined by those most directly involved
    B. focus on management weakness rather than management strength
    C. only show variable costs
    D. show in detail why losses are occurring

7. Standards on which budgets are developed should be based PRIMARILY on

   A. a general consensus
   B. agency wishes
   C. analytical studies
   D. historical performance

8. The income, cost, and expense goals making up a budget are aimed at achieving a predetermined objective but do not necessarily measure the lowest possible costs.
   This is PRIMARILY so because

   A. budget committees are accounting-oriented and are not sympathetic with the supervisor's personnel problems
   B. budget committees fail to recognize the difference between direct and indirect costs
   C. the level of expenditures provided for in a budget by budget committees is frequently an arbitrary rather than a scientifically determined amount
   D. budget committees spend considerable time evaluating data to the point that the material gathered is not representative or current

9. You, as a unit head, have been asked to submit budget estimates of staff, equipment, and supplies in terms of programs for your unit for the coming fiscal year.
   In addition to their use in planning, such unit budget estimates can be BEST used to

   A. reveal excessive costs in operations
   B. justify increases in the debt limit
   C. analyze employee salary adjustments
   D. predict the success of future programs

10. Which of the following is the BEST reason for budgeting a new calculating machine for an office?

    A. The clerks in the office often make mistakes in adding.
    B. The machine would save time and money.
    C. It was budgeted last year but never received.
    D. All the other offices have calculating machines.

11. As an aspect of the managerial function, a budget is described BEST as a

    A. set of qualitative management controls over productivity
    B. tool based on historical accounting reports
    C. type of management plan expressed in quantitative terms
    D. precise estimate of future quantitative and qualitative contingencies

12. Which one of the following is *generally* accepted as the MAJOR immediate advantage of installing a system of program budgeting? It

    A. encourages managers to relate their decisions to the agency's long-range goals
    B. is a replacement for the financial or fiscal budget
    C. decreases the need for managers to make trade-offs in the decision-making process
    D. helps to adjust budget figures to provide for unexpected developments

13. Of the following, the BEST means for assuring necessary responsiveness of a budgetary program to changing conditions is by

    A. overestimating budgetary expenditures by 15% and assigning the excess to unforeseen problem areas
    B. underestimating budgetary expenditures by at least 20% and setting aside a reserve account in the same amount
    C. reviewing and revising the budget at regular intervals so that it retains its character as a current document
    D. establishing *budget by exception* policies for each division in the agency

14. According to expert thought in the area of budgeting, participation in the preparation of a government agency's budget should GENERALLY involve

    A. only top management
    B. only lower levels of management
    C. all levels of the organization
    D. only a central budget office or bureau

15. Of the following, the MOST useful guide to analysis of budget estimates for the coming fiscal year is a comparison with

    A. appropriations as amended for the current fiscal year
    B. manpower requirements for the previous two years
    C. initial appropriations for the current fiscal year
    D. budget estimates for the preceding five years,

16. Line managers often request more funds for their units than are actually required to attain their current objectives.
    Which one of the following is the MOST important reason for such inflated budget requests? The

    A. expectation that budget examiners will exercise their prerogative of budget cutting
    B. line manager's interest in improving the performance of his unit is thereby indicated to top management
    C. expectation that such requests will make it easier to obtain additional funds in future years
    D. opinion that it makes sense to obtain additional funds and decide later how to use them

17. Integrating budgeting with program planning and evaluation in a city agency is GENERALLY considered to be

    A. *undesirable*; budgeting must focus on the fiscal year at hand, whereas planning must concern itself with developments over a period of years
    B. *desirable*; budgeting facilitates the choice-making process by evaluating the financial implications of agency programs and forcing cost comparisons among them
    C. *undesirable*; accountants and statisticians with the required budgetary skills have little familiarity with the substantive programs that the agency is conducting
    D. *desirable*; such a partnership increases the budgetary skills of planners, thus promoting more effective use of public resources

18. In government budgeting, the problem of relating financial transactions to the fiscal year in which they are budgeted is BEST met by

    A. determining the cash balance by comparing how much money has been received and how much has been paid out
    B. applying net revenue to the fiscal year in which they are collected as offset by relevant expenses
    C. adopting a system whereby appropriations are entered when they are received and expenditures are entered when they are paid out
    D. entering expenditures on the books when the obligation to make the expenditure is made

19. If the agency's bookkeeping system records income when it is received and expenditures when the money is paid out, this system is USUALLY known as a _____ system.

    A. cash   B. flow-payment
    C. deferred   D. fiscal year income

20. An audit, as the term applies to budget execution, is MOST NEARLY a

    A. procedure based on the budget estimates
    B. control exercised by the executive on the legislature in the establishment of program priorities
    C. check on the legality of expenditures and is based on the appropriations act
    D. requirement which must be met before funds can be spent

21. In government budgeting, there is a procedure known as *allotment.*
    Of the following statements which relate to allotment, select the one that is MOST generally considered to be correct. Allotment

    A. increases the practice of budget units coming back to the legislative branch for supplemental appropriations
    B. is simply an example of red tape
    C. eliminates the requirement of timing of expenditures
    D. is designed to prevent waste

22. In government budgeting, the establishment of the schedules of allotments is MOST generally the responsibility of the

    A. budget unit and the legislature
    B. budget unit and the executive
    C. budget unit only
    D. executive and the legislature

23. Of the following statements relating to preparation of an organization's budget request, which is the MOST generally valid precaution?

    A. Give specific instructions on the format of budget requests and required supporting data.
    B. Because of the complexity of preparing a budget request, avoid argumentation to support the requests
    C. Put requests in whatever format is desirable.
    D. Consider that final approval will be given to initial estimates.

Question 24.

DIRECTIONS: Answer Question 24 on the basis of the following information.

Sample Budget

Environmental Safety
   Air Pollution Protection
      Personal Services $20,000,000
      Contractual Services   4,000,000
      Supplies and Materials   4,000,000
      Capital Outlay   2,000,000
        Total Air Pollution Protection $30,000,000

   Water Pollution Protection
      Personal Services $23,000,000
      Supplies and Materials   4,500,000
      Capital Outlay   20,500,000
        Total Water Pollution Protection $48,000,000
   Total Environmental Safety $78,000,000

24. Based on the above budget, which is the MOST valid statement?

   A. Environmental Safety, Air Pollution Protection, and Water Pollution Protection could all be considered program elements.
   B. The object listings included water pollution protection and capital outlay.
   C. Examples of the program element listings in the above are personal services and supplies and materials.
   D. Contractual Services and Environmental Safety were the program element listings.

25. Which of the following is NOT an advantage of a program budget over a line-item budget?
A program budget

   A. allows us to set up priority lists in deciding what activities we will spend our money on
   B. gives us more control over expenditures than a line-item budget
   C. is more informative in that we know the broad purposes of spending money
   D. enables us to see if one program is getting much less money than the others

26. Of the following statements which relate to the budget process in a well-organized government, select the one that is MOST NEARLY correct.

   A. The budget cycle is the step-by-step process which is repeated each and every fiscal year.
   B. Securing approval of the budget does not take place within the budget cycle.
   C. The development of a new budget and putting it into effect is a two-step process known as the budget cycle.
   D. The fiscal period, usually a fiscal year, has no relation to the budget cycle.

27. If a manager were asked what PPBS stands for, he would be right if he said

    A. public planning budgeting system
    B. planning programming budgeting system
    C. planning projections budgeting system
    D. programming procedures budgeting system

Questions 28-29

DIRECTIONS: Answer Questions 28 and 29 on the basis of the following information.

Sample Budget

	Amount
Refuse Collection	
Personal Services	$ 30,000
Contractual Services	5,000
Supplies and Materials	5,000
Capital Outlay	10,000
	$ 50,000
Residential Collections	
Dwellings – 1 pickup per week	1,000
Tons of refuse collected per year	375
Cost of collections per ton	$ 8
Cost per dwelling pickup per year	$ 3
Total annual cost	$ 3,000

28. The sample budget shown is a simplified example of a _____ budget.

    A. factorial
    B. performance
    C. qualitative
    D. rational

29. The budget shown in the sample differs CHIEFLY from line-item and program budgets in that it includes

    A. objects of expenditure but not activities or functions
    B. only activities, functions, and controls
    C. activities and functions, but not objects of expenditure
    D. levels of service

30. Performance budgeting focuses PRIMARY attention upon which one of the following? The

    A. things to be acquired, such as supplies and equipment
    B. general character and relative importance of the work to be done or the service to be rendered
    C. list of personnel to be employed, by specific title
    D. separation of employee performance evaluations from employee compensation

KEY (CORRECT ANSWERS)

1.	A	16.	A
2.	B	17.	B
3.	C	18.	D
4.	A	19.	A
5.	D	20.	C
6.	A	21.	D
7.	C	22.	C
8.	C	23.	A
9.	A	24.	A
10.	B	25.	B
11.	C	26.	A
12.	A	27.	B
13.	C	28.	B
14.	C	29.	D
15.	A	30.	B

TEST 2

DIRECTIONS: Each question or incomplete statement is followed by several suggested answers or completions. Select the one that BEST answers the question or completes the statement. *PRINT THE LETTER OF THE CORRECT ANSWER IN THE SPACE AT THE RIGHT.*

1. Of the following, the FIRST step in the installation and operation of a performance budgeting system generally should be the

    A. identification of program costs in relationship to the accounting system and operating structure
    B. identification of the specific end results of past programs in other jurisdictions
    C. identification of work programs that are meaningful for management purposes
    D. establishment of organizational structures each containing only one work program

    1.___

2. Of the following, the MOST important purpose of a system of quarterly allotments of appropriated funds generally is to enable the

    A. head of the judicial branch to determine the legality of agency requests for budget increases
    B. operating agencies of government to upgrade the quality of their services without increasing costs
    C. head of the executive branch to control the rate at which the operating agencies obligate and expend funds
    D. operating agencies of government to avoid payment for services which have not been properly rendered by employees

    2.___

3. In the preparation of the agency's budget, the agency's central budget office has two responsibilities: program review and management improvement.
   Which one of the following questions concerning an operating agency's program is MOST closely related to the agency budget officer's program review responsibility?

    A. Can expenditures for supplies, materials, or equipment be reduced?
    B. Will improved work methods contribute to a more effective program?
    C. What is the relative importance of this program as compared with other programs?
    D. Will a realignment of responsibilities contribute to a higher level of program performance?

    3.___

Questions 4-9.

DIRECTIONS: Questions 4 through 9 are to be answered only on the basis of the information contained in the charts below which relate to the budget allocations of City X, a small suburban community. The charts depict the annual budget allocations by Department and by Expenditures over a five-year period.

CITY X BUDGET IN MILLIONS OF DOLLARS

TABLE I. Budget Allocations by Department

Department	1997	1998	1999	2000	2001
Public Safety	30	45	50	40	50
Health and Welfare	50	75	90	60	70
Engineering	5	8	10	5	8
Human Resources	10	12	20	10	22
Conservation and Environment	10	15	20	20	15
Education and Development	15	25	35	15	15
TOTAL BUDGET	120	180	225	150	180

TABLE II. Budget Allocations by Expenditures

Category	1997	1998	1999	2000	2001
Raw Materials and Machinery	36	63	68	30	98
Capital Outlay	12	27	56	15	18
Personal Services	72	90	101	105	64
TOTAL BUDGET	120	180	225	150	160

4. The year in which the SMALLEST percentage of the total annual budget was allocated to the Department of Education and Development is

   A. 1997　　B. 1998　　C. 2000　　D. 2001

5. Assume that in 2000 the Department of Conservation and Environment divided its annual budget into the three categories of expenditures and in exactly the same proportion as the budget shown in Table II for the year 2000. The amount allocated for capital outlay in the Department of Conservation and Environment's 2000 budget was MOST NEARLY _____ million.

   A. $2　　B. $4　　C. $6　　D. $10

6. From the year 1998 to the year 2000, the sum of the annual budgets for the Departments of Public Safety and Engineering showed an overall _____ million.

   A. decline of $8　　B. increase of $7
   C. decline of $15　　D. increase of $22

7. The LARGEST dollar increase in departmental budget allocations from one year to the next was in

   A. Public Safety from 1997 to 1998
   B. Health and Welfare from 1997 to 1998
   C. Education and Development from 1999 to 2000
   D. Human Resources from 1999 to 2000

8. During the five-year period, the annual budget of the Department of Human Resources was greater than the annual budget for the Department of Conservation and Environment in _____ of the years.

   A. none　　B. one　　C. two　　D. three

9. If the total City X budget increases at the same rate from 2001 to 2002 as it did from 2000 to 2001, the total City X budget for 2002 will be MOST NEARLY _____ million.

   A. $180   B. $200   C. $210   D. $215

10. The one of the following which is LEAST important in developing a budget for the next fiscal year for project maintenance is the

   A. adequacy of the current year's budget
   B. changes in workload that can be anticipated
   C. budget restrictions indicated in a memorandum covering budget preparations
   D. staff reassignments which are expected during the next fiscal year

11. The performance budget used by the department places MOST emphasis on

   A. building facilities   B. equipment costs
   C. personnel costs   D. services rendered

12. The LARGEST part of the expenditures of the department is for

   A. equipment   B. maintenance
   C. operating materials   D. personnel services

13. The department function which requires the GREATEST expenditure of funds is

   A. refuse collection   B. refuse disposal
   C. snow removal   D. street cleaning

14. A FIRST step in budget preparation is *usually*

   A. a realistic attempt to satisfy all unit requests
   B. forecasting the amount of various kinds of work to be done during the coming budget year
   C. an effort to increase work output
   D. appraising the quality of work done in the previous year

15. There are various types of budgets which are used to measure different government activities.
    The type of budget which *particularly* measures input of resource as compared with output of service is the _____ budget.

   A. capital   B. traditional   C. performance   D. program

16. The budget for a given cost during a given period was $100,000. The actual cost for the period was $90,000. Based upon these facts, one should say that the responsible manager has done a better than expected job in controlling the cost if the cost is

   A. variable and actual production equaled budgeted production
   B. a discretionary fixed cost and actual production equaled budgeted production
   C. variable and actual production was 90% of budgeted production
   D. variable and actual production was 80% of budgeted production

17. In most municipal budgeting systems involving capital and operating budgets, the leasing or renting of facilities is usually shown in

    A. the operating budget
    B. the capital budget
    C. a separate schedule
    D. either budget

17.____

18. New York City's budgeting procedure is unusual in that budget appropriations are considered in two parts, as follows: _____ budget and _____ budget.

    A. capital; income
    B. expense; income
    C. revenue; expense
    D. expense; capital

18.____

19. Budget planning is MOST useful when it achieves

    A. cost control
    B. forecast of receipts
    C. performance review
    D. personnel reduction

19.____

20. After a budget has been developed, it serves to

    A. assist the accounting department in posting expenditures
    B. measure the effectiveness of department managers
    C. provide a yardstick against which actual costs are measured
    D. provide the operating department with total expenditures to date

20.____

21. A budget is a plan whereby a goal is set for future operations. It affords a medium for comparing actual expenditures with planned expenditures.
    The one of the following which is the MOST accurate statement on the basis of this statement is that

    A. the budget serves as an accurate measure of past as well as future expenditures
    B. the budget presents an estimate of expenditures to be made in the future
    C. budget estimates should be based upon past budget requirements
    D. planned expenditures usually fall short of actual expenditures

21.____

22. If one attempts to list the advantages of the management-by-exception principle as it is used in connection with the budgeting process, several distinct advantages could be cited.
    Which of the following is NOT an advantage of this principle as it applies to the budgeting process? Management-by-exception

    A. saves time
    B. identifies critical problem areas
    C. focuses attention and concentrates effort
    D. escalates the frequency and importance of budget-related decisions

22.____

23. Of the following statements that relate to a budget, select the one that is MOST accurate.

    A. A budget is made up by an organization to plan its future activities.
    B. A budget specifies how much the organization to which it relates estimates it will spend over a certain period of time.
    C. A budget specifies in dollars and cents how much is spent in a particular time period.
    D. All plans dealing with money are budgets.

23.____

24. Of the following, the one which is NOT a contribution that a budget makes to organizational programming is that a budget

   A. enables a comparison of what actually happened with what was expected
   B. stresses the need to forecast specific goals and eliminates the need to focus on tasks needed to accomplish goals
   C. may illustrate duplication of effort between interdependent activities
   D. shows the relationship between various organizational segments

25. A line-item budget is a GOOD control budget because

   A. it clearly specifies how the items being purchased will be used
   B. expenditures can be shown primarily for contractual services
   C. it clearly specifies what the money is buying
   D. it clearly specifies the services to be provide

KEY (CORRECT ANSWERS)

1.	C	11.	D
2.	C	12.	D
3.	C	13.	A
4.	D	14.	B
5.	A	15.	C
6.	A	16.	A
7.	B	17.	A
8.	B	18.	D
9.	D	19.	A
10.	D	20.	C

21.	B
22.	D
23.	B
24.	B
25.	C

EXAMINATION SECTION
TEST 1

DIRECTIONS: Each question or incomplete statement is followed by several suggested answers or completions. Select the one that BEST answers the question or completes the statement. *PRINT THE LETTER OF THE CORRECT ANSWER IN THE SPACE AT THE RIGHT.*

1. In performing a systems study, the analyst may find it necessary to prepare an accurate record of working statistics from departmental forms, questionnaires, and information gleaned in interviews.
   Which one of the following statements dealing with the statistical part of the study is the MOST valid?

   A. The emphasis of every survey is data collection.
   B. Data should not be represented in narrative form.
   C. The statistical report should include the titles of personnel required for each processing task.
   D. In gathering facts, the objective of a systems study should be the primary consideration.

   1.____

2. The most direct method of obtaining information about activities in the area under study is by observation. There are several general rules for an analyst that are essential for observing and being accepted as an observer.
   The one of the following statements relating to this aspect of an analyst's responsibility that is most valid in the initial phase is that the analyst should NOT

   A. limit himself to observing only; he may criticize operations and methods
   B. prepare himself for what he is about to observe
   C. obtain permission of the department's management to actually perform some of the clerical tasks himself
   D. offer views of impending charges regarding new staff requirements, equipment, or procedures

   2.____

3. The active concern of the systems analyst is the study and documentation of what he observes as it exists. Before attempting the actual study and documentation, the analyst should comply with certain generally accepted procedures.
   Of the following, the step the analyst should *generally* take FIRST is to

   A. define the problem and prepare a statement of objectives
   B. confer with the project director concerning persons to be interviewed
   C. accumulate data from all available sources within the area under study
   D. meet with operations managers to enlist their cooperation

   3.____

4. During the course of any systems study, the analyst will have to gather some statistics if the operation model is to be realistic and meaningful.
   With respect to the statistical report part of the study, it is MOST valid to say that

   A. it must follow a standard format since there should be no variation from one study to the next
   B. the primary factor to be considered is the volume of work in the departmental unit at each stage of completion
   C. only variations that occur during peak and slow periods should be recorded
   D. unless deadlines in the departmental units studied by the analyst occur constantly, they should not be taken into account

   4.____

5. In systems analysis, the interview is one of the analyst's major sources of information. In conducting an interview, he should strive for immediate rapport with the operations manager or department head with whom he deals.
With respect to his responsibility in this area, it is considered LEAST appropriate for the analyst to

   A. explain the full background of the study and the scope of the investigation
   B. emphasize the importance of achieving the stated objectives and review the plan of the project
   C. assume that the attitudes of the workers are less important than those of the executives
   D. request the manager's assistance in the form of questions, suggestions, and general cooperation

6. Large, complex endeavors often take a long time to implement. The following statements relate to long lead times imposed by large-scale endeavors.
Select the one usually considered to be LEAST valid.

   A. Where there are external sponsors who provide funds or political support, they should be provided with some demonstration of what is being accomplished.
   B. Long lead times simplify planning and diminish the threat of obsolescence by assuring that objectives will be updated by the time the project is nearing completion.
   C. During the period when no tangible results are forthcoming, techniques must be found to assess progress.
   D. Employees, particularly scientific personnel, should feel a sense of accomplishment or they may shy away from research which involves long-term commitments.

7. In traditional management theory, administrators are expected to collect and weigh facts and probabilities, make an optimal decision and see that it is carried out.
In the management of large-scale development projects, such a clear sequence of action is *generally* NOT possible because of

   A. their limited duration
   B. the static and fixed balance of power among interest groups
   C. continuous suppression of new facts
   D. constantly changing constraints and pressures

Questions 8-10.

DIRECTIONS: One of the most valuable parts of the systems package is the systems flowchart, a technique that aids understanding of the work flow. A flowchart should depict all the intricacies of the work flow from start to finish in order to give the onlooker a solid picture at a glance. The table below contains symbols used by the analyst in flowcharting. In answering Questions 8 through 10, refer to the following figures.

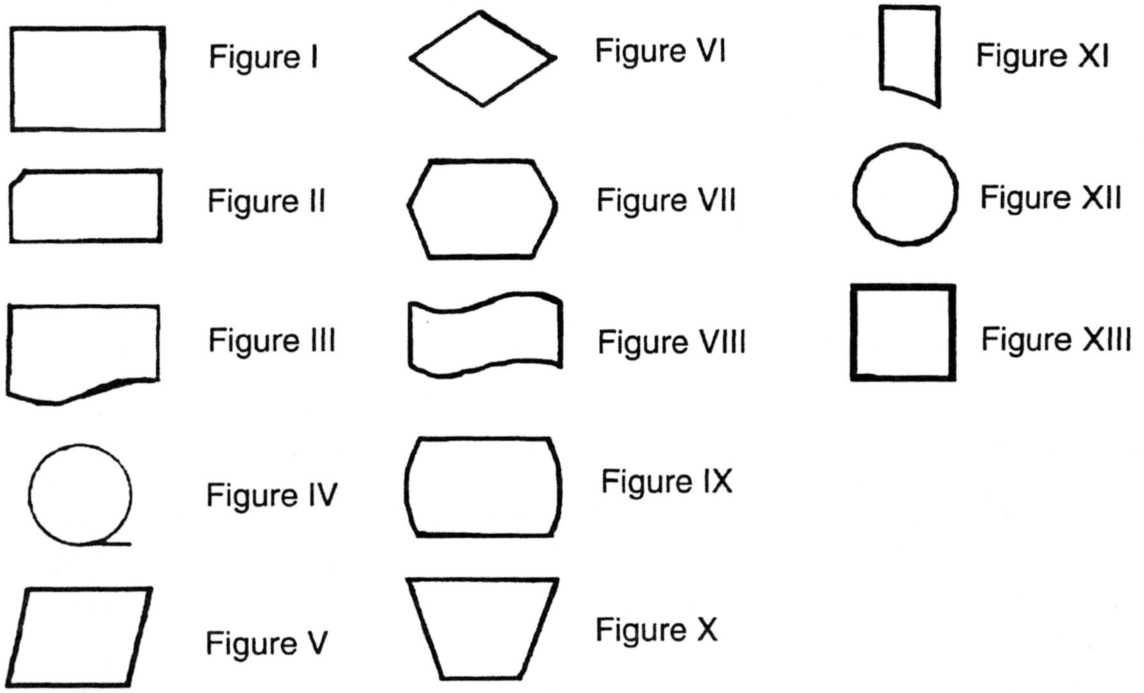

Figure I
Figure II
Figure III
Figure IV
Figure V
Figure VI
Figure VII
Figure VIII
Figure IX
Figure X
Figure XI
Figure XII
Figure XIII

8. The symbol that is COMMONLY used to specify clerical procedures which are not essential to the main processing function and yet are part of the overall procedure is represented by Figure

   A. III   B. VI   C. XII   D. XIII

9. An analyst wishes to designate the following activities:
   File reports; Calculate average; Attach labels.
   The MOST APPROPRIATE symbol to use is represented by Figure

   A. V   B. VI   C. VII   D. II

10. A *Report, Journal,* or *Record* should be represented by Figure

    A. I   B. III   C. IX   D. XI

Question 11.

DIRECTIONS: The following figures are often used in program and systems flowcharting.

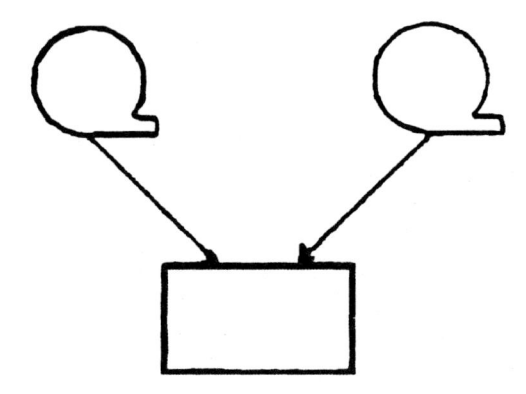

11. The above figures represent

   A. two magnetic tapes incorporated in a processing function
   B. two report papers to be put in a cabinet in chronological order
   C. two transmittal tapes—both externally generated—routed to a vault
   D. an auxiliary operation involving two sequential decisions

12. When research and analysis of government programs, e.g., pest control, drug rehabilitation, etc., is sponsored and conducted within a government unit, the scope of the analysis should *generally* be _____ the scope of the authority of the manager to whom the analyst is responsible.

   A. less than
   B. less than or equal to
   C. greater than or equal to
   D. greater than

13. In recent years, there has been an increasing emphasis on outputs–the goods and services that a program produces. This emphasis on outputs imposes an information requirement. The one of the following which would MOST likely NOT be considered output information in a hospital or health care program is the

   A. number of patients cared for
   B. number of days patients were hospitalized
   C. budgeted monies for hospital beds
   D. quality of the service

14. Which one of the following statements pertaining to management information systems is generally considered to be LEAST valid?

   A. A management information system is a network of related subsystems developed according to an integrated scheme for evaluating the activities of an agency.
   B. A management information system specifies the content and format, the preparation and integration of information for all various functions within an agency that will best satisfy needs at various levels of management.
   C. To operate a successful management information system, an agency will require a complex electronic computer installation.
   D. The five elements which compose a management information system are: data input, files, data processing, procedures, and data output.

15. In the field of records management, electronic equipment is being used to handle office paperwork or data processing. With respect to such use, of the following, it is MOST valid to say that

    A. electronic equipment is not making great strides in the achievement of speed and economy in office paperwork
    B. electronic equipment accelerates the rate at which office paperwork is completed
    C. paperwork problems can be completely solved through mechanization
    D. introduction of electronic data processing equipment cuts down on the paper consumed in office processes

16. A reports control program evaluates the reporting requirements of top management so that reviews can be made of the existing reporting system to determine its adequacy. Of the following statements pertaining to reports control, which is the MOST likely to be characteristic of such a program?

    A. Only the exception will be reported
    B. Preparation of daily reports will be promoted
    C. Executives will not delegate responsibility for preparing reports
    D. Normal conditions are reported

17. Which of the following types of work measurement techniques requires the HIGHEST degree of training and skill of technicians and supervisors and is MOST likely to involve the HIGHEST original cost?

    A. Work sampling
    B. Predetermined time standards
    C. The time study (stopwatch timing)
    D. Employee reporting

18. Which of the following types of work measurement techniques *generally* requires the LEAST amount of time to measure and establish standards?

    A. Work sampling
    B. Predetermined time standards
    C. The time study (stopwatch timing)
    D. Employee reporting

19. Assume that you, as an analyst, have been assigned to formally organize small work groups within a city department to perform a special project. After studying the project, you find you must choose between two possible approaches–either task teams or highly functionalized groups.
    What would be one of the advantages of choosing the task-team approach over the highly functionalized organization?

    A. Detailed, centralized planning would be encouraged.
    B. Indifference to city goals and restrictions on output would be lessened.
    C. Work would be divided into very specialized areas.
    D. Superiors would be primarily concerned with seeing that subordinates do not deviate from the project.

20. In systems theory, there is a *what-if* method of treating uncertainty that explores the effect on the alternatives of environmental change. This method is generally referred to as _____ analysis.

   A. sensitivity
   B. contingency
   C. a fortiori
   D. systems

KEY (CORRECT ANSWERS)

1.	D	11.	A
2.	D	12.	B
3.	A	13.	C
4.	B	14.	C
5.	C	15.	B
6.	B	16.	A
7.	D	17.	B
8.	D	18.	A
9.	A	19.	B
10.	B	20.	B

TEST 2

DIRECTIONS: Each question or incomplete statement is followed by several suggested answers or completions. Select the one that BEST answers the question or completes the statement. *PRINT THE LETTER OF THE CORRECT ANSWER IN THE SPACE AT THE RIGHT.*

1. Which of the following systems exists at the strategic level of an organization? 1.____

    A. Decision support system (DSS)
    B. Executive support system (ESS)
    C. Knowledge work system (KWS)
    D. Management information system (MIS)

2. The functions of knowledge workers in an organization generally include each of the following EXCEPT 2.____

    A. updating knowledge
    B. managing documentation of knowledge
    C. serving as internal consultants
    D. acting as change agents

3. Which of the following is not a management benefit associated with end-user development of information systems? 3.____

    A. Reduced application backlog
    B. Increased user satisfaction
    C. Simplified testing and documentation procedures
    D. Improved requirements determination

4. Assume that an analyst is preparing an analysis of a departmental program. His investigation leads him to a potential problem relating to the program. The analyst thinks the potential problem is so serious that he cannot rely on preventive actions to remove the cause or significantly reduce the probability of its occurrence.
Of the following, the MOST appropriate way for the analyst to promptly handle this serious matter described above would be to 4.____

    A. apply systematic afterthought to the achievement of objectives by analysis of the problem
    B. compare actual performance with the expected standard of performance
    C. prepare contingency actions to be adopted immediately if the problem does occur
    D. identify, locate, and describe the deviation from the standard

5. Assume that an analyst is directed to investigate a problem relating to organizational behavior in his agency and to prepare a report thereon. After reviewing the preliminary draft, his superior cautions him to overcome his tendency to misuse and overgeneralize his interpretation of existing knowledge.
Which one of the following statements appearing in the draft is MOST *usually* considered to be a common distortion of behavioral science knowledge? 5.____

    A. Pay—even incentive pay—isn't very important anymore.
    B. There are nonrational aspects to people's behavior.
    C. The informal system exerts much control over organizational participants.
    D. Employees have many motives.

Questions 6-10.

DIRECTIONS: Each of Questions 6 through 10 consists of a statement which contains one word that is incorrectly used because it is not in keeping with the meaning that the quotation is evidently intended to convey. Determine which word is incorrectly used. Then select from the words lettered A, B, C, or D the word which, when substituted for the incorrectly used word, would BEST help to convey the meaning of the statement.

6. While the utilization of cost-benefit analysis in decision-making processes should be encouraged, it must be well understood that there are many limitations on the constraints of the analysis. One must be cautioned against using cost-benefit procedures automatically and blindly. Still, society will almost certainly be better off with the application of cost-benefit methods than it would be without them. As some authorities aptly point out, an important advantage of a cost-benefit study is that it forces those responsible to quantify costs and benefits as far as possible rather than rest content with vague qualitative judgments or personal hunches. Also, such an analysis has the very valuable by-product of causing questions to be asked which would otherwise not have been raised. Finally, even if cost-benefit analysis cannot give the right answer, it can sometimes play the purely negative role of screening projects and rejecting those answers which are obviously less promising.

A. precise
C. applicability
B. externally
D. unresponsiveness

7. The programming method used by the government should attempt to assess the costs and benefits of individual projects, in comparison with private and other public alternatives. The program, then, consists of the most meritorious projects that the budget will design. Meritorious projects excluded from the budget provide arguments for increasing its size. There are difficulties inherent in the specific project approach. The attempt is to apply profit criteria in public projects analogous to those used in evaluating private projects. This involves comparison of monetary values of present and future costs and benefits. But, in many important cases, such as highways, parkways, and bridges, the product of the government's investment does not directly enter the market economy. Consequently, evaluation requires imputation of market values. For example, the returns on a bridge have been estimated by attempting to value the time saved by users. Such measurements necessarily contain a strong, element of artificiality.

A. annulled   B. expedient   C. accommodate   D. marginally

8. Consider the problem of budgeting for activities designed to alleviate poverty and rooted unemployment. Are skill retraining efforts better or worse investments than public works? Are they better or worse than subsidies or other special incentives to attract new industry? Or, at an even more fundamental level, is a dollar invested in an attempt to rehabilitate a mature, technologically displaced, educationally handicapped, unemployed man a better commitment than a comparable dollar invested in supporting the educational and technical preparation of his son for employment in a different line of work? The questions may look unreasonable, even unanswerable. But the fact is that they are implicitly answered in any budget decision in the defined problem area. The only subordinate issue is whether the answer rests on intuition and guess, or on a budget system that presents relevant information so organized as to contribute to rational analysis, planning, and decision-making.

A. incomplete
C. significant
B. relevant
D. speculate

9. Choices among health programs, on the basis of cost-benefit analysis, raise another set of ethical problems. Measuring discounted lifetime earnings does not reveal the value of alleviating pain and suffering; some diseases have a high death rate, others are debilitating, others are merely uncomfortable. In general, choices among health and education programs that are predicated on discounted lifetime earnings will structure the choice against those who have low earnings, those whose earnings will materialize only at some future point in time, or those whose participation in the labor force is limited. It may be an appropriate economic policy to reduce expenditures in areas that maximize the future level of national income. But the maximization of social welfare may dictate attention to considerations, such as equality of opportunity, that transcend the limitations of values defined in such narrow terms.

    A. concentrate   B. divergent   C. enforcing   D. favorably

9._____

10. Without defined and time-phased objectives, it is difficult to be critical of administrative performance. To level a charge of waste or malperformance at the managers of a public program is, of course, one of the more popular pastimes of any administration's loyal opposition. But it is a rare experience to find such a charge documented by the kind of precise cost-effectiveness measures that are the common test of the quality of management performance in a well-run organization. Those who take a professional view of management responsibility are even more concerned about the acceptance of the kind of information that would enable a manager to assess the progress and quality of his own performance and, as appropriate, to initiate corrective action before outside criticism can even start.

    A. absence   B. rebut   C. withdraw   D. impeded

10._____

11. What is the relationship between the cost of inputs and the value of outputs when the results obtained from a program can be measured in money? _____ ratio.

    A. Value administrative-cost   B. Break-even point
    C. Variable-direct   D. Cost-benefit

11._____

12. Some writers in the field of public expenditure have noted a disturbing tendency inherent in cost-benefit analysis. Which one of the following statements MOST accurately expresses their concern over the use of cost-benefit analysis? It

    A. encourages the attachment of monetary values to intangibles
    B. has a built-in neglect of measurable outcomes while emphasizing the nonmeasurable
    C. consciously exaggerates social values and overstates political values
    D. encourages emphasis of those costs and benefits that cannot be measured rather than those that can

12._____

13. In private industry, budgetary control begins logically with an estimate of sales and the income therefrom.
Of the following, the term used in government which is MOST analogous to that of sales in private industry is

    A. borrowed funds   B. the amount appropriated
    C. general overhead   D. surplus funds

13._____

14. When constructing graphs of causally related variables, how should the variables be placed to conform to conventional use?

   A. The independent variable should be placed on the vertical axis and the dependent variable on the horizontal axis.
   B. The dependent variable should be placed on the vertical axis and the independent variable on the horizontal axis.
   C. Independent variables should be placed on both axes.
   D. Dependent variables should be placed on both axes.

Questions 15–18.

DIRECTIONS: Answer Questions 15 through 18 on the basis of the following graph describing the output of computer operators.

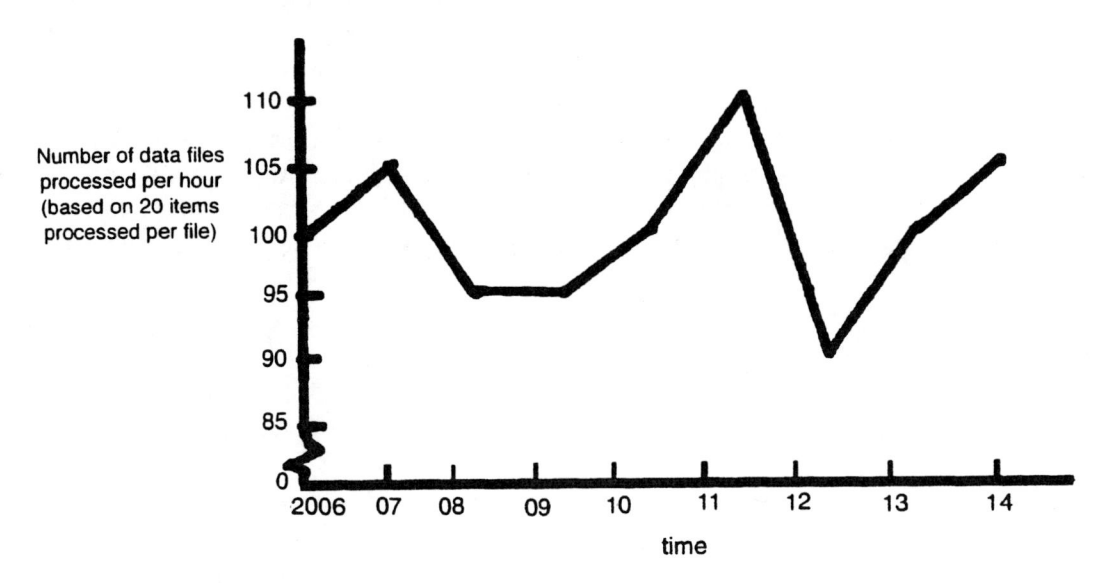

15. Of the following, during what four-year period did the AVERAGE OUTPUT of computer operators *fall below* 100 data files per hour?

   A. 2007-10   B. 2008-11   C. 2010-13   D. 2011-14

16. The AVERAGE PERCENTAGE CHANGE in output over the previous year's output for the years 2009 to 2012 is MOST NEARLY

   A. 2   B. 0   C. -5   D. -7

17. The DIFFERENCE between the actual output for 2012 and the projected figure based upon the average increase from 2006 to 2011 is MOST NEARLY

   A. 18   B. 20   C. 22   D. 24

18. Assume that after constructing the above graph, you, an analyst, discovered that the average number of items processed per file in 2012 was 25 (instead of 20) because of the complex nature of the work performed during that period.
The AVERAGE OUTPUT in files per hour for the period 2010 to 2013, expressed in terms of 20 items per file, would then be APPROXIMATELY

    A. 95 B. 100 C. 105 D. 110

18._____

19. Assume that Unit S's production fluctuated substantially from one year to another. In 2009, Unit S's production was 100% greater than in 2008; in 2010, it was 25% less than in 2009; and in 2011, it was 10% greater than in 2010. On the basis of this information, it is CORRECT to conclude that Unit S's production in 2011 exceeded its production in 2008 by

    A. 50% B. 65% C. 75% D. 90%

19._____

20. Statistical sampling is often used in administrative operations primarily because it enables

    A. administrators to make staff selections
    B. decisions to be made based on mathematical and scientific fact
    C. courses of action to be determined by electronic data processing or computer programs
    D. useful predictions to be made from relatively small samples

20._____

KEY (CORRECT ANSWERS)

1. B
2. B
3. C
4. C
5. A

6. C
7. C
8. C
9. A
10. A

11. D
12. A
13. B
14. B
15. A

16. B
17. C
18. C
19. B
20. D

EXAMINATION SECTION
TEST 1

DIRECTIONS: Each question or incomplete statement is followed by several suggested answers or completions. Select the one that BEST answers the question or completes the statement. *PRINT THE LETTER OF THE CORRECT ANSWER IN THE SPACE AT THE RIGHT.*

1. Of the following factors, which one is LEAST important in determining the size of staff needed in conducting an organization survey?
   The

   A. effectiveness of the personnel in supplying data for the study
   B. extent of report writing anticipated
   C. number of field locations and headquarters staff units to be covered
   D. number of individuals to be interviewed as part of fact finding

   1.____

2. In planning a systems survey, which one of the following is MOST important in carrying out an effective survey after the purpose and scope of the survey has been determined?
   The

   A. format of the survey report
   B. methods and techniques to be employed
   C. personality problems which may materialize
   D. exact starting and completion dates

   2.____

3. Which of the following is the BEST way of organizing a final report?

   A. Begin and end the report with a summary of conclusions showing how conclusions were changed as a result of findings and recommendations
   B. Begin the report with an overall summary and then place findings and recommendations in several sections
   C. Intertwine findings and conclusions in such a manner as to make the report readable and interesting
   D. Place the findings and recommendations in separate sections avoiding conclusions to the maximum extent possible

   3.____

4. Which of the following disadvantages is the MOST serious in making reports verbally rather than in writing?

   A. An effective analyst may not be a good public speaker.
   B. Verbal reports are conveniently forgotten.
   C. It may not generate actions and follow-through by recipients.
   D. There is a lack of permanent record to which one may later refer.

   4.____

5. Following a management survey, which of the following represents the MOST serious pitfall which may be made in recommending improvements?

   A. Failure to convince people of the benefits to be derived from the recommendations
   B. Failure to freely discuss recommendations with those who must live with them
   C. Tendency of the survey team to put their own personalities into the report
   D. Tendency to deal in personalities instead of dealing with objectives and sound management practices

   5.____

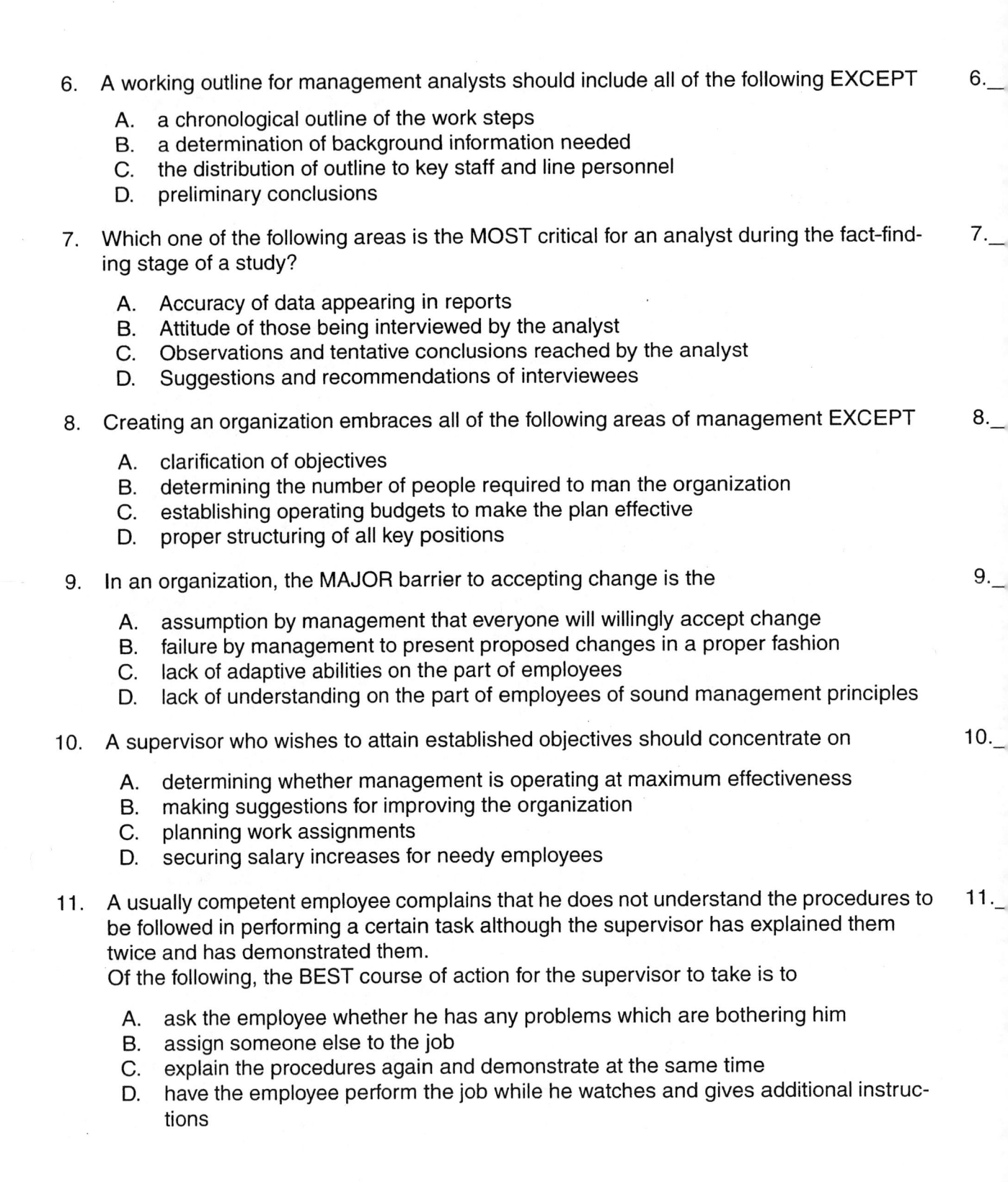

6. A working outline for management analysts should include all of the following EXCEPT

    A. a chronological outline of the work steps
    B. a determination of background information needed
    C. the distribution of outline to key staff and line personnel
    D. preliminary conclusions

7. Which one of the following areas is the MOST critical for an analyst during the fact-finding stage of a study?

    A. Accuracy of data appearing in reports
    B. Attitude of those being interviewed by the analyst
    C. Observations and tentative conclusions reached by the analyst
    D. Suggestions and recommendations of interviewees

8. Creating an organization embraces all of the following areas of management EXCEPT

    A. clarification of objectives
    B. determining the number of people required to man the organization
    C. establishing operating budgets to make the plan effective
    D. proper structuring of all key positions

9. In an organization, the MAJOR barrier to accepting change is the

    A. assumption by management that everyone will willingly accept change
    B. failure by management to present proposed changes in a proper fashion
    C. lack of adaptive abilities on the part of employees
    D. lack of understanding on the part of employees of sound management principles

10. A supervisor who wishes to attain established objectives should concentrate on

    A. determining whether management is operating at maximum effectiveness
    B. making suggestions for improving the organization
    C. planning work assignments
    D. securing salary increases for needy employees

11. A usually competent employee complains that he does not understand the procedures to be followed in performing a certain task although the supervisor has explained them twice and has demonstrated them.
    Of the following, the BEST course of action for the supervisor to take is to

    A. ask the employee whether he has any problems which are bothering him
    B. assign someone else to the job
    C. explain the procedures again and demonstrate at the same time
    D. have the employee perform the job while he watches and gives additional instructions

12. GENERALLY, in order to be completely qualified as a supervisor, a person   12.____

    A. should be able to perform exceptionally well at least one of the jobs he supervises and have some knowledge of the others
    B. must have an intimate working knowledge of all facets of the jobs which he supervises
    C. should know the basic principles and procedures of the jobs he supervises
    D. need know little or nothing of the jobs which he supervises as long as he knows the principles of supervision

13. Which of the following contributes MOST to the problem of waste and inefficiency in offices?   13.____

    A. Cost control is a budget function primarily.
    B. Most organizations do not have soundly conceived budgets.
    C. Procedures improvement staffs have not as yet gained acceptance among white collar workers.
    D. Supervisors generally are uninterested in making improvements.

14. Which of the following contributes MOST to the great number of duplicate reports and double-checking procedures frequently found in offices?   14.____
    The

    A. desire for protection
    B. desire to improve problem solving
    C. intent to *manage by exception*
    D. need for budget data

15. Which one of the following BEST identifies the narrow technician as compared with the broad-gauged analyst?   15.____
    He

    A. analyzes the activities of an agency
    B. attempts to form sound relationships with departmental personnel
    C. focuses attention on forms design and appearance
    D. follows work flow from one bureau to another by charting operational steps

16. The percentage of budget funds allocated to fixed overhead costs can be MOST effectively reduced by   16.____

    A. a soundly conceived *promotion from within* policy
    B. increasing the amount of work performed
    C. relocating to areas closer to the center of cities
    D. tightening the *fixed cost* portion of the budget

17. The term *span of control* USUALLY refers to   17.____

    A. individuals reporting to a common supervisor
    B. individuals with whom one individual has contact in the course of performing his assigned duties
    C. levels of supervision in an organization
    D. percentage of time in an organization devoted to supervisory duties

18. For an analyst, which of the following is generally LEAST important in conducting a management survey?

   A. Ability of employees to understand goals of the survey
   B. Attitude of supervisors of employees
   C. Availability of employees for interviews
   D. Cooperation of employees

19. Of the following, morale in an agency is generally MOST significantly affected by

   A. agency policies and procedures
   B. agency recognition of executives supporting agency goals
   C. the extent to which an agency meets its announced goals
   D. the number of management surveys conducted in an agency

20. Which of the following BEST describes the principle of *management by exception?*

   A. Allocating executive time and effort in direct relation to the dollar values of the budget
   B. Decentralizing management and dealing primarily with problem areas
   C. Measuring only direct costs
   D. Setting goals and objectives and managing only these

21. A WEAKNESS of many budgetary systems today is that they

   A. are subjectively determined by those most directly involved
   B. focus on management weakness rather than management strength
   C. only show variable costs
   D. show in detail why losses are occurring

22. Standards on which budgets are developed should be based PRIMARILY on

   A. a general consensus
   B. agency wishes
   C. analytical studies
   D. historical performance

23. The income, cost, and expense goals making up a budget are aimed at achieving a predetermined objective but do not necessarily measure the lowest possible costs. This is PRIMARILY so because

   A. budget committees are accounting-oriented and are not sympathetic with the supervisor's personnel problems
   B. budget committees fail to recognize the difference between direct and indirect costs
   C. the level of expenditures provided for in a budget by budget committees is frequently an arbitrary rather than a scientifically determined amount
   D. budget committees spend considerable time evaluating data to the point that the material gathered is not representative or current

24. Linear programming has all of the following characteristics EXCEPT: It 24.____
    A. is concerned with an optimum position in relation to some objective
    B. involves the selection among alternatives or the appropriate combination of alternatives
    C. not only requires that variables be qualitative but also rests on the assumption that the relations among the variables are minimized
    D. takes into account constraints or limits within which the decision is to be reached

25. In the PERT planning system, the time in which a non-critical task can slip schedule without holding up a project is USUALLY called 25.____
    A. constraint   B. duration time
    C. dead time   D. float or slack

26. The Produc-trol board and Schedugraphs are commercial variations of the _____ chart. 26.____
    A. flow   B. Gantt
    C. layout   D. multiple activity

27. The item which cannot be analyzed by such schematic techniques as the frequency polygon and the histogram is the 27.____
    A. age of accounts receivable
    B. morale and cohesiveness of work groups
    C. number of accidents in a plant
    D. wage pattern

28. An essential employee benefit of work measurement which FREQUENTLY is the key to the successful implementation of such a program is 28.____
    A. equitable work distribution
    B. facilitation of the development of budgets
    C. measurement and control of office productivity
    D. prevention of unfair work distribution

29. An organizational arrangement whereby different employees perform different work steps upon the same work items at the same time is called the _____ method. 29.____
    A. functional
    B. homogenous
    C. parallel or linear arrangement
    D. unit assembly

30. Frequently, opposition to a management survey stems from an executive's feeling that he might be considered responsible for the unsatisfactory conditions that the project is aimed at correcting. 30.____
    To overcome this type of opposition, the analyst should GENERALLY
    A. avoid the issue altogether
    B. face the situation *head on* and, if the executive is responsible, tell him so
    C. offer a reasonable explanation for those conditions early enough in the discussion to forestall any implication of criticism
    D. place the blame for the unsatisfactory conditions at the lowest level in the organization to avoid incriminating the boss

31. Which of the following situations is LEAST likely to require a management survey?

    A. Changes in policy
    B. Management requests for additional manpower
    C. Legislation mandating changes in operating procedures
    D. Significantly lower costs than anticipated

32. The efficiency of a procedure is often influenced by the practices or performance of departments that play no direct part in carrying it out.
    In view of this, the analyst must

    A. disregard the practices or performance of departments that play no direct part in the procedure
    B. do the very best job within the department studied to compensate for the outside problems
    C. ask for assistance in solving the problems created by this situation
    D. study and evaluate the external factors to the extent that they bear on the problem

33. Which one of the following is NOT a key step in staff delegation and development?

    A. Evaluation of the completed job
    B. Preparation of a subordinate to accept additional duties
    C. Review of daily progress
    D. Selection of a suitable job to be delegated

34. Which one of the following is NOT an essential characteristic of effective delegation?

    A. In delegating, the supervisor is no longer responsible.
    B. The individual to whom authority is delegated must be accountable for fulfillment of the task.
    C. The individual to whom authority is delegated must clearly understand this authority.
    D. The individual to whom authority is delegated must get honest recognition for a job well done.

35. Whenever a manager must determine how long an operation should take, he is involved with the problem of setting a time standard.
    To PROPERLY set time standards, the manager must distinguish between

    A. estimation processes and evaluation processes
    B. performance of the slowest employee and performance of the fastest employee
    C. stop watch study and work sampling
    D. synthetic and arbitrary systems

36. Assuming a report is needed, which approach USUALLY facilitates implementation?
    A

    A. draft report submitted to key people for review, discussion, modification, and then resubmission in final form
    B. report in final form which sets forth alternate recommended solutions
    C. report which sets forth the problems and the recommended solution in conformance with the desires of those most directly involved
    D. visual presentation with minimal report writing

37. Of the following elements, which is the LEAST important in writing a survey report? 37.____
A

   A. definite course of action to be followed
   B. listing of benefits to be gained through implementation
   C. review of opinions as differentiated from facts
   D. summary of conclusions

38. Physical appearance and accuracy are important features in gaining acceptance to rec- 38.____
ommendations. Which one of the following might be OVERLOOKED in preparing a
report which is to have wide distribution?

   A. A comprehensive index
   B. An attractive binder
   C. Proper spacing and page layout
   D. Charts and tables

39. The elimination of meaningless reports, although reducing the total information output, 39.____
IMPROVES the management process by

   A. determining the number of employees required to perform the work assigned
   B. identifying the difference between direct and indirect costs
   C. increasing the effectiveness of executives
   D. limiting the budget to variable costs

40. In determining whether or not to use a computerized system as opposed to a manual 40.____
system, which of the following would normally have the MOST influence on the decision?
The

   A. availability of analysts and programmers to design and install the system
   B. availability of computer time
   C. basic premise that all computerized systems are superior to manual systems
   D. volume and complexity of transactions required

KEY (CORRECT ANSWERS)

1.	A	11.	D	21.	A	31.	D
2.	B	12.	C	22.	C	32.	D
3.	B	13.	C	23.	C	33.	C
4.	D	14.	A	24.	C	34.	A
5.	D	15.	C	25.	D	35.	A
6.	D	16.	B	26.	B	36.	A
7.	C	17.	A	27.	B	37.	C
8.	C	18.	A	28.	A	38.	B
9.	B	19.	A	29.	D	39.	C
10.	C	20.	B	30.	C	40.	D

TEST 2

DIRECTIONS: Each question or incomplete statement is followed by several suggested answers or completions. Select the one that BEST answers the question or completes the statement. *PRINT THE LETTER OF THE CORRECT ANSWER IN THE SPACE AT THE RIGHT.*

1. The one of the following that is NOT normally involved in the development of a management information system is

    A. determination of the best method of preparing and presenting the required information
    B. determination of line and staff relationships within the various units of the organizational structure
    C. determination of what specific information is needed for decision-making and control
    D. identification of the critical aspects of the business, i.e., the end results and other elements of performance which need to be planned and controlled

2. The long-term growth in size and complexity of both business and government has increased management's dependence on more formal written summaries of operating results in place of the informal, on-the-spot observations and judgments of smaller organizations.
   In addition, there is a growing management need to

    A. increase the complexity of those phases of the management process which have previously been simplified
    B. increase the speed and accuracy of giant computers
    C. measure the effectiveness of managerial performance
    D. reduce alcoholism by greatly limiting personal contacts between the various levels of management within the organization

3. Of the following, it is MOST essential that a management information system provide information needed for

    A. determining computer time requirements
    B. developing new office layouts
    C. drawing new organization charts
    D. planning and measuring results

4. The PRIMARY purpose of control reports is to

    A. compare actual performance with planned results
    B. determine staffing requirements
    C. determine the work flow
    D. develop a new budget

5. Which one of the following has the GREATEST negative impact on communications in a large organization?

    A. Delays in formulating variable policies relating to communications
    B. Failure to conduct comprehensive courses in communications skills
    C. Failure to get information to those who need it
    D. Unclear organizational objectives

6. Major random access devices for a computer include all of the following EXCEPT

   A. magnetic disks
   B. magnetic drums
   C. magnetic plastic tapes
   D. mass storage devices

7. The type of computer configuration in which the data are processed at one time after they have been made a matter of record is known as

   A. batching   B. in line   C. off line   D. real time

8. A computer configuration system in which the input or output equipment is directly connected and operates under control of the computer is known as

   A. off line
   B. on line
   C. random access
   D. real time

9. The PRINCIPAL distinction between a digital computer and an analogue computer is one

   A. counts while the other measures electrical current
   B. is an IBM monopoly while the other is an Apple monopoly
   C. is used primarily in manufacturing while the other is used primarily for billing
   D. system is based on cards while the other is based on discs

10. ALL digital computers are generally considered to consist of four major sections. The one of the following which is NOT a major section is

    A. buffer
    B. control
    C. processing
    D. storage

11. Of the following, administrative control is PRIMARILY dependent upon

    A. adequate information
    B. a widespread spy network
    C. strict supervisors
    D. strong sanctions

12. Meticulous care must be exercised in writing the methodology section of the research report so that

    A. another investigator will achieve the same results if he repeats the study
    B. the interpretation of the findings cannot be challenged
    C. the report will be well balanced
    D. the rules of scientific logic are clearly indicated

13. When data are grouped into a frequency distribution, the *true mode* by definition is the _____ in the distribution

    A. 50% point
    B. largest single range
    C. point of greatest concentration
    D. smallest single range

14. Which of the following is LEAST likely to be a potential benefit arising from the use of electronic data processing systems?

    A. Analysis of more data and analysis of data in greater depth than manual systems
    B. Increased speed and accuracy in information processing
    C. Lower capital expenditures for office equipment
    D. Reduced personnel costs in tabulating and reporting functions

15. A *grapevine* is BEST defined as

    A. a harmful method of communication
    B. a system of communication operative below the executive level
    C. an informal communication system of no functional importance to an organization
    D. the internal and non-systematic channel of communication within an organization

16. Of the following, the symbol shown at the right, as used in a systems flow chart, means

    A. document
    B. manual operation
    C. planning
    D. process

17. The mean age of a sample group drawn from population X is 37.5 years and the standard error of the mean is 5.9. There is a 99% probability that the computed mean age of other samples drawn from population X would fall within the range of

    A. 31.6 – 43.4
    B. 26.0 – 52.7
    C. 22.2 – 52.8
    D. 20.0 – 55.0

18. After a budget has been developed, it serves to

    A. assist the accounting department in posting expenditures
    B. measure the effectiveness of department managers
    C. provide a yardstick against which actual costs are measured
    D. provide the operating department with total expenditures to date

19. In order to insure that work measurement or time study results will be consistent from one study to another, and reflect a fair day's work, the performance of the clerks must be rated or levelled.
    Which of the following is LEAST likely to be included among the techniques for determining the performance level or for rating the study?

    A. Predetermined times
    B. Published rating tables
    C. Sampling studies
    D. Training films

20. Of the following, the BEST practice to follow when training a new employee is to

    A. encourage him to feel free to ask questions at any time
    B. immediately demonstrate how fast his job can be done so he will know what is expected of him
    C. let him watch other employees for a week or two
    D. point out mistakes after completion so he will learn by experience

21. An IMPORTANT aspect to keep in mind during the decision-making process is that 21.____

    A. all possible alternatives for attaining goals should be sought out and considered
    B. considering various alternatives only leads to confusion
    C. once a decision has been made, it cannot be retracted
    D. there is only one correct method to reach any goal

22. Implementation of accountability REQUIRES 22.____

    A. a leader who will not hesitate to take punitive action
    B. an established system of communication from the bottom to the top
    C. explicit directives from leaders
    D. too much expense to justify it

23. Of the following, the MAJOR difference between systems and procedures analysis and work simplification is: 23.____

    A. The former complicates organizational routine and the latter simplifies it
    B. The former is objective and the latter is subjective
    C. The former generally utilizes expert advice and the latter is a *do-it-yourself* improvement by supervisors and workers
    D. There is no difference other than in name

24. Systems development is concerned with providing 24.____

    A. a specific set of work procedures
    B. an overall framework to describe general relationships
    C. definitions of particular organizational functions
    D. organizational symbolism

25. Organizational systems and procedures should be 25.____

    A. developed as problems arise as no design can anticipate adequately the requirements of an organization
    B. developed jointly by experts in systems and procedures and the people who are responsible for implementing them
    C. developed solely by experts in systems and procedures
    D. eliminated whenever possible to save unnecessary expense

26. The CHIEF danger of a decentralized control system is that 26.____

    A. excessive reports and communications will be generated
    B. problem areas may not be detected readily
    C. the expense will become prohibitive
    D. this will result in too many *chiefs*

27. Of the following, management guides and controls clerical work PRINCIPALLY through

    A. close supervision and constant checking of personnel
    B. spot checking of clerical procedures
    C. strong sanctions for clerical supervisors
    D. the use of printed forms

28. Which of the following is MOST important before conducting fact-finding interviews?

    A. Becoming acquainted with all personnel to be interviewed
    B. Explaining the techniques you plan to use
    C. Explaining to the operating officials the purpose and scope of the study
    D. Orientation of the physical layout

29. Of the following, the one that is NOT essential in carrying out a comprehensive work improvement program is

    A. standards of performance
    B. supervisory training
    C. work count/task list
    D. work distribution chart

30. Which of the following control techniques is MOST useful on large, complex systems projects?

    A. A general work plan
    B. Gantt chart
    C. Monthly progress report
    D. PERT chart

31. The action which is MOST effective in gaining acceptance of a study by the agency which is being studied is

    A. a directive from the agency head to install a study based on recommendations included in a report
    B. a lecture-type presentation following approval of the procedures
    C. a written procedure in narrative form covering the proposed system with visual presentations and discussions
    D. procedural charts showing the *before* situation, forms, steps, etc. to the employees affected

32. Which of the following is NOT an advantage in the use of oral instructions as compared with written instructions? Oral instruction(s)

    A. can easily be changed
    B. is superior in transmitting complex directives
    C. facilitate exchange of information between a superior and his subordinate
    D. with discussions make it easier to ascertain understanding

33. Which organization principle is MOST closely related to procedural analysis and improvement?

    A. Duplication, overlapping, and conflict should be eliminated.
    B. Managerial authority should be clearly defined.
    C. The objectives of the organization should be clearly defined.
    D. Top management should be freed of burdensome detail.

34. Which one of the following is the MAJOR objective of operational audits? 34._____

   A. Detecting fraud
   B. Determining organization problems
   C. Determining the number of personnel needed
   D. Recommending opportunities for improving operating and management practices

35. Of the following, the formalization of organization structure is BEST achieved by 35._____

   A. a narrative description of the plan of organization
   B. functional charts
   C. job descriptions together with organization charts
   D. multi-flow charts

36. Budget planning is MOST useful when it achieves 36._____

   A. cost control
   B. forecast of receipts
   C. performance review
   D. personnel reduction

37. The UNDERLYING principle of sound administration is to 37._____

   A. base administration on investigation of facts
   B. have plenty of resources available
   C. hire a strong administrator
   D. establish a broad policy

38. Although questionnaires are not the best survey tool the management analyst has to use, there are times when a good questionnaire can expedite the *fact-finding* phase of a management survey. 38._____
    Which of the following should be AVOIDED in the design and distribution of the questionnaire?

   A. Questions should be framed so that answers can be classified and tabulated for analysis.
   B. Those receiving the questionnaire must be knowledgeable enough to accurately provide the information desired.
   C. The questionnaire should enable the respondent to answer in a narrative manner.
   D. The questionnaire should require a minimum amount of writing.

39. Of the following, the formula which is used to calculate the arithmetic mean from data grouped in a frequency distribution is: 39._____
    M =

   A. $\dfrac{n}{\Sigma fx}$ B. $N(\Sigma fx)$ C. $\dfrac{\Sigma fx}{N}$ D. $\dfrac{\Sigma x}{fN}$

40. Arranging large groups of numbers in frequency distributions 40._____

   A. gives a more composite picture of the total group than a random listing
   B. is misleading in most cases
   C. is unnecessary in most instances
   D. presents the data in a form whereby further manipulation of the group is eliminated

KEY (CORRECT ANSWERS)

1.	B	11.	A	21.	A	31.	C
2.	C	12.	A	22.	B	32.	B
3.	D	13.	C	23.	C	33.	A
4.	A	14.	C	24.	B	34.	D
5.	C	15.	D	25.	B	35.	C
6.	C	16.	B	26.	B	36.	A
7.	A	17.	C	27.	D	37.	A
8.	B	18.	C	28.	C	38.	C
9.	A	19.	C	29.	B	39.	C
10.	A	20.	A	30.	D	40.	A

EXAMINATION SECTION
TEST 1

DIRECTIONS: Each question or incomplete statement is followed by several suggested answers or completions. Select the one that BEST answers the question or completes the statement. *PRINT THE LETTER OF THE CORRECT ANSWER IN THE SPACE AT THE RIGHT.*

1. In many instances, managers deliberately set up procedures and routines that more than one department or more than one employee is required to complete and verify an entire operation or transaction.
   The MAIN reason for establishing such routines is *generally* to

   A. minimize the chances of gaps and deficiencies in feedback of information to management
   B. expand the individual employee's vision and concern for broader organizational objectives
   C. provide satisfaction of employees' social and egoistic needs through teamwork and horizontal communications
   D. facilitate internal control designed to prevent errors, whether intentional or accidental

   1._____

2. Committees—sometimes referred to as boards, commissions, or task forces—are widely used in government to investigate certain problems or to manage certain agencies.
   Of the following, the MOST serious limitation of the committee approach to management in government is that

   A. it reflects government's inability to delegate authority effectively to individual executives
   B. committee members do not usually have similar backgrounds, experience, and abilities
   C. it promotes horizontal communication at the expense of vertical communication
   D. the spreading out of responsibility to a committee often results in a willingness to settle for weak, compromise solutions

   2._____

3. Of the following, the BEST reason for replacing members of committees on a staggered or partial basis rather than replacing all members simultaneously is that this practice

   A. gives representatives of different interest groups a chance to contribute their ideas
   B. encourages continuity of policy since retained members are familiar with previous actions
   C. prevents interpersonal frictions from building up and hindering the work of the group
   D. improves the quality of the group's recommendations and decisions by stimulating development of new ideas

   3._____

4. Assume that in considering a variety of actions to take to solve a given problem, a manager decides to take no action at all.
   According to generally accepted management practice, such a decision would be

   4._____

A. *proper,* because under normal circumstances, it is better to make no decision
B. *improper,* because inaction would be rightly construed as shunning one's responsibilities
C. *proper,* since this would be a decision which might produce more positive results than the other alternatives
D. *improper,* since such a solution would delay corrective action and exacerbate the problem

5. Some writers in the field of management assume that when a newly promoted manager has been informed by his superior about the subordinates he is to direct and the extent of his authority, that is all that is necessary. However, thereafter, this new manager should realize that, for practical purposes, his authority will be effective ONLY when

   A. he accepts full responsibility for the actions of his subordinates
   B. his subordinates are motivated to carry out their assignments
   C. it derives from acceptable personal attributes rather than from his official position
   D. he exercises it in an authoritarian manner

6. A newly appointed manager is assigned to assist the head of a small developing agency handling innovative programs. Although this manager is a diligent worker, he does not delegate authority to middle- and lower-echelon supervisors. The MOST important reason why it would be desirable to change this attitude toward delegation is because otherwise

   A. he may have to assume more responsibility for the actions of his subordinates than is implied in the authority delegated to him
   B. his subordinates will tend to produce innovative solutions on their own
   C. the agency will become a decentralized type of organization in which he cannot maintain adequate controls
   D. he may not have time to perform other essential tasks

7. All types of organizations and all functions within them are to varying degrees affected today by the need to understand the application of computer systems to management practices.
   The one of the following purposes for which such systems would be MOST useful is to

   A. lower the costs of problem-solving by utilizing data that is already in the agency's control system correlated with new data
   B. stabilize basic patterns of the organization into long-term structures and relationships
   C. give instant solutions to complex problems
   D. affect savings in labor costs for office tasks involving non-routine complex problems

8. Compared to individual decision-making, group decision-making is burdened with the DISADVANTAGE of

   A. making snap judgments
   B. pressure to examine all relevant elements of the problem
   C. greater motivation needed to implement the decision
   D. the need to clarify problems for the group participants

9. Assume that a manager in an agency, faced with a major administrative problem, has developed a number of alternative solutions to the problem.
Which of the following would be MOST effective in helping the manager make the best decision?

   A. *Experience,* because a manager can distill from the past the fundamental reasons for success or failure since the future generally duplicates the past
   B. *Experimentation,* because it is the method used in scientific inquiry and can be tried out economically in limited areas
   C. *Research analysis,* because it is generally less costly than most other methods and involves the interrelationships among the more critical factors that bear upon the goal sought
   D. *Value forecasting,* because it assigns numerical significance to the values of alternative tangible and intangible choices and indicates the degree of risk involved in each choice

10. Management information systems operate more effectively for managers than mere data tabulating systems because information systems

    A. eliminate the need for managers to tell information processors what is required
    B. are used primarily for staff rather than line functions
    C. are less expensive to operate than manual methods of data collection
    D. present and utilize data in a meaningful form

11. Project-type organizations are in widespread use today because they offer a number of advantages.
The MOST important purpose of the project organization is to

    A. secure a higher degree of coordination than could be obtained in a conventional line structure
    B. provide an orderly way of phasing projects in and out of organizations
    C. expedite routine administrative processes
    D. allow for rapid assessment of the status of any given project and its effect on agency productivity

12. A manager adjusts his plans for future activity by reviewing information about the performance of his subordinates. This is an application of the process of

    A. human factor impact   B. coordinated response
    C. feedback communication   D. reaction control

13. From the viewpoint of the manager in an agency, the one of the following which is the MOST constructive function of a status system or a rank system based on employee performance is that the system

    A. makes possible effective communication, thereby lessening social distances between organizational levels
    B. is helpful to employees of lesser ability because it provides them with an incentive to exceed their capacities
    C. encourages the employees to attain or exceed the goals set for them by the organization
    D. diminishes friction in assignment and work relation-ships of personnel

14. Some managers ask employees who have been newly hired by their agency and then assigned to their divisions or units such questions as: *What are your personal goals? What do you expect from your job? Why do you want to work for this organization?* For a manager to ask these questions is GENERALLY considered

   A. *inadvisable;* these questions should have been asked prior to hiring the employee
   B. *inadvisable;* the answers will arouse subjective prejudices in the manager before he sees what kind of work the employee can do
   C. *advisable;* this approach indicates to the employee that the manager is interested in him as an individual
   D. *advisable;* the manager can judge how much of a disparity exists between the employee's goals and the agency's goals

15. Assume that you have prepared a report to your superior recommending a reorganization of your staff to eliminate two levels of supervision. The total number of employees would remain the same, with the supervisors of the two eliminated levels taking on staff assignments.
In your report, which one of the following should NOT be listed as an expected result of such a reorganization?

   A. Fewer breakdowns and distortions in communications to staff
   B. Greater need for training
   C. Broader opportunities for development of employee skills
   D. Fewer employee errors due to exercise of closer supervision and control

16. *Administration* has often been criticized as being unproductive in the sense that it seems far removed from the end products of an organization.
According to modern management thought, this criticism, for the most part, is

   A. *invalid,* because administrators make it possible for subordinates to produce goods or services by directing coordinating, and controlling their activities
   B. *valid,* because most subordinates usually do the work required to produce goods and services with only general direction from their immediate superiors
   C. *invalid,* because administrators must see to all of the details associated with the production of services
   D. *valid,* because administrators generally work behind the scenes and are mainly concerned with long-range planning

17. A manager must be able to evaluate the relative importance of his decisions and establish priorities for carrying them out.
Which one of the following factors bearing on the relative importance of making a decision would indicate to a manager that he can delegate that decision to a subordinate or give it low priority? The

   A. decision concerns a matter on which strict confiden-tiality must be maintained
   B. community impact of the decision is great
   C. decision can be easily changed
   D. decision commits the agency to a heavy expenditure of funds

18. Suppose that you are responsible for reviewing and submitting to your superior the monthly reports from ten field auditors. Despite your repeated warnings to these auditors, most of them hand in their reports close to or after the deadline dates, so that you have no time to return them for revision and find yourself working overtime to make the necessary corrections yourself.
The deadline dates for the auditors' reports and your report cannot be changed.
Of the following, the MOST probable cause for this con-tinuing situation is that

    A. these auditors need retraining in the writing of this type of report
    B. possible disciplinary action as a result of the delay by the auditors has not been impressed upon them
    C. the auditors have had an opportunity to provide you with feedback to explain the reasons for the delays
    D. you, as the manager, have not used disciplinary measures of sufficient severity to change their behavior

19. Assume that an agency desiring to try out a *management-by-objectives* program has set down the guidelines listed below to implement this activity.
Which one of these guidelines is MOST likely to present obstacles to the success of this type of program?

    A. Specific work objectives should be determined by top management for employees at all levels.
    B. Objectives should be specific, attainable, and preferably measurable as to units, costs, ratios, time, etc.
    C. Standards of performance should be either qualitative or quantitative, preferably quantitative.
    D. There should be recognition and rewards for success-ful achievement of objectives.

20. Of the following, the MOST meaningful way to express productivity where employees work a standard number of hours each day is in terms of the relationship between man-

    A. hours expended and number of work-units needed to produce the final product
    B. days expended and goods and services produced
    C. days and energy expended
    D. days expended and number of workers

21. Agencies often develop productivity indices for many of their activities.
Of the following, the MOST important use for such indices is *generally* to

    A. measure the agency's output against its own past performance
    B. improve quality standards while letting productivity remain unchanged
    C. compare outputs of the agency with outputs in private industry
    D. determine manpower requirements

22. The MOST outstanding characteristic of staff authority, such as that of a public relations officer in an agency, as compared with line authority, is *generally* accepted to be

    A. reliance upon personal attributes
    B. direct relationship to the primary objectives of the organization
    C. absence of the right to direct or command
    D. responsibility for attention to technical details

23. In the traditional organization structure, there are often more barriers to upward communication than to downward communication.
From the viewpoint of a manager whose goal is to overcome obstacles to communication, this situation should be

    A. *accepted;* the downward system is the more important since it is highly directive, giving necessary orders, instructions, and procedures
    B. *changed;* the upward system should receive more emphasis than the downward system, which represents stifling bureaucratic authority
    C. *accepted;* it is generally conceded that upward systems supply enough feedback for control purposes necessary to the organization's survival
    D. *changed;* research has generally verified the need for an increase in upward communications to supply more information about employees' ideas, attitudes, and performance

24. A principal difficulty in productivity measurement for local government services is in defining and measuring output, a problem familiar to managers. A measurement that merely looks good, but which may be against the public interest, is another serious problem. Managers should avoid encouraging employees to take actions that lead to such measurements.
In accordance with the foregoing statement, it would be MOST desirable for a manager to develop a productivity measure that

    A. correlates the actual productivity measure with impact on benefit to the citizenry
    B. does not allow for a mandated annual increase in productivity
    C. firmly fixes priorities for resource allocations
    D. uses numerical output, by itself, in productivity incentive plans

25. For a manager, the MOST significant finding of the Hawthorne studies and experiments is that an employee's productivity is affected MOST favorably when the

    A. importance of tasks is emphasized and there is a logical arrangement of work functions
    B. physical surroundings and work conditions are improved
    C. organization has a good public relations program
    D. employee is given recognition and allowed to participate in decision-making

KEY (CORRECT ANSWERS)

1. D
2. D
3. B
4. C
5. B

6. D
7. A
8. D
9. C
10. D

11. A
12. C
13. C
14. A
15. D

16. A
17. C
18. D
19. A
20. B

21. A
22. C
23. D
24. A
25. D

TEST 2

DIRECTIONS: Each question or incomplete statement is followed by several suggested answers or completions. Select the one that BEST answers the question or completes the statement. *PRINT THE LETTER OF THE CORRECT ANSWER IN THE SPACE AT THE RIGHT.*

1. Which one of the following is generally accepted by managers as the MOST difficult aspect of a training program in staff supervision?

    A. Determining training needs of the staff
    B. Evaluating the effectiveness of the courses
    C. Locating capable instructors to teach the courses
    D. Finding adequate space and scheduling acceptable times for all participants

2. Assume that, as a manager, you have decided to start a job enrichment program with the purpose of making jobs more varied and interesting in an effort to increase the motivation of a certain group of workers in your division. Which one of the following should generally NOT be part of this program?

    A. Increasing the accountability of these individuals for their own work
    B. Granting additional authority or job freedom to these employees in their job activities
    C. Mandating increased monthly production goals for this group of employees
    D. Giving each of these employees a complete unit of work

3. Both employer and employee have an important stake in effective preparation for retirement.
   According to modern management thinking, the one of the following which is probably the MOST important aspect of a sound pre-retirement program is to

    A. make assignments that utilize the employee's abilities fully
    B. reassign the employee to a less demanding position in the organization for the last year or two he is on the job
    C. provide the employee with financial data and other facts that would be pertinent to his retirement planning
    D. encourage the employee to develop interests and hobbies which are connected with the job

4. The civil service system generally emphasizes a policy of *promotion-from-within.* Employees in the direct line of promotion in a given occupational group are eligible for promotion to the next higher title in that occupational group.
   Which one of the following is LEAST likely to occur as a result of this policy and practice?

    A. Training time will be saved since employees in higher-level positions are already familiar with many agency rules, regulations, and procedures.
    B. The recruitment section will be able to show prospective employees that there are distinct promotional opportunities.
    C. Employees will be provided with a clear-cut picture as to their possible career ladder.
    D. Employees will be encouraged to seek broad-based training and education to enhance their promotability.

5. From a management point of view, the MAIN drawback of seniority as opposed to merit as a basis for granting pay increases to workers is that a pay increase system based on seniority

   A. is favored by unions
   B. upsets organizational status relationships
   C. may encourage mediocre performance by employees
   D. is more difficult to administer than a merit plan

6. One of the actions that is often taken against employees in the non-uniformed forces who are accused of misconduct on the job is suspension without pay.
   The MOST justifiable reason for taking such action is to

   A. ease an employee out of the agency
   B. enable an investigation to be conducted into the circumstances of the offense where doubt exists about the guilt of the employee
   C. improve the performance of the employee when he returns to the job
   D. punish the employee by imposing a hardship on him

7. A manager has had difficulty in getting good clerical employees to staff a filing section under his supervision. To add to his problems, one of his most competent senior clerks requests a transfer to the accounting division so that he can utilize his new accounting skill, which he is acquiring by going to college at night. The manager attempts to keep the senior clerk in his filing section by calling the director of personnel and getting him to promise not to authorize any transfer. GENERALLY, this manager's action is

   A. *desirable;* he should not help his staff to develop themselves if it means losing good people
   B. *undesirable;* he should recommend that the senior clerk get a raise in the hope of preventing him from transferring to another section
   C. *desirable;* it shows that the manager is concerned about the senior clerk's future performance
   D. *undesirable;* it is good policy to transfer employees to the type of work they are interested in and for which they are acquiring training

8. One of your subordinates, a unit supervisor, comes to you, the division chief, because he feels that he is working out of title, and he suggests that his competitive class position should be reclassified to a higher title.
   Which one of the following statements that the subordinate has made is generally LEAST likely to be a valid support for his suggestion?

   A. The work he is doing conforms to the general statement of duties and responsibilities as described in the class specification for the next higher title in his occupational group.
   B. Most of the typical tasks he performs are listed in the class specification for a title with a higher salary range and are not listed for his current title.
   C. His education and experience qualifications far exceed the minimum requirements for the position he holds.
   D. His duties and responsibilities have changed recently and are now similar to those of his supervisor.

9. Assume that a class specification for a competitive title used exclusively by your agency is outdated, and that no examination for the title has been given since the specification was issued.
Of the following, the MOST appropriate action for your agency to take is to

   A. make the necessary changes and submit the revised class specification to the city civil service commission
   B. write the personnel director to recommend that the class specification be updated, giving the reasons and suggested revisions
   C. prepare a revised class specification and submit it to the office of management and budget for their approval
   D. secure approval of the state civil service commission to update the class specification, and then submit the revised specification to the city civil service commission

10. Assume that an appropriate eligible list has been established and certified to your agency for a title in which a large number of provisionals are serving in your agency.
In order to obtain permission from the personnel director to retain some of them beyond the usual time limit set by rules (two months) following certification of the list, which one of the following conditions MUST apply?

   A. The positions are sensitive and require investigation of eligibles prior to appointment.
   B. Replacement of all provisionals within two months would impair essential public service.
   C. Employees are required to work rotating shifts, including nights and weekends.
   D. The duties of the positions require unusual physical effort and endurance.

11. Under the federally-funded Comprehensive Employment and Training Act (CETA), the hiring by the city of non-civil servants for CETA jobs is PROHIBITED when the

   A. applicants are unemployed because of seasonal lay-offs in private industry
   B. applicants do not meet U.S. citizenship and city residence requirements
   C. jobs have minimum requirements of specialized professional or technical training and experience
   D. jobs are comparable to those performed by laid-off civil servants

12. Assume you are in charge of the duplicating service in your agency. Since employees assigned to this operation lack a sense of accomplishment because the work is highly specialized and repetitive, your superior proposes to enlarge the jobs of these workers and asks you about your reaction to this strategy.
The MOST appropriate response for you to make is that job enlargement would be

   A. *undesirable,* PRIMARILY because it would increase production costs
   B. *undesirable,* PRIMARILY because it would diminish the quality of the output
   C. *desirable,* PRIMARILY because it might make it possible to add an entire level of management to the organizational structure of your agency
   D. *desirable,* PRIMARILY because it might make it possible to decrease the amount of supervision the workers will require

13. According to civil service law, layoff or demotion must be made in inverse order of seniority among employees permanently serving in the same title and layoff unit. Which one of the following is now the CORRECT formula for computing seniority?
Total continuous service in the

A. competitive class *only*
B. competitive, non-competitive, or labor class
C. classified or unclassified services
D. competitive, non-competitive, exempt, and labor classes

14. Under which of the following conditions would an appoint-ing officer be permitted to consider the sex of a candidate in making an employment decision?
When

    A. the duties of the position require considerable physical effort or strength
    B. the duties of the position are considered inherently dangerous
    C. separate toilet facilities and dressing rooms for the sexes are unavailable and/or cannot be provided in any event
    D. the public has indicated a preference to be served by persons of a specified sex

15. Assume that an accountant under your supervision signs out to the field to make an agency audit. It is later discovered that, although he had reported himself at work until 5 P.M. that day, he had actually left for home at 3:30 P.M. Although this accountant has worked for the city for ten years and has had an excellent performance record, he is demoted to a lower title in punishment for this breach of duty.
According to generally accepted thinking on personnel management, the disciplinary action taken in this case should be considered

    A. *appropriate;* a lesser penalty might encourage repetition of the offense
    B. *inappropriate;* the correct penalty for such a breach of duty should be dismissal
    C. *appropriate;* the accountant's abilities may be utilized better in the new assignment
    D. *inappropriate;* the impact of a continuing stigma and loss of salary is not commensurate with the offense committed

16. Line managers often request more funds for their units than are actually required to attain their current objectives.
Which one of the following is the MOST important reason for such inflated budget requests?
The

    A. expectation that budget examiners will exercise their prerogative of budget cutting
    B. line manager's interest in improving the performance of his unit is thereby indicated to top management
    C. expectation that such requests will make it easier to obtain additional funds in future years
    D. opinion that it makes sense to obtain additional funds and decide later how to use them

17. Integrating budgeting with program planning and evaluation in a city agency is GENERALLY considered to be

    A. *undesirable;* budgeting must focus on the fiscal year at hand, whereas planning must concern itself with developments over a period of years
    B. *desirable;* budgeting facilitates the choice-making process by evaluating the financial implications of agency programs and forcing cost comparisons among them
    C. *undesirable;* accountants and statisticians with the required budgetary skills have little familiarity with the substantive programs that the agency is conducting
    D. *desirable;* such a partnership increases the budgetary skills of planners, thus promoting more effective use of public resources

18. As an aspect of the managerial function, a budget is described BEST as a

    A. set of qualitative management controls over productivity
    B. tool based on historical accounting reports
    C. type of management plan expressed in quantitative terms
    D. precise estimate of future quantitative and qualitative contingencies

19. Which one of the following is *generally* accepted as the MAJOR immediate advantage of installing a system of program budgeting?
    It

    A. encourages managers to relate their decisions to the agency's long-range goals
    B. is a replacement for the financial or fiscal budget
    C. decreases the need for managers to make trade-offs in the decision-making process
    D. helps to adjust budget figures to provide for unexpected developments

20. Of the following, the BEST means for assuring necessary responsiveness of a budgetary program to changing conditions is by

    A. overestimating budgetary expenditures by 15% and assigning the excess to unforeseen problem areas
    B. underestimating budgetary expenditures by at least 20% and setting aside a reserve account in the same amount
    C. reviewing and revising the budget at regular intervals so that it retains its character as a current document
    D. establishing *budget by exception* policies for each division in the agency

21. According to expert thought in the area of budgeting, participation in the preparation of a government agency's budget should GENERALLY involve

    A. only top management
    B. only lower levels of management
    C. all levels of the organization
    D. only a central budget office or bureau

22. Of the following, the MOST useful guide to analysis of budget estimates for the coming fiscal year is a com-parison with

    A. appropriations as amended for the current fiscal year
    B. manpower requirements for the previous two years
    C. initial appropriations for the current fiscal year
    D. budget estimates for the preceding five years

23. A manager assigned to analyze the costs and benefits associated with a program which the agency head proposes to undertake may encounter certain factors which cannot be measured in dollar terms.
    In such a case, the manager should GENERALLY

    A. ignore the factors which cannot be quantified
    B. evaluate the factors in accordance with their degree of importance to the overall agency goals

C. give the factors weight equal to the weight given to measurable costs and benefits
D. assume that non-measurable costs and benefits will balance out against one another

24. If city employees believe that they are receiving adverse treatment in terms of training and disciplinary actions because of their national origin, they may file charges of discrimination with the Federal government's

    A. Human Rights Commission
    B. Public Employee Relations Board
    C. Equal Employment Opportunity Commission
    D. United States Department of Commerce

24.____

25. Under existing employment statutes, the city is obligated, as an employer, to take *affirmative action* in certain instances.
This requirement has been imposed to ensure that

    A. employees who are members of minority groups, or women, be given special opportunities for training and promotion even though they are not available to other employees
    B. employees or applicants for employment are treated without regard to race, color, religion, sex, or national origin
    C. proof exists to show that the city has acted with good intentions in any case where it has disregarded this requirement
    D. men and women are treated alike except where State law provides special hour or working conditions for women

25.____

KEY (CORRECT ANSWERS)

1. B
2. C
3. C
4. D
5. C

6. B
7. D
8. C
9. B
10. B

11. D
12. D
13. D
14. C
15. D

16. A
17. B
18. C
19. A
20. C

21. C
22. A
23. B
24. C
25. B

EXAMINATION SECTION
TEST 1

DIRECTIONS: Each question or incomplete statement is followed by several suggested answers or completions. Select the one that BEST answers the question or completes the statement. *PRINT THE LETTER OF THE CORRECT ANSWER IN THE SPACE AT THE RIGHT.*

1. When a supervisor in a large office introduces a change in the regular office procedure, it is USUAL to expect

    A. immediate acceptance by office staff, unless the change is unnecessary
    B. an immediate production increase, since new procedures are more stimulating than old ones
    C. a temporary production loss, even if the change is really an overall improvement
    D. resistance to the change only if it has been put into writing

    1.____

2. A supervisor evaluates the performance of subordinates and then applies measures, where needed, which result in bringing performance up to desired standards.
Which of the following functions of management might he BEST be described as performing?

    A. Organizing   B. Controlling   C. Directing   D. Planning

    2.____

3. Assume that, as a supervisor, you have been assigned responsibility for a new and complex project which entails collection and analysis of data. You have prepared general written instructions which explain the project and procedures to be followed by several statisticians.
Which of the procedures below would be MOST advisable for you, as the supervisor, to follow?

    A. Distribute the instructions to your subordinates to come to you with any important questions
    B. Distribute the instructions and advise subordinates to come to you with any important questions
    C. Meet with subordinates as a group and explain the project using the written instructions as a handout
    D. Delegate responsibility for further explanation of the project to an immediate qualified subordinate to free you for concentration on research design

    3.____

4. Supervisors have an obligation to make careful and thorough appraisals and reports of probationary employees. Of the following, the MOST important justification for this statement is that the probationary period

    A. should be used for positive development of the employee's understanding of the organization
    B. is the most effective period for changing a new employee's knowledges, skills, and attitudes
    C. insures that the employee will meet work standard requirements on future assignments
    D. should be considered as the final step in the selection process

    4.____

5. Many studies of management indicate that a principal reason for failure of supervisors lies in their ability to delegate duties effectively.
Which one of the following practices by a supervisor would NOT be a block to successful delegation?

   A. Instructing the delegatee to follow a set procedure in carrying out the assignment
   B. Maintaining point by point control over the process delegated
   C. Transferring ultimate responsibility for the duties assigned to the delegatee
   D. Requiring the delegatee to keep the delegator informed of his progress

6. Crosswise communication occurs between personnel at lower or middle levels of different organizational units. It often speeds information and improves understanding, but has certain dangers.
Of the following proposed policies, which would NOT be important as a safeguard in crosswise communication?

   A. Supervisors should agree as to how crosswise communication should occur.
   B. Crosswise relationships must exist only between employees of equal status.
   C. Subordinates must keep their superiors informed about their interdepartmental communications.
   D. Subordinates must refrain from making commitments beyond their authority.

7. *Systems* theory has given us certain principles which are as applicable to organizational and social activities as they are to those of science. With regard to the training of employees in an organization, which of the following is likely to be most consistent with the modern *systems* approach?
Training can be effective ONLY when it is

   A. related to the individual abilities of the employees
   B. done on all levels of the organizational hierarchy
   C. evaluated on the basis of experimental and control groups
   D. provided on the job by the immediate supervisor

8. The management of a large agency, before making a decision as to whether or not to computerize its operations, should have a feasibility study made.
Of the following, the one which is LEAST important to include in such a study is

   A. the current abilities of management and staff to use a computer
   B. projected workloads and changes in objectives of functional units in the agency
   C. the contributions expected of each organizational unit towards achievement of agency objectives
   D. the decision-making activity and informational needs of each management function

9. Managing information covers the creation, collection, processing, storage and transmission of information that appears in a variety of forms. A supervisor responsible for a statistical unit can be considered, in many respects, an information manager.
Of the following, which would be considered the LEAST important aspect of the information manager's job?

   A. Establishing better information standards and formats
   B. Reducing the amount of unnecessary paper work performed
   C. Producing progressively greater numbers of informational reports
   D. Developing a greater appreciation for information among management members

10. Because of the need for improvement in information systems throughout industry and government, various techniques for improving these systems have been developed. Of these, *systems simulation* is a technique for improving systems which

    A. creates new ideas and concepts through the use of a computer
    B. deals with time controlling of interrelated systems which make up an overall project
    C. permits experimentation with various ideas to see what results might be obtained
    D. does not rely on assumptions which condition the value of the results

10.____

11. The one of the following which it is NOT advisable for a supervisor to do when dealing with individual employees is to

    A. recognize a person's outstanding service as well as his mistakes
    B. help an employee satisfy his need to excel
    C. encourage an efficient employee to seek better opportunities even if this action may cause the supervisor to lose a good worker
    D. take public notice of an employee's mistakes so that fewer errors will be made in the future

11.____

12. Suppose that you are in a department where you are given the responsibility for teaching seven new assistants a number of routine procedures that all assistants should know.
Of the following, the BEST method for you to follow in teaching these procedures is to

    A. separate the slower learners from the faster learners and adapt your presentation to their level of ability
    B. instruct all the new employees in a group without attempting to assess differences in learning rates
    C. restrict your approach to giving them detailed written instructions in order to save time
    D. avoid giving the employees written instructions in order to force them to memorize job procedures quickly

12.____

13. Suppose that you are a supervisor to whom several assistants must hand in work for review. You notice that one of the assistants gets very upset whenever you discover an error in his work, although all the assistants make mistakes from time to time.
Of the following, it would be BEST for you to

    A. arrange discreetly for the employee's work to be reviewed by another supervisor
    B. ignore his reaction since giving attention to such behavior increases its intensity
    C. suggest that the employee seek medical help since he has such great difficulty in accepting normal criticism
    D. try to build the employee's self-confidence by emphasizing those parts of his work that are done well

13.____

14. Suppose you are a supervisor responsible for supervising a number of assistants in an agency where each assistant receives a manual of policies and procedures when he first reports for work. You have been asked to teach your subordinates a new procedure which requires knowledge of several items of policy and procedure found in the manual. The one of the following techniques which it would be BEST for you to employ is to

    A. give verbal instructions which include a review of the appropriate standard procedures as well as an explanation of new tasks
    B. give individual instruction restricted to the new procedure to each assistant as the need arises
    C. provide written instructions for new procedural elements and refer employees to their manuals for explanation of standard procedures
    D. ask employees to review appropriate sections of their manual and then explain those aspects of the new procedure which the manual did not cover

15. Suppose that you are a supervisor in charge of a unit in which changes in work procedures are about to be instituted. The one of the following which you, as the supervisor, should anticipate as being MOST likely to occur during the changeover is

    A. a temporary rise in production because of interest in the new procedures
    B. uniform acceptance of these procedures on the part of your staff
    C. varying interpretations of the new procedures by your staff
    D. general agreement among staff members that the new procedures are advantageous

16. Suppose that a supervisor and one of the assistants under his supervision are known to be friends who play golf together on weekends.
    The maintenance of such a friendship on the part of the supervisor is GENERALLY

    A. *acceptable* as long as this assistant continues to perform his duties satisfactorily
    B. *unacceptable* since the supervisor will find it difficult to treat the assistant as a subordinate
    C. *acceptable* if the supervisor does not favor this assistant above other employees
    D. *unacceptable* because the other assistants will resent the friendship regardless of the supervisor's behavior on the job

17. Suppose that you are a supervisor assigned to review the financial records of an agency which has recently undergone a major reorganization.
    Which of the following would it be best for you to do FIRST?

    A. Interview the individual in charge of agency financial operations to determine whether the organizational changes affect the system of financial review
    B. Discuss the nature of the reorganization with your own supervisor to anticipate and plan a new financial review procedure.
    C. Carry out the financial review as usual, and adjust your methods to any problems arising from the reorganization.
    D. Request a written report from the agency head explaining the nature of the reorganization and recommending changes in the system of financial review.

18. Suppose that a newly assigned supervisor finds that he must delegate some of his duties to subordinates in order to get the work done.
Which one of the following would NOT be a block to his delegating these duties effectively?

    A. Inability to give proper directions as to what he wants done
    B. Reluctance to take calculated risks
    C. Lack of trust in his subordinates
    D. Retaining ultimate responsibility for the delegated work

19. A supervisor sometimes performs the staff function of preparing and circulating reports among bureau chiefs. Which of the following is LEAST important as an objective in designing and writing such reports?

    A. Providing relevant information on past, present, and future actions
    B. Modifying his language in order to insure goodwill among the bureau chiefs
    C. Helping the readers of the report to make appropriate decisions
    D. Summarizing important information to help readers see trends or outstanding points.

20. Suppose you are a supervisor assigned to prepare a report to be read by all bureau chiefs in your agency.
The MOST important reason for avoiding highly technical accounting terminology in writing this report is to

    A. ensure the accuracy and relevancy of the text
    B. insure winning the readers' cooperation
    C. make the report more interesting to the readers
    D. make it easier for the readers to understand

21. Which of the following conditions is MOST likely to cause low morale in an office?

    A. Different standards of performance for individuals in the same title
    B. A requirement that employees perform at full capacity
    C. Standards of performance that vary with titles of employees
    D. Careful attention to the image of the division or department

22. A wise supervisor or representative of management realizes that, in the relationship between supervisor and subordinates, all power is not on the side of management, and that subordinates do sometimes react to restrictive authority in such a manner as to seriously retard management's objectives. A wise supervisor does not stimulate such reactions.
In the subordinate's attempt to retaliate against an unusually authoritative management style, which of the following actions would generally be LEAST successful for the subordinate? He

    A. joins with other employees in organizations to deal with management
    B. obviously delays in carrying out instructions which are given in an arrogant or incisive manner
    C. performs assignments exactly as instructed even when he recognizes errors in instructions
    D. holds back the flow of feedback information to superiors

23. Which of the following is the MOST likely and costly effect of vague and indefinite instructions given to subordinates by a supervisor?

    A. Misunderstanding and ineffective work on the part of the subordinates
    B. A necessity for the supervisor to report identical instructions with each assignment
    C. A failure of the supervisor to adequately keep the attention of subordinates
    D. Inability of subordinates to assist each other in the absence of the supervisor

24. At the professional level, there is a kind of informal authority which exercises itself even though no delegation of authority has taken place from higher management. It occurs within the context of knowledge required and professional competence in a special area. An example of the kind of authority described in this statement is MOST clearly exemplified in the situation where a senior supervisor influences associates and subordinates by virtue of the

    A. salary level fixed for his particular set of duties
    B. amount of college training he possesses
    C. technical position he has gained and holds on the work team
    D. initiative and judgment he has demonstrated to his supervisor

25. An assistant under your supervision attempts to conceal the fact that he has made an error.
    Under this circumstance, it would be BEST for you, as the supervisor, to proceed on the assumption that

    A. this evasion indicates something wrong in the fundamental relationship between you and the assistant
    B. this evasion is not deliberate, if the error is subsequently corrected by the assistant
    C. this evasion should be overlooked if the error is not significant
    D. detection and correction of errors will come about as an automatic consequence of internal control procedures

KEY (CORRECT ANSWERS)

1.	C	11.	D
2.	B	12.	B
3.	C	13.	D
4.	D	14.	A
5.	D	15.	C
6.	B	16.	C
7.	B	17.	A
8.	A	18.	D
9.	C	19.	B
10.	C	20.	D

21. A
22. B
23. A
24. C
25. A

TEST 2

DIRECTIONS: Each question or incomplete statement is followed by several suggested answers or completions. Select the one that BEST answers the question or completes the statement. *PRINT THE LETTER OF THE CORRECT ANSWER IN THE SPACE AT THE RIGHT.*

1. The unit which you supervise has a number of attorneys, accountants, examiners, statisticians, and clerks who prepare some of the routine papers required to be filed.
   In order to be certain that nothing goes out of your office that is improper, you have instituted a system that requires that you review and initial all moving papers, memoranda of law and briefs that are prepared. As a result, you put in a great deal of overtime and even must take work home with you frequently.
   A situation such as this is

   A. inevitable if you are to keep proper controls over the quality of the office work product
   B. indicative of the fact that the agency must provide an additional position within your office for an assistant supervisor who would do all the reviewing, leaving you free for other pressing administrative work and to handle the most difficult work in your unit
   C. the logical result of an ever-increasing case load
   D. symptomatic of poor supervision and management

   1._

2. Your unit has been assigned a new employee who has never worked for the city.
   To orient him to his job in your unit, of the following, the BEST procedure is first to

   A. assign him to another employee to whatever work that employee gives him so that he can become familiar with your work and at the same time be productive
   B. give him copies of the charter and code provisions affecting your operations plus any in-office memoranda or instructions that are available and have him read them
   C. assign him to work on a relatively simple problem and then, after he has finished it, tell him politely what he did wrong
   D. explain to him the duties of his position and the functions of the office

   2._

3. A bureau chief who supervises other supervisors makes it a practice to assign them more cases than they can possibly handle.
   This approach is

   A. *right,* because it results in getting more work done than would otherwise be the case
   B. *right,* because it relieves the bureau chief making the assignments of the responsibility of getting the work done
   C. *wrong,* because it builds resistance on the part of those called upon to handle the case load
   D. *wrong,* because superiors lose track of cases

   3._

4. Assume you are a supervisor and are expected to exercise *authority* over subordinates.
   Which of the following BEST defines *authority?* The

   A. ability to control the nature of the contribution a subordinate is desirous of making
   B. innate inability to get others to do for you what you want to get done irrespective of their own wishes
   C. legal right conferred by the agency to control the actions of others
   D. power to determine a subordinate's attitude toward his agency and his superiors

   4._

5. Paternalistic leadership stresses a paternal or fatherly influence in the relationships between the leader and the group and is manifest in a watchful care for the comfort and welfare of the followers.
Which one of the following statements regarding paternalistic leadership is MOST accurate?

   A. Employees who work well under paternalistic leadership come to expect such leadership even when the paternal leader has left the organization.
   B. Most disputes arising out of supervisor-subordinate relationships develop because group leaders do not understand the principles of paternalistic leadership.
   C. Paternalistic leadership frequently destroys office relationships because most employees are turned into non-thinking dependent robots.
   D. Paternalistic leadership is rarely, if ever, successful because employees resent paternalistic leadership which they equate with weakness.

6. Employees who have extensive dealings with members of the public should have, as much as possible, *real acceptance* of all people and a willingness to serve everyone impartially and objectively.
Assuming that this statement is correct, the one of the following which would be the BEST demonstration of *real acceptance* is

   A. condoning antisocial behavior
   B. giving the appearance of agreeing with everyone encountered
   C. refusing to give opinions on anyone's behavior
   D. understanding the feelings expressed through a person's behavior

7. Assume that the agency chief has requested you to help plan a public relations program because of recent complaints from citizens about the unbecoming conduct and language of various groups of city employees who have dealings with the public.
In carrying out this assignment, the one of the following steps which should be undertaken FIRST is to

   A. study the characteristics of the public clientele dealt with by employees in your agency
   B. arrange to have employees attend several seminars on human relations
   C. develop several procedures for dealing with the public and allow the staff to choose the one which is best
   D. find out whether the employees in your agency may oppose any plan proposed by you

8. The one of the following statements which BEST expresses the relationship between the morale of government employees and the public relations aspects of their work is:

   A. There is little relationship between employee morale and public relations, chiefly because public opinion is shaped primarily by response to departmental policy formulation.
   B. Employee morale is closely related to public relations, chiefly because the employee's morale will largely determine the manner in which he deals with the public.
   C. There is little relationship between employee morale and public relations, chiefly because public relations is primarily a function of the agency's public relations department.
   D. Employee morale is closely related to public relations, chiefly because employee morale indicates the attitude of the agency's top officials toward the public.

9. As a supervisor, you are required to deal extensively with the public. The agency chief has indicated that he is considering holding a special in-service training course for employees in communications skills.
Holding this training course would be

   A. *advisable,* chiefly because government employees should receive formal training in public relations skills
   B. *inadvisable,* chiefly because the public regards such training as a *waste of the tax-payers' money*
   C. *advisable,* chiefly because such training will enable the employee to aid in drafting departmental press releases
   D. *inadvisable,* chiefly because of the great difficulty involved in developing such skills through formal instruction

10. Assume that you have extensive contact with the public. In dealing with the public, sensitivity to an individual's attitudes is important because these attitudes can be used to predict behavior.
However, the MAIN reason that attitudes CANNOT successfully predict all behavior is that

   A. attitudes are highly resistant to change
   B. an individual acquires attitudes as a function of growing up in a particular cultural environment
   C. attitudes are only one of many factors which determine a person's behavior
   D. an individual's behavior is not always observable

11. Rotation of employees from assignment to assignment is sometimes advocated by management experts.
Of the following, the MOST probable advantage to the organization of this practice is that it leads to

   A. higher specialization of duties so that excessive identification with the overall organization is reduced
   B. increased loyalty of employees to their immediate supervisors
   C. greater training and development of employees
   D. intensified desire of employees to obtain additional, outside formal education

12. Usually, a supervisor should attempt to standardize the work for which he is responsible.
The one of the following which is a BASIC reason for doing this is to

   A. eliminate the need to establish priorities
   B. permit the granting of exceptions to rules and special circumstances
   C. facilitate the taking of action based on applicable standards
   D. learn the identity of outstanding employees

13. The differences between line and staff authority are often quite ambiguous.
Of the following, the ESSENTIAL difference is that

   A. *line authority* is exercised by first-level supervisors; *staff authority* is exercised by higher-level supervisors and managerial staff
   B. *staff authority* is the right to issue directives; *line authority* is entirely consultative
   C. *line authority* is the power to make decisions regarding intra-agency matters; *staff authority* involves decisions regarding inter-agency matters
   D. *staff authority* is largely advisory; *line authority* is the right to command

14. Modern management theory stresses work-centered motivation as one way of increasing the productivity of employees.
The one of the following which is PARTICULARLY characteristic of such motivation is that it

   A. emphasizes the crucial role of routinization of procedures
   B. stresses the satisfaction to be found in performing work
   C. features the value of wages and fringe benefits
   D. uses a firm but fair method of discipline

15. The agency's informal communications network is called the *grapevine*.
If employees are learning about important organizational developments primarily through the grapevine, this is MOST likely an indication that

   A. official channels of communication are not functioning so efficiently as they should
   B. supervisory personnel are making effective use of the grapevine to communicate with subordinates
   C. employees already have a clear understanding of the agency's policies and procedures
   D. upward formal channels of communication within the agency are informing management of employee grievances

16. Of the following, a flow chart is BEST described as a chart which shows

   A. the places through which work moves in the course of the job process
   B. which employees perform specific functions leading to the completion of a job
   C. the schedules for production and how they eliminate waiting time between jobs
   D. how work units are affected by the actions of related work units

17. Evaluation of the results of training is necessary in order to assess its value.
Of the following, the BEST technique for the supervisor to use in determining whether the training under consideration actually resulted in the desired modification of the behavior of the employee concerned is through

   A. inference   B. job analysis
   C. observation   D. simulation

18. The usual distinction between line and staff authority is that staff authority is mainly advisory, whereas line authority is the right to command. However, a third category has been suggested–prescriptive–to distinguish those personnel whose functions may be formally defined as staff but in practice exercise considerable authority regarding decisions relating to their specialties.
The one of the following which indicates the MAJOR purpose of creating this third category is to

   A. develop the ability of each employee to perform a greater number of tasks
   B. reduce line-staff conflict
   C. prevent over-specialization of functions
   D. encourage decision-making by line personnel

19. It is sometimes considered desirable to train employees to a standard of proficiency higher than that deemed necessary for actual job performance.
The MOST likely reason for such overtraining would be to

    A. eliminate the need for standards
    B. increase the value of refresher training
    C. compensate for previous lack of training
    D. reduce forgetting or loss of skill

20. Assume that you have been directed to immediately institute various new procedures in the handling of records.
Of the following, the BEST method for you to use to insure that your subordinates know exactly what to do is to

    A. circulate a memorandum explaining the new procedures and have your subordinates initial it
    B. explain the new procedures to one or two subordinates and ask them to tell the others
    C. have a meeting with your subordinates to give them copies of the procedures and discuss it with them
    D. post the new procedures where they can be referred to by all those concerned

21. A supervisor decided to hold a problem-solving conference with his entire staff and distributed an announcement and agenda one week before the meeting.
Of the following, the BEST reason for providing each participant with an agenda is that

    A. participants will feel that something will be accomplished
    B. participants may prepare for the conference
    C. controversy will be reduced
    D. the top man should state the expected conclusions

22. In attempting to motivate employees, rewards are considered preferable to punishment PRIMARILY because

    A. punishment seldom has any effect on human behavior
    B. punishment usually results in decreased production
    C. supervisors find it difficult to punish
    D. rewards are more likely to result in willing cooperation

23. In an attempt to combat the low morale in his organization, a high-level supervisor publicized an *open-door* policy to allow employees who wished to do so to come to him with their complaints.
Which of the following is LEAST likely to account for the fact that no employee came in with a complaint?

    A. Employees are generally reluctant to go over the heads of their immediate supervisors.
    B. The employees did not feel that management would help them.
    C. The low morale was not due to complaints associated with the job.
    D. The employees felt that, they had more to lose than to gain.

24. It is MOST desirable to use written instructions rather than oral instructions for a particular job when 24.____

   A. a mistake on the job will not be serious
   B. the job can be completed in a short time
   C. there is no need to explain the job minutely
   D. the job involves many details

25. You have been asked to prepare for public distribution a statement dealing with a controversial matter. 25.____
Of the following approaches, the one which would usually be MOST effective is to present your department's point of view

   A. as tersely as possible with no reference to any other matters
   B. developed from ideas and facts well known to most readers
   C. and show all the statistical data and techniques which were used in arriving at it
   D. in such a way that the controversial parts are omitted

KEY (CORRECT ANSWERS)

1.	D	11.	C
2.	D	12.	C
3.	C	13.	D
4.	C	14.	B
5.	A	15.	A
6.	D	16.	A
7.	A	17.	C
8.	B	18.	B
9.	A	19.	D
10.	C	20.	C

21.	B
22.	D
23.	C
24.	D
25.	B

TEST 3

DIRECTIONS: Each question or incomplete statement is followed by several suggested answers or completions. Select the one that BEST answers the question or completes the statement. *PRINT THE LETTER OF THE CORRECT ANSWER IN THE SPACE AT THE RIGHT.*

1. An administrator who supervises other supervisors makes it a practice to set deadline dates for completion of assignments.
   A NATURAL consequence of setting deadline dates is that

   A. supervisors will usually wait until the deadline date before they give projects their wholehearted attention
   B. projects are completed sooner than if no deadline dates are set
   C. such dates are ignored even though they are conspicuously posted
   D. the frequency of errors sharply increases resulting in an inability to meet deadlines

2. Assume that you are chairing a meeting of the members of your staff. You throw out a question to the group. No one answers your question immediately, so that you find yourself faced with silence.
   In the circumstances, it would probably be BEST for you to

   A. ask the member of the group who appears to be least attentive to repeat the question
   B. change the topic quickly
   C. repeat the question carefully, pronouncing each word, and if there is still no response, repeat the question an additional time
   D. wait for an answer since someone will usually say something to break the tension

3. Assume that you are holding a meeting with the members of your staff. John, a member of the unit, keeps sidetracking the subject of the discussion by bringing up extraneous matters. You deal with the situation by saying to him after he has raised an immaterial point, "That's an interesting point John, but can you show me how it ties in with what we're talking about?"
   Your approach in this situation would GENERALLY be considered

   A. *bad;* you have prevented the group from discussing not only extraneous matters but pertinent material as well
   B. *bad;* you have seriously humiliated John in front of the entire group
   C. *good;* you have pointed out how the discussion is straying from the main topic
   D. *good;* you have prevented John from presenting extraneous matters at future meetings

4. Assume that a senior supervisor is asked to supervise a group of staff personnel. The work of one of these staff men meets minimum standards of acceptability. However, this staff man constantly looks for something at which to take offense. In any conversation with either a fellow staff man or with a superior, he views the slightest criticism as a grave insult.
   In this case, the senior supervisor should

   A. advise the staff man that the next time he refuses to accept criticism, he will be severely reprimanded
   B. ask members of the group for advice on how to deal with this staff man
   C. make it a practice to speak calmly, slowly, and deliberately to this staff man and question him frequently to make sure that there is no breakdown in communications
   D. recognize that professional help may be required and that this problem may not be conducive to a solution by a supervisor

5. Assume that you discover that one of the staff in preparing certain papers has made a serious mistake which has become obvious.
   In dealing with this situation, it would be BEST for you to begin by

   A. asking the employee how the mistake happened
   B. asking the employee to read through the papers to see whether he can correct the mistake
   C. pointing out to the employee that, while an occasional error is permissible, frequent errors can prove a source of embarrassment to all concerned
   D. pointing to the mistake and asking the employee whether he realizes the consequences of the mistake

6. You desire to develop teamwork among the members of your staff. You are assigned a case which will require that two of the staff work together if the papers are to be prepared in time. You decided to assign two employees, whom you know to be close friends, to work on these papers. Your action in this regard would GENERALLY be considered

   A. *bad;* friends working together tend to do as little as they can get away with
   B. *bad;* people who are friends socially often find that the bonds of friendship disintegrate in work situations
   C. *good;* friends who are permitted to work together show their appreciation by utilizing every opportunity to reinforce the group leader's position of authority
   D. *good;* the evidence suggests that more work can be done in this way

7. You notice that all of the employees, without exception, take lunch hours which in your view are excessively long. You call each of them to your desk and point out that unless this practice is brought to a stop, appropriate action will be taken.
   The way in which you handled this problem would GENERALLY be considered

   A. *proper,* primarily because a civil servant, no matter what his professional status, owes the public a full day's work for a full day's pay
   B. *proper,* primarily because employees need to have a clear picture of the rewards and penalties that go with public employment
   C. *improper,* primarily because group problems require group discussion which need not be formal in character
   D. *improper,* primarily because professional personnel resent having such matters as lunch hours brought to their attention.

8. In communicating with superiors or subordinates, it is well to bear in mind a phenomenon known as the *halo effect.* An example of this *halo effect* occurs when we

   A. employ informal language in a formal setting as a means of attracting attention
   B. ignore the advice of someone we distrust without evaluating the advice
   C. ask people to speak up who have a tendency to speak softly or occasionally indistinctly
   D. react to a piece of good work by inquiring into the motivations of those who did the work

9. Which of the following dangers is MOST likely to arise when a work group becomes too tightly knit? The

    A. group may appoint an informal leader who gradually sets policies and standards for the group to the detriment of the agency
    B. group may be reluctant to accept new employees as members
    C. quantity and quality of work produced may tend to diminish sharply despite the group's best efforts
    D. group may focus too strongly on employee benefits at inappropriate times

10. The overall managerial problem has become more complex because each group of management specialists will tend to view the interests of the enterprise in terms which are compatible with the survival or the increase of its special function. That is, each group will have a trained capacity for its own function and a *trained incapacity* to see its relation to the whole.
    The *trained incapacity* to which the foregoing passage refers PROBABLY results from

    A. an imbalance in the number of specialists as compared with the number of generalists
    B. development by each specialized group of a certain dominant value or goal that shapes its entire way of doing things
    C. low morale accompanied by lackadaisical behavior by large segments of the managerial staff
    D. supervisory failure to inculcate pride in workmanship

11. Of the following, the MOST important responsibility of a supervisor in charge of a section is to

    A. establish close personal relationships with each of his subordinates in the section
    B. insure that each subordinate in the section knows the full range of his duties and responsibilities
    C. maintain friendly relations with his immediate supervisor
    D. protect his subordinates from criticism from any source

12. The BEST way to get a good work output from employees is to

    A. hold over them the threat of disciplinary action or removal
    B. maintain a steady, unrelenting pressure on them
    C. show them that you can do anything they can do faster and better
    D. win their respect and liking so they want to work for you

13. Supervisors should GENERALLY

    A. lean more toward management than toward their subordinates
    B. lean neither toward subordinates nor management
    C. lean more toward their subordinates than toward their management
    D. maintain a proper balance between management and subordinates

14. For a supervisor in charge of a section to ask occasionally the opinion of a subordinate concerning a problem is   14._____

    A. *desirable;* but it would be even better if the subordinate were consulted routinely on every problem
    B. *desirable;* subordinates may make good suggestions and will be pleased by being consulted
    C. *undesirable;* subordinats may be resentful if their advice is not followed
    D. *undesirable;* the supervisor should not attempt to shift his responsibilities to subordinates

15. The PRIMARY responsibility of a supervisor is to   15._____

    A. gain the confidence and make friends of all his subordinates
    B. get the work done properly
    C. satisfy his superior and gain his respect
    D. train the men in new methods for doing the work

16. In starting a work simplification study, the one of the following steps that should be taken FIRST is to   16._____

    A. break the work down into its elements
    B. draw up a chart of operations
    C. enlist the interest and cooperation of the personnel
    D. suggest alternative procedures

17. Of the following, the MOST important value of a manual of procedures is that it usually   17._____

    A. eliminates the need for on-the-job training
    B. decreases the span of control which can be exercised by individual supervisory personnel
    C. outlines methods of operation for ready reference
    D. provides concrete examples of work previously performed by employees

18. Reprimanding a subordinate when he has done something wrong should be done PRIMARILY in order to   18._____

    A. deter others from similar acts
    B. improve the subordinate in future performance
    C. maintain discipline
    D. uphold departmental rules

19. Most of the training of new employees in a public agency is USUALLY accomplished by   19._____

    A. formal classes   B. general orientation
    C. internship   D. on-the-job activities

20. You find that delivery of a certain item cannot possibly be made to a using agency by the date the using agency requested.
    Of the following, the MOST advisable course of action for you to take FIRST is to

    A. cancel the order and inform the using agency
    B. discuss the problem with the using agency
    C. notify the using agency to obtain the item through direct purchase
    D. schedule the delivery for the earliest possible date

21. Assume that one of your subordinates has gotten into the habit of regularly and routinely referring every small problem which arises in his work to you.
    In order to help him overcome this habit, it is generally MOST advisable for you to

    A. advise him that you do not have time to discuss each problem with him and that he should do whatever he wants
    B. ask your subordinate for his solution and approve any satisfactory approach that he suggests
    C. refuse to discuss such routine problems with him
    D. tell him that he should consider looking for another position if he does not feel competent to solve such routine problems

22. The BEST of the following reasons for developing understudies to supervisory staff is that this practice

    A. assures that capable staff will not leave their jobs since they are certain to be promoted
    B. helps to assure continued efficiency when persons in important positions leave their jobs
    C. improves morale by demonstrating to employees the opportunities for advancement
    D. provides an opportunity for giving on-the-job training

23. When a supervisor delegates some of his work to a subordinate, the

    A. supervisor retains final responsibility for the work
    B. supervisor should not check on the work until it has been completed
    C. subordinate assumes full responsibility for the successful completion of the work
    D. subordinate is likely to lose interest and get less satisfaction from the work

24. Sometimes it is necessary to give out written orders or to post written or typed information on a bulletin board rather than to merely give spoken orders. The supervisor must decide how he will do it.
    In which of the following situations would it be BETTER for him to give written rather than spoken orders?

    A. He is going to reassign a man from one unit to another under his supervision.
    B. His staff must be informed of a permanent change in a complicated operating procedure.
    C. A man must be transferred from a clerical unit to an operating unit.
    D. He must order a group of staff men to do a difficult and tedious inventory job to which most of them are likely to object.

25. Of the following symbolic patterns, which one is NOT representative of a normal direction in which formal organizational communications flow.   25._____

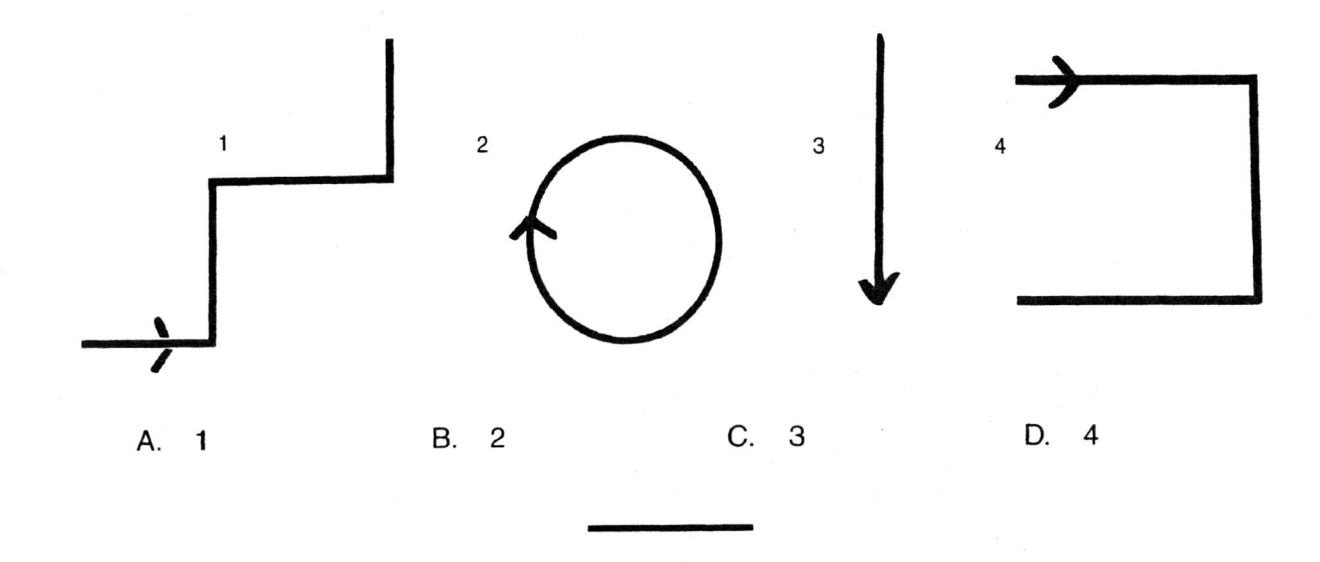

A. 1   B. 2   C. 3   D. 4

KEY (CORRECT ANSWERS)

1.	B		11.	B
2.	D		12.	D
3.	C		13.	D
4.	D		14.	B
5.	A		15.	B
6.	D		16.	C
7.	C		17.	C
8.	B		18.	B
9.	B		19.	D
10.	B		20.	B

21. B
22. B
23. A
24. B
25. B

EXAMINATION SECTION
TEST 1

DIRECTIONS: Each question or incomplete statement is followed by several suggested answers or completions. Select the one that BEST answers the question or completes the statement. *PRINT THE LETTER OF THE CORRECT ANSWER IN THE SPACE AT THE RIGHT.*

1. *Which one* of the following generalizations is *most likely* to be INACCURATE and lead to judgmental errors in communication?

    A. A supervisor must be able to read with understanding
    B. Misunderstanding may lead to dislike
    C. Anyone can listen to another person and understand what he means
    D. It is usually desirable to let a speaker talk until he is finished

    1.____

2. Assume that, as a supervisor, you have been directed to inform your subordinates about the implementation of a new procedure which will affect their work. While communicating this information, you should do all of the following EXCEPT

    A. obtain the approval of your subordinates regarding the new procedure
    B. explain the reason for implementing the new procedure
    C. hold a staff meeting at a time convenient to most of your subordinates
    D. encourage a productive discussion of the new procedure

    2.____

3. Assume that you are in charge of a section that handles requests for information on matters received from the public. One day, you observe that a clerk under your supervision is using a method to log-in requests for information that is different from the one specified by you in the past. Upon questioning the clerk, you discover that instructions changing the old procedure were delivered orally by your supervisor on a day on which you were absent from the office.
Of the following, the *most appropriate* action for you to take is to

    A. tell the clerk to revert to the old procedure at once
    B. ask your supervisor for information about the change
    C. call your staff together and tell them that no existing procedure is to be changed unless you direct that it be done
    D. write a memo to your supervisor suggesting that all future changes in procedure are to be in writing and that they be directed to you

    3.____

4. At the first meeting with your staff after appointment as a supervisor, you find considerable indifference and some hostility among the participants.
Of the following, the *most appropriate* way to handle this situation is to

    A. disregard the attitudes displayed and continue to make your presentation until you have completed it
    B. discontinue your presentation but continue the meeting and attempt to find out the reasons for their attitudes
    C. warm up your audience with some good natured statements and anecdotes and then proceed with your presentation
    D. discontinue the meeting and set up personal interviews with the staff members to try to find out the reason for their attitude

    4.____

5. In order to start the training of a new employee, it has been a standard practice to have him read a manual of instructions or procedures.
This method is currently being replaced by the _____ method.

   A. audio-visual
   B. conference
   C. lecture
   D. programmed instruction

6. Of the following subjects, the *one* that can usually be *successfully* taught by a first-line supervisor who is training his subordinates is:

   A. Theory and philosophy of management
   B. Human relations
   C. Responsibilities of a supervisor
   D. Job skills

7. Assume that as a supervisor you are training a clerk who is experiencing difficulty learning a new task.
Which one of the following would be the LEAST effective approach to take when trying to solve this problem? To

   A. ask questions which will reveal the clerk's understanding of the task
   B. take a different approach in explaining the task
   C. give the clerk an opportunity to ask questions about the task
   D. make sure the clerk knows you are watching his work closely

8. One school of management and supervision involves participation by employees in the setting of group goals and in the sharing of responsibility for the operation of the unit. If this philosophy were applied to a unit consisting of professional and clerical personnel, one should expect

   A. the professional and clerical personnel to participate with equal effectiveness in operating areas and policy areas
   B. the professional personnel to participate with greater effectiveness than the clerical personnel in policy areas
   C. the clerical personnel to participate with greater effectiveness than the professional personnel in operating areas
   D. greater participation by clerical personnel but with less responsibility for their actions

9. With regard to productivity, high morale among employees *generally* indicates a

   A. history of high productivity
   B. nearly absolute positive correlation with high productivity
   C. predisposition to be productive under facilitating leadership and circumstances
   D. complacency which has little effect on productivity

10. Assume that you are going to organize the professionals and clerks under your supervision into work groups or teams of two or three employees.
Of the following, the step which is LEAST likely to foster the successful development of each group is to

   A. allow friends to work together in the group
   B. provide special help and attention to employees with no friends in their group
   C. frequently switch employees from group to group
   D. rotate jobs within the group in order to strengthen group identification

11. Following are four statements which might be made by an employee to his supervisor during a performance evaluation interview.
Which of the statements BEST provides a basis for developing a plan to improve the employee's performance?

    A. *I understand that you are dissatisfied with my work and I will try harder in the future.*
    B. *I feel that I've been making too many careless clerical errors recently.*
    C. *I am aware that I will be subject to disciplinary action if my work does not improve within one month.*
    D. *I understand that this interview is simply a requirement of your job, and not a personal attack on me.*

12. Three months ago, Mr. Smith and his supervisor, Mrs. Jones, developed a plan which was intended to correct Mr. Smith's inadequate job performance. Now, during a follow-up interview, Mr. Smith, who thought his performance had satisfactorily improved, has been informed that Mrs. Jones is still dissatisfied with his work.
Of the following, it is *most likely* that the disagreement occurred because, when formulating the plan, they did NOT

    A. set realistic goals for Mr. Smith Is performance
    B. set a reasonable time limit for Mr. Smith to effect his improvement in performance
    C. provide for adequate training to improve Mr. Smith's skills
    D. establish performance standards for measuring Mr. Smith's progress

13. When a supervisor delegates authority to subordinates, there are usually many problems to overcome, such as inadequately trained subordinates and poor planning.
All of the following are means of increasing the effectiveness of delegation EXCEPT:

    A. Defining assignments in the light of results expected
    B. Maintaining open lines of communication
    C. Establishing tight controls so that subordinates will stay within the bounds of the area of delegation
    D. Providing rewards for successful assumption of authority by a subordinate

14. Assume that one of your subordinates has arrived late for work several times during the current month. The last time he was late you had warned him that another unexcused lateness would result in formal disciplinary action.
If the employee arrives late for work again during this month, the FIRST action you should take is to

    A. give the employee a chance to explain this lateness
    B. give the employee a written copy of your warning
    C. tell the employee that you are recommending formal disciplinary action
    D. tell the employee that you will give him only one more chance before recommending formal disciplinary action

15. In trying to decide how many subordinates a manager can control directly, one of the determinants is how much the manager can reduce the frequency and time consumed in contacts with his subordinates.
Of the following, the factor which LEAST influences the number and direction of these contacts is:

   A. How well the manager delegates authority
   B. The rate at which the organization is changing
   C. The control techniques used by the manager
   D. Whether the activity is line or staff

16. Systematic rotation of employees through lateral transfer within a government organization to provide for managerial development is

   A. *good,* because systematic rotation develops specialists who learn to do many jobs well
   B. *bad,* because the outsider upsets the status quo of the existing organization
   C. *good,* because rotation provides challenge and organizational flexibility
   D. *bad,* because it is upsetting to employees to be transferred within a service

17. Assume that you are required to provide an evaluation of the performance of your subordinates.
Of the following factors, it is MOST important that the performance evaluation include a rating of each employees

   A. initiative B. productivity C. intelligence D. personality

18. When preparing performance evaluations of your subordinates, *one* way to help assure that you are rating each employee fairly is to

   A. prepare a list of all employees and all the rating factors and rate all employees on one rating factor before going on to the next factor
   B. prepare a list of all your employees and all the rating factors and rate each employee on all factors before going on to the next employee
   C. discuss all the ratings you anticipate giving with another supervisor in order to obtain an unbiased opinion
   D. discuss each employee with his co-workers in order to obtain peer judgment of worth before doing any rating

19. A managerial plan which would include the GREATEST control is a plan which is

   A. spontaneous and geared to each new job that is received
   B. detailed and covering an extended time period
   C. long-range and generalized, allowing for various interpretations
   D. specific and prepared daily

20. Assume that you are preparing a report which includes statistical data covering increases in budget allocations of four agencies for the past ten years.
For you to represent the statistical data pictorially or graphically within the report is a

   A. *poor idea,* because you should be able to make statistical data understandable through the use of words
   B. *good idea,* because it is easier for the reader to understand pictorial representation rather than quantities of words conveying statistical data
   C. *poor idea,* because using pictorial representation in a report may make the report too expensive to print
   D. *good idea,* because a pictorial representation makes the report appear more attractive than the use of many words to convey the statistical data

---

KEY (CORRECT ANSWERS)

1.	C	11.	A
2.	A	12.	B
3.	B	13.	C
4.	D	14.	A
5.	D	15.	D
6.	D	16.	C
7.	D	17.	B
8.	B	18.	A
9.	C	19.	B
10.	C	20.	B

TEST 2

DIRECTIONS: Each question or incomplete statement is followed by several suggested answers or completions. Select the one that BEST answers the question or completes the statement. *PRINT THE LETTER OF THE CORRECT ANSWER IN THE SPACE AT THE RIGHT.*

1. Research studies have shown that supervisors of groups with high production records USUALLY

    A. give detailed instructions, constantly check on progress, and insist on approval of all decisions before implementation
    B. do considerable paperwork and other work similar to that performed by subordinates
    C. think of themselves as team members on the same level as others in the work group
    D. perform tasks traditionally associated with managerial functions

2. Mr. Smith, a bureau chief, is summoned by his agency's head in a conference to discuss Mr. Jones, an accountant who works in one of the divisions of his bureau. Mr. Jones has committed an error of such magnitude as to arouse the agency head's concern.
After agreeing with the other conferees that a severe reprimand would be the appropriate punishment, Mr. Smith should

    A. arrange for Mr. Jones to explain the reasons for his error to the agency head
    B. send a memorandum to Mr. Jones, being careful that the language emphasizes the nature of the error rather than Mr. Jones' personal faults
    C. inform Mr. Jones' immediate supervisor of the conclusion reached at the conference, and let the supervisor take the necessary action
    D. suggest to the agency head that no additional action be taken against Mr. Jones because no further damage will be caused by the error

3. Assume that Ms. Thomson, a unit chief, has determined that the findings of an internal audit have been seriously distorted as a result of careless errors. The audit had been performed by a group of auditors in her unit and the errors were overlooked by the associate accountant in charge of the audit. Ms. Thomson has decided to delay discussing the matter with the associate accountant and the staff who performed the audit until she verifies certain details, which may require prolonged investigation.
Ms. Thomson's method of handling this situation is

    A. *appropriate;* employees should not be accused of wrongdoing until all the facts have been determined
    B. *inappropriate;* the employees involved may assume that the errors were considered unimportant
    C. *appropriate;* employees are more likely to change their behavior as a result of disciplinary action taken after a *cooling off* period
    D. *inappropriate;* the employees involved may have forgotten the details and become emotionally upset when confronted with the facts

4. After studying the financial situation in his agency, an administrative accountant decides to recommend centralization of certain accounting functions which are being performed in three different bureaus of the organization.
The one of the following which is *most likely* to be a DISADVANTAGE if this recommendation is implemented is that

   A. there may be less coordination of the accounting procedure because central direction is not so close to the day-to-day problems as the personnel handling them in each specialized accounting unit
   B. the higher management levels would not be able to make emergency decisions in as timely a manner as the more involved, lower-level administrators who are closer to the problem
   C. it is more difficult to focus the attention of the top management in order to resolve accounting problems because of the many other activities top management is involved in at the same time
   D. the accuracy of upward and inter-unit communication may be reduced because centralization may require insertion of more levels of administration in the chain of command

5. Of the following assumptions about the role of conflict in an organization, the *one* which is the MOST accurate statement of the approach of modern management theorists is that conflict

   A. can usually be avoided or controlled
   B. serves as a vital element in organizational change
   C. works against attainment of organizational goals
   D. provides a constructive outlet for problem employees

6. Which of the following is generally regarded as the BEST approach for a supervisor to follow in handling grievances brought by subordinates?

   A. Avoid becoming involved personally
   B. Involve the union representative in the first stage of discussion
   C. Settle the grievance as soon as possible
   D. Arrange for arbitration by a third party

7. Assume that supervisors of similar-sized accounting units in city, state, and federal offices were interviewed and observed at their work. It was found that the ways they acted in and viewed their roles tended to be very similar, regardless of who employed them.
Which of the following is the BEST explanation of this similarity?

   A. A supervisor will ordinarily behave in conformance to his own self-image
   B. Each role in an organization, including the supervisory role, calls for a distinct type of personality
   C. The supervisory role reflects an exceptionally complex pattern of human response
   D. The general nature of the duties and responsibilities of the supervisory position determines the role

8. Which of the following is NOT consistent with the findings of recent research about the characteristics of successful top managers?

   A. They are *inner-directed* and not overly concerned with pleasing others
   B. They are challenged by situations filled with high risk and ambiguity
   C. They tend to stay on the same job for long periods of time
   D. They consider it more important to handle critical assignments successfully than to do routine work well

9. As a supervisor you have to give subordinate operational guidelines.
   Of the following, the BEST reason for providing them with information about the overall objectives within which their operations fit is that the subordinates will

   A. be more likely to carry out the operation according to your expectations
   B. know that there is a legitimate reason for carrying out the operation in the way you have prescribed
   C. be more likely to handle unanticipated problems that may arise without having to take up your time
   D. more likely to transmit the operating instructions correctly to their subordinates

10. A supervisor holds frequent meetings with his staff.
    Of the following, the BEST approach he can take in order to elicit productive discussions at these meetings is for him to

    A. ask questions of those who attend
    B. include several levels of supervisors at the meetings
    C. hold the meetings at a specified time each week
    D. begin each meeting with a statement that discussion is welcomed

11. Of the following, the MOST important action that a supervisor can take to increase the productivity of a subordinate is to

    A. increase his uninterrupted work time
    B. increase the number of reproducing machines available in the office
    C. provide clerical assistance whenever he requests it
    D. reduce the number of his assigned tasks

12. Assume that, as a supervisor, you find that you often must countermand or modify your original staff memos. If this practice continues, *which one* of the following situations is MOST likely to occur? The

    A. staff will not bother to read your memos B. office files will become cluttered
    C. staff will delay acting on your memos   D. memos will be treated routinely

13. In making management decisions the committee approach is often used by managers.
    Of the following, the BEST reason for using this approach is to

    A. prevent any one individual from assuming too much authority
    B. allow the manager to bring a wider range of experience and judgment to bear on the problem
    C. allow the participation of all staff members, which will make them feel more committed to the decisions reached
    D. permit the rapid transmission of information about decisions reached to the staff members concerned

14. In establishing standards for the measurement of the performance of a management project team, it is MOST important for the project manager to

   A. identify and define the objectives of the project
   B. determine the number of people who will be assigned to the project team
   C. evaluate the skills of the staff who will be assigned to the project team
   D. estimate fairly accurately the length of time required to complete each phase of the project

15. It is virtually impossible to tell an employee either that he is not so good as another employee or that he does not measure up to a desirable level of performance, without having him feel threatened, rejected, and discouraged.
In accordance with the foregoing observation, a supervisor who is concerned about the performance of the less efficient members of his staff should realize that

   A. he might obtain better results by not discussing the quality and quantity of their work with them, but by relying instead on the written evaluation of their performance to motivate their improvement
   B. since he is required to discuss their performance with them, he should do so in words of encouragement and in so friendly a manner as to not destroy their morale
   C. he might discuss their work in a general way, without mentioning any of the specifics about the quality of their performance, with the expectation that they would understand the full implications of his talk
   D. he should make it a point, while telling them of their poor performance, to mention that their work is as good as that of some of the other employees in the unit

16. Some advocates of management-by-objectives procedures in public agencies have been urging that this method of operations be expanded to encompass all agencies of the government, for one or more of the following reasons, not all of which may be correct:

   I. The MBO method is likely to succeed because it embraces the practice of setting near-term goals for the subordinate manager, reviewing accomplishments at an appropriate time, and repeating this process indefinitely
   II. Provision for authority to perform the tasks assigned as goals in the MBO method is normally not needed because targets are set in quantitative or qualitative terms and specific times for accomplishment are arranged in short-term, repetitive intervals
   III. Many other appraisal-of-performance programs failed because both supervisors and subordinates resisted them, while the MBO approach is not instituted until there is an organizational commitment to it
   IV. Personal accountability is clearly established through the MBO approach because verifiable results are set up in the process of formulating the targets

   Which of the choices below includes ALL of the foregoing statements that are CORRECT?

   A. I and III
   B. II and IV
   C. I,II,III,IV
   D. I,III,IV

17. In preparing an organizational structure, the PRINCIPAL guideline for locating staff units is to place them

    A. all under a common supervisor
    B. as close as possible to the activities they serve
    C. as close to the chief executive as possible without over-extending his span of control
    D. at the lowest operational level

18. The relative importance of any unit in a department can be LEAST reliably judged by the

    A. amount of office space allocated to the unit
    B. number of employees in the unit
    C. rank of the individual who heads the unit
    D. rank of the individual to whom the unit head reports directly

19. Those who favor Planning-Programming-Budgeting Systems (PPBS) as a new method of governmental financial administration emphasize that PPBS

    A. applies statistical measurements which correlate highly with criteria
    B. makes possible economic systems analysis, including an explicit examination of alternatives
    C. makes available scarce government resources which can be coordinated on a government-wide basis and shared between local units of government
    D. shifts the emphasis in budgeting methods to an automated system of data processing

20. The term applied to computer processing which processes data concurrently with a given activity and provides results soon enough to influence the selection of a course of action is

    A. realtime processing   B. batch processing
    C. random access processing   D. integrated data processing

---

KEY (CORRECT ANSWERS)

1.	D	11.	A
2.	C	12.	C
3.	B	13.	B
4.	D	14.	A
5.	B	15.	B
6.	C	16.	D
7.	D	17.	B
8.	C	18.	B
9.	C	19.	B
10.	A	20.	A

EXAMINATION SECTION
TEST 1

DIRECTIONS: Each question or incomplete statement is followed by several suggested answers or completions. Select the one that BEST answers the question or completes the statement. *PRINT THE LETTER OF THE CORRECT ANSWER IN THE SPACE AT THE RIGHT.*

1. Professional staff members in large organizations are sometimes frustrated by a lack of vital work-related information because of the failure of some middle-management supervisors to pass along unrestricted information from top management.
   All of the following are considered to be reasons for such failure to pass along information EXCEPT the supervisors'

   A. belief that information affecting procedures will be ignored unless they are present to supervise their subordinates
   B. fear that specific information will require explanation or justification
   C. inclination to regard the possession of information as a symbol of higher status
   D. tendency to treat information as private property

2. Increasingly in government, employees' records are being handled by automated data processing systems. However, employees frequently doubt a computer's ability to handle their records properly.
   Which of the following is the BEST way for management to overcome such doubts?

   A. Conduct a public relations campaign to explain the savings certain to result from the use of computers
   B. Use automated data processing equipment made by the firm which has the best repair facilities in the industry
   C. Maintain a clerical force to spot check on the accuracy of the computer's record-keeping
   D. Establish automated data processing systems that are objective, impartial, and take into account individual factors as far as possible

3. Some management experts question the usefulness of offering cash to individual employees for their suggestions.
   Which of the following reasons for opposing cash awards is MOST valid?

   A. Emphasis on individual gain deters cooperative effort.
   B. Money spent on evaluating suggestions may outweigh the value of the suggestions.
   C. Awards encourage employees to think about unusual methods of doing work.
   D. Suggestions too technical for ordinary evaluation are usually presented.

4. The use of outside consultants, rather than regular staff, in studying and recommending improvements in the operations of public agencies has been criticized.
   Of the following, the BEST argument in favor of using regular staff is that such staff can better perform the work because they

   A. are more knowledgeable about operations and problems
   B. can more easily be organized into teams consisting of technical specialists
   C. may wish to gain additional professional experience
   D. will provide reports which will be more interesting to the public since they are more experienced

5. One approach to organizational problem-solving is to have all problem-solving authority centralized at the top of the organization.
However, from the viewpoint of providing maximum service to the public, this practice is UNWISE chiefly because it

   A. reduces the responsibility of the decision-makers
   B. produces delays
   C. reduces internal communications
   D. requires specialists

6. Research has shown that problem-solving efficiency is optimal when the motivation of the problem-solver is at a moderate rather than an extreme level.
Of the following, probably the CHIEF reason for this is that the problem-solver

   A. will cause confusion among his subordinates when his motivation is too high
   B. must avoid alternate solutions that tend to lead him up blind alleys
   C. can devote his attention to both the immediate problem as well as to other relevant problems in the general area
   D. must feel the need to solve the problem but not so urgently as to direct all his attention to the need and none to the means of solution

7. Don't be afraid to make mistakes. Many organizations are paralyzed from the fear of making mistakes. As a result, they don't do the things they should; they don't try new and different ideas.
For the effective supervisor, the MOST valid implication of this statement is that

   A. mistakes should not be encouraged, but there are some unavoidable risks in decision-making
   B. mistakes which stem from trying new and different ideas are usually not serious
   C. the possibility of doing things wrong is limited by one's organizational position
   D. the fear of making mistakes will prevent future errors

8. The duties of an employee under your supervision may be either routine, problem-solving, innovative, or creative. Which of the following BEST describes duties which are both innovative and creative?

   A. Checking to make sure that work is done properly
   B. Applying principles in a practical manner
   C. Developing new and better methods of meeting goals
   D. Working at two or more jobs at the same time

9. According to modern management theory, a supervisor who uses as little authority as possible and as much as is necessary would be considered to be using a mode that is

   A. autocratic   B. inappropriate
   C. participative   D. directive

10. Delegation involves establishing and maintaining effective working arrangements between a supervisor and the persons who report to him.
Delegation is MOST likely to have taken place when the

    A. entire staff openly discusses common problems in order to reach solutions satisfactory to the supervisor
    B. performance of specified work is entrusted to a capable person, and the expected results are mutually understood
    C. persons assigned to properly accomplish work are carefully evaluated and given a chance to explain shortcomings
    D. supervisor provides specific written instructions in order to prevent anxiety on the part of inexperienced persons

11. Supervisors often are not aware of the effect that their behavior has on their subordinates.
The one of the following training methods which would be BEST for changing such supervisory behavior is

    A. essential skills training
    B. off-the-job training
    C. sensitivity training
    D. developmental training

12. A supervisor, in his role as a trainer, may have to decide on the length and frequency of training sessions.
When the material to be taught is new, difficult, and lengthy, the trainer should be guided by the principle that for BEST results in such circumstances, sessions should be

    A. longer, relatively fewer in number, and held on successive days
    B. shorter, relatively greater in number, and spaced at intervals of several days
    C. of average length, relatively fewer in number, and held at intermittent intervals
    D. of random length and frequency, but spaced at fixed intervals

13. Employee training which is based on realistic simulation, sometimes known as *game play* or *role play*, is sometimes preferable to learning from actual experience on the job. Which of the following is NOT a correct statement concerning the value of simulation to trainees?

    A. Simulation allows for practice in decision-making without any need for subsequent discussion.
    B. Simulation is intrinsically motivating because it offers a variety of challenges.
    C. Compared to other, more traditional training techniques, simulation is dynamic.
    D. The simulation environment is nonpunitive as compared to real life.

14. Programmed instruction as a method of training has all of the following advantages EXCEPT:

    A. Learning is accomplished in an optimum sequence of distinct steps
    B. Trainees have wide latitude in deciding what is to be learned within each program
    C. The trainee takes an active part in the learning process
    D. The trainee receives immediate knowledge of the results of his response

15. In a work-study program, trainees were required to submit weekly written performance reports in order to insure that work assignments fulfilled the program objectives. Such reports would also assist the administrator of the work-study program PRIMARILY to

    A. eliminate personal counseling for the trainees
    B. identify problems requiring prompt resolution
    C. reduce the amount of clerical work for all concerned
    D. estimate the rate at which budgeted funds are being expended

16. Which of the following would be MOST useful in order to avoid misunderstanding when preparing correspondence or reports?

    A. Use vocabulary which is at an elementary level
    B. Present each sentence as an individual paragraph
    C. Have someone other than the writer read the material for clarity
    D. Use general words which are open to interpretation

17. Which of the following supervisory methods would be MOST likely to train subordinates to give a prompt response to memoranda in an organizational setting where most transactions are informal?

    A. Issue a written directive setting forth a schedule of strict deadlines
    B. Let it be known, informally, that those who respond promptly will be rewarded
    C. Follow up each memorandum by a personal inquiry regarding the receiver's reaction to it
    D. Direct subordinates to furnish a precise explanation for ignoring memos

18. Conferences may fail for a number of reasons. Still, a conference that is an apparent failure may have some benefit.
    Which of the following would LEAST likely be such a benefit? It may

    A. increase for most participants their possessiveness about information they have
    B. produce a climate of good will and trust among many of the participants
    C. provide most participants with an opportunity to learn things about the others
    D. serve as a unifying force to keep most of the individuals functioning as a group

19. Assume that you have been assigned to study and suggest improvements in an operating unit of a delegate agency whose staff has become overwhelmed with problems, has had inadequate resources, and has become accustomed to things getting worse. The staff is indifferent to cooperating with you because they see no hope of improvement.
    Which of the following steps would be LEAST useful in carrying out your assignment?

    A. Encourage the entire staff to make suggestions to you for change
    B. Inform the staff that management is somewhat dissatisfied with their performance
    C. Let staff know that you are fully aware of their problems and stresses
    D. Look for those problem areas where changes can be made quickly

20. Which of the following statements about employer-employee relations is NOT considered to be correct by leading managerial experts?

    A. An important factor in good employer-employee relations is treating workers respectfully.
    B. Employer-employee relations are profoundly influenced by the fundamentals of human nature.
    C. Good employer-employee relations must stem from top management and reach downward.
    D. Employee unions are usually a major obstacle to establishing good employer-employee relations.

21. In connection with labor relations, the term *management rights* GENERALLY refers to

    A. a managerial review level in a grievance system
    B. statutory prohibitions that bar monetary negotiations
    C. the impact of collective bargaining on government
    D. those subjects which management considers to be non-negotiable

22. Barriers may exist to the utilization of women in higher level positions. Some of these barriers are attitudinal in nature.
    Which of the following is MOST clearly attitudinal in nature?

    A. Advancement opportunities which are vertical in nature and thus require seniority
    B. Experience which is inadequate or irrelevant to the needs of a dynamic and progressive organization
    C. Inadequate means of early identification of employees with talent and potential for advancement
    D. Lack of self-confidence on the part of some women concerning their ability to handle a higher position

23. Because a reader reacts to the meaning he associates with a word, we can never be sure what emotional impact a word may carry or how it may affect our readers.
    The MOST logical implication of this statement for employees who correspond with members of the public is that

    A. a writer should try to select a neutral word that will not bias his writing by its hidden emotional meaning
    B. simple language should be used in writing letters denying requests so that readers are not upset by the denial
    C. every writer should adopt a writing style which he finds natural and easy
    D. whenever there is any doubt as to how a word is defined, the dictionary should be consulted

24. A public information program should be based on clear information about the nature of actual public knowledge and opinion. One way of learning about the views of the public is through the use of questionnaires.
    Which of the following is of LEAST importance in designing a questionnaire?

    A. A respondent should be asked for his name and address.
    B. A respondent should be asked to choose from among several statements the one which expresses his views.
    C. Questions should ask for responses in a form suitable for processing.
    D. Questions should be stated in familiar language.

25. Assume that you have accepted an invitation to speak before an interested group about a problem. You have brought with you for distribution a number of booklets and other informational material.
Of the following, which would be the BEST way to use this material?

   A. Distribute it before you begin talking so that the audience may read it at their leisure.
   B. Distribute it during your talk to increase the likelihood that it will be read.
   C. Hold it until the end of your talk, then announce that those who wish may take or examine the material.
   D. Before starting the talk, leave it on a table in the back of the room so that people may pick it up as they enter.

25. ___

KEY (CORRECT ANSWERS)

1.	A	11.	C
2.	D	12.	B
3.	A	13.	A
4.	A	14.	B
5.	B	15.	B
6.	D	16.	C
7.	A	17.	C
8.	C	18.	A
9.	C	19.	B
10.	B	20.	D

21. D
22. D
23. A
24. A
25. C

TEST 2

DIRECTIONS: Each question or incomplete statement is followed by several suggested answers or completions. Select the one that BEST answers the question or completes the statement. *PRINT THE LETTER OF THE CORRECT ANSWER IN THE SPACE AT THE RIGHT.*

1. Of the following, the FIRST step in planning an operation is to

    A. obtain relevant information
    B. identify the goal to be achieved
    C. consider possible alternatives
    D. make necessary assignments

2. A supervisor who is extremely busy performing routine tasks is MOST likely making INCORRECT use of what basic principle of supervision?

    A. Homogeneous Assignment
    B. Span of Control
    C. Work Distribution
    D. Delegation of Authority

3. Controls help supervisors to obtain information from which they can determine whether their staffs are achieving planned goals.
Which one of the following would be LEAST useful as a control device?

    A. Employee diaries
    B. Organization charts
    C. Periodic inspections
    D. Progress charts

4. A certain employee has difficulty in effectively performing a particular portion of his routine assignments, but his overall productivity is average.
As the direct supervisor of this individual, your BEST course of action would be to

    A. attempt to develop the man's capacity to execute the problematical facets of his assignments
    B. diversify the employee's work assignments in order to build up his confidence
    C. reassign the man to less difficult tasks
    D. request in a private conversation that the employee improve his work output

5. A supervisor who uses persuasion as a means of supervising a unit would GENERALLY also use which of the following practices to supervise his unit?

    A. Supervise and control the staff with an authoritative attitude to indicate that he is a *take-charge* individual
    B. Make significant changes in the organizational operations so as to improve job efficiency
    C. Remove major communication barriers between himself, subordinates, and management
    D. Supervise everyday operations while being mindful of the problems of his subordinates

6. Whenever a supervisor in charge of a unit delegates a routine task to a capable subordinate, he tells him exactly how to do it.
This practice is GENERALLY

    A. *desirable,* chiefly because good supervisors should be aware of the traits of their subordinates and delegate responsibilities to them accordingly
    B. *undesirable,* chiefly because only non-routine tasks should be delegated
    C. *desirable,* chiefly because a supervisor should frequently test the willingness of his subordinates to perform ordinary tasks
    D. *undesirable,* chiefly because a capable subordinate should usually be allowed to exercise his own discretion in doing a routine job

7. The one of the following activities through which a supervisor BEST demonstrates leadership ability is by

   A. arranging periodic staff meetings in order to keep his subordinates informed about professional developments in the field
   B. frequently issuing definite orders and directives which will lessen the need for subordinates to make decisions in handling any tasks assigned to them
   C. devoting the major part of his time to supervising subordinates so as to stimulate continuous improvement
   D. setting aside time for self-development and research so as to improve the skills, techniques, and procedures of his unit

8. The following three statements relate to the supervision of employees:
   I. The assignment of difficult tasks that offer a challenge is more conducive to good morale than the assignment of easy tasks
   II. The same general principles of supervision that apply to men are equally applicable to women
   III. The best retraining program should cover all phases of an employee's work in a general manner

   Which of the following choices list ALL of the above statements that are generally correct?

   A. II, III
   B. I
   C. I, II
   D. I, II, III

9. Which of the following examples BEST illustrates the application of the *exception principle* as a supervisory technique?

   A. A complex job is divided among several employees who work simultaneously to complete the whole job in a shorter time.
   B. An employee is required to complete any task delegated to him to such an extent that nothing is left for the superior who delegated the task except to approve it.
   C. A superior delegates responsibility to a subordinate but retains authority to make the final decisions.
   D. A superior delegates all work possible to his subordinates and retains that which requires his personal attention or performance.

10. Assume that you are a supervisor. Your immediate superior frequently gives orders to your subordinates without your knowledge.
    Of the following, the MOST direct and effective way for you to handle this problem is to

    A. tell your subordinates to take orders only from you
    B. submit a report to higher authority in which you cite specific instances
    C. discuss it with your immediate superior
    D. find out to what extent your authority and prestige as a supervisor have been affected

11. In an agency which has as its primary purpose the protection of the public against fraudulent business practices, which of the following would GENERALLY be considered an *auxiliary* or *staff* rather than a *line* function?

    A. Interviewing victims of frauds and advising them about their legal remedies
    B. Daily activities directed toward prevention of fraudulent business practices
    C. Keeping records and statistics about business violations reported and corrected
    D. Follow-up inspections by investigators after corrective action has been taken

12. A supervisor can MOST effectively reduce the spread of false rumors through the *grapevine* by

   A. identifying and disciplining any subordinate responsible for initiating such rumors
   B. keeping his subordinates informed as much as possible about matters affecting them
   C. denying false rumors which might tend to lower staff morale and productivity
   D. making sure confidential matters are kept secure from access by unauthorized employees

12.____

13. A supervisor has tried to learn about the background, education, and family relationships of his subordinates through observation, personal contact, and inspection of their personnel records.
These supervisory actions are GENERALLY

   A. *inadvisable,* chiefly because they may lead to charges of favoritism
   B. *advisable,* chiefly because they may make him more popular with his subordinates
   C. *inadvisable,* chiefly because his efforts may be regarded as an invasion of privacy
   D. *advisable,* chiefly because the information may enable him to develop better understanding of each of his subordinates

13.____

14. In an emergency situation, when action must be taken immediately, it is BEST for the supervisor to give orders in the form of

   A. direct commands which are brief and precise
   B. requests, so that his subordinates will not become alarmed
   C. suggestions which offer alternative courses of action
   D. implied directives, so that his subordinates may use their judgment in carrying them out

14.____

15. When demonstrating a new and complex procedure to a group of subordinates, it is ESSENTIAL that a supervisor

   A. go slowly and repeat the steps involved at least once
   B. show the employees common errors and the consequences of such errors
   C. go through the process at the usual speed so that the employees can see the rate at which they should work
   D. distribute summaries of the procedure during the demonstration and instruct his subordinates to refer to them afterwards

15.____

16. After a procedures manual has been written and distributed,

   A. continuous maintenance work is necessary to keep the manual current
   B. it is best to issue new manuals rather than make changes in the original manual
   C. no changes should be necessary
   D. only major changes should be considered

16.____

17. Of the following, the MOST important criterion of effective report writing is

    A. eloquence of writing style
    B. the use of technical language
    C. to be brief and to the point
    D. to cover all details

18. The use of electronic data processing

    A. has proven unsuccessful in most organizations
    B. has unquestionable advantages for all organizations
    C. is unnecessary in most organizations
    D. should be decided upon only after careful feasibility studies by individual organizations

19. The PRIMARY purpose of work measurement is to

    A. design and install a wage incentive program
    B. determine who should be promoted
    C. establish a yardstick to determine extent of progress
    D. set up a spirit of competition among employees

20. The action which is MOST effective in gaining acceptance of a study by the agency which is being studied is

    A. a directive from the agency head to install a study based on recommendations included in a report
    B. a lecture-type presentation following approval of the procedures
    C. a written procedure in narrative form covering the proposed system with visual presentations and discussions
    D. procedural charts showing the *before* situation, forms, steps, etc., to the employees affected

21. Which organization principle is MOST closely related to procedural analysis and improvement?

    A. Duplication, overlapping, and conflict should be eliminated.
    B. Managerial authority should be clearly defined.
    C. The objectives of the organization should be clearly defined.
    D. Top management should be freed of burdensome detail.

22. Which one of the following is the MAJOR objective of operational audits?

    A. Detecting fraud
    B. Determining organization problems
    C. Determining the number of personnel needed
    D. Recommending opportunities for improving operating and management practices

23. Of the following, the formalization of organization structure is BEST achieved by

    A. a narrative description of the plan of organization
    B. functional charts
    C. job descriptions together with organization charts
    D. multi-flow charts

24. Budget planning is MOST useful when it achieves 24.____

    A. cost control   B. forecast of receipts
    C. performance review   D. personnel reduction

25. GENERALLY, in applying the principle of delegation in dealing with subordinates, a supervisor 25.____

    A. allows his subordinates to set up work goals and to fix the limits within which they can work
    B. allows his subordinates to set up work goals and then gives detailed orders as to how they are to be achieved
    C. makes relatively few decisions by himself and frames his orders in broad, general terms
    D. provides externalized motivation for his subordinates

KEY (CORRECT ANSWERS)

1.	B	11.	C
2.	D	12.	B
3.	B	13.	D
4.	A	14.	A
5.	D	15.	A
6.	D	16.	A
7.	C	17.	C
8.	C	18.	D
9.	D	19.	C
10.	C	20.	C

21.	A
22.	D
23.	C
24.	A
25.	C

EXAMINATION SECTION
TEST 1

DIRECTIONS: Each question or incomplete statement is followed by several suggested answers or completions. Select the one that BEST answers the question or completes the statement. *PRINT THE LETTER OF THE CORRECT ANSWER IN THE SPACE AT THE RIGHT.*

1. The one of the following which is the CHIEF reason for the difference between the administration of justice agencies and that of other units in public administration is that

    A. correctional institutions are concerned with security
    B. some defendants are proven to be innocent after trial
    C. the administration of justice is much more complicated than other aspects of public administration
    D. correctional institutions produce services their *clients* or *customers* fail to understand or ask for

   1.____

2. Of the following, the MOST important reason why employees resist change is that

    A. they have not received adequate training in preparation for the change
    B. experience has shown that when new ideas don't work, employees get blamed and not the individuals responsible for the new ideas
    C. new ideas and methods almost always represent a threat to the security of the individuals involved
    D. new ideas often are not practical and disrupt operations unnecessarily

   2.____

3. Stress situations are ideal for building up a backlog of knowledge about an employee's behavior. Not only does it inform the supervisor of many aspects of a person's behavior patterns, but it is also vitally important to have foreknowledge of how people behave under stress.
   The one of the following which is NOT implied by this passage is that

    A. a person under stress may give some indication of his unsuitability for work in an institution
    B. putting people under stress is the best means of determining their usual patterns of behavior
    C. stress situations may give important clues about performance in the service
    D. there is a need to know about a person's reaction to situations *when the chips are down*

   3.____

4. There are situations requiring a supervisor to give direct orders to subordinates assigned to work under the direct control of other supervisors.
   Under which of the following conditions would this shift of command responsibility be MOST appropriate?

    A. Emergency operations require the cooperative action of two or more organizational units.
    B. One of the other supervisors is not doing his job, thus defeating the goals of the organization.
    C. The subordinates are performing their assigned tasks in the absence of their own supervisor.
    D. The subordinates ask a superior officer who is not their own supervisor how to perform an assignment given them by their supervisor.

   4.____

5. The one of the following which BEST differentiates staff supervision from line supervision is that

   A. staff supervision has the authority to immediately correct a line subordinate's action
   B. staff supervision is an advisory relationship
   C. line supervision goes beyond the normal boundaries of direct supervision within a *command*
   D. line supervision does not report findings and make recommendations

6. Decision-making is a rational process calling for a *suspended judgment* by the supervisor until all the facts have been ascertained and analyzed, and the consequences of alternative courses of action studied; *then* the decision maker

   A. acts as both judge and jury and selects what he believes to be the best of the alternative plans
   B. consults with those who will be most directly involved to obtain a recommendation as to the most appropriate course of action
   C. reviews the facts which he has already analyzed, reduces his thoughts to writing, and selects that course of action which can have the fewest negative consequences if his thinking contains an error
   D. stops, considers the matter for at least a 24-hour period, before referring it to a superior for evaluation

7. Decision-making can be defined as the

   A. delegation of authority and responsibility to persons capable of performing their assigned duties with moderate or little supervision
   B. imposition of a supervisor's decision upon a work group
   C. technique of selecting the course of action with the most desired consequences, and the least undesired or unexpected consequences
   D. process principally concerned with improvement of procedures

8. A supervisor who is not well-motivated and has no desire to accept basic responsibilities will

   A. compromise to the extent of permitting poor performance for lengthy periods without correction
   B. get good performance from his work group if the employees are satisfied with their pay and other working conditions
   C. not have marginal workers in his work group if the work is interesting
   D. perform adequately as long as the work of his group consists of routine operations

9. A supervisor is more than a bond or connecting link between two levels of employees. He has joint responsibility which must be shared with both management and with the work group.
Of the following, the item which BEST expresses the meaning of this statement is:

   A. A supervisor works with both management and the work group and must reconcile the differences between them.
   B. In management, the supervisor is solely concerned with efforts directing the work of his subordinates.
   C. The supervisory role is basically that of a liaison man between management and the work force.
   D. What a supervisor says and does when confronted with day-to-day problems depends upon his level in the organization.

10. Operations research is the observation of operations in business or government, and it utilizes both hypotheses and controlled experiments to determine the outcome of decisions. In effect, it reproduces the future impact on the decision in a clinical environment suited to intensive study.
Operations research has

   A. been more promising than applied research in the ascertaining of knowledge for the purpose of decision-making
   B. never been amenable to fact analysis on the grand scale
   C. not been used extensively in government
   D. proven to be the only rational and logical approach to decision-making on long-range problems

11. Assume that a civilian makes a complaint regarding the behavior of a certain worker to the supervisor of the worker. The supervisor regards the complaint as unjustified and unreasonable.
In these circumstances, the supervisor

   A. must make a written note of the complaint and forward it through channels to the unit or individual responsible for complaint investigations
   B. should assure the complainant that disciplinary action will be appropriate to the seriousness of the alleged offense
   C. should immediately summon the worker if he is available so that the latter may attempt to straighten out the difficulty
   D. should inform the complainant that his complaint appears to be unjustified and unreasonable

12. Modern management usually establishes a personal history folder for an employee at the time of hiring. Disciplinary matters appear in such personal history folders. Employees do not like the idea of disciplinary actions appearing in their permanent personal folders.
Authorities believe that

   A. after a few years have passed since the commission of the infraction, disciplinary actions should be removed from folders
   B. disciplinary actions should remain in folders; it is not the records but the use of records that requires detailed study
   C. most personnel have not had disciplinary action taken against them and would resent the removal of disciplinary actions from such folders
   D. there is no point in removing disciplinary actions from personal history folders since employees who have been guilty of infractions should not be allowed to forget their infractions

13. While supervisors should not fear the acceptance of responsibility, they

   A. generally seek out responsibility that subordinates should exercise, particularly when the supervisors do not have sufficient work to do
   B. must be on guard against the abuse of authority that often accompanies the acceptance of total responsibility
   C. should avoid responsibility that is customarily exercised by their superiors
   D. who are anxious for promotions accept responsibility but do not exercise the authority warranted by the responsibility

14. Planning is part of the decision-making process. By planning is meant the development of details of alternative plans of action.
   The key to *effective* planning is

   A. careful research to determine whether a tentative plan has been tried at some time in the past
   B. participation by employees in planning, preferably those employees who will be involved in putting the selected plan into action
   C. speed; poor plans can be discarded after they are put into effect while good plans usually are not put into effect because of delays
   D. writing the plan up in considerable detail and then forwarding the plan, through channels, to the executive officer having final approval of the plan

15. Equating strict discipline with punitive measures and lax discipline with rehabilitation creates a false dichotomy. The one of the statements given below that would BEST follow from the belief expressed in this statement is that discipline

   A. is important for treatment
   B. militates against treatment programs
   C. is not an important consideration in institutions where effective rehabilitation programs prevail
   D. minimizes the need for punitive measures if it is strict

16. If training starts at the lower level of command, it is like planting a seed in tilled ground but removing the sun and rain. Seeds cannot grow unless they have help from above.
   Of the following, the MOST appropriate conclusion to be drawn from this statement is that

   A. the head of an institution may not delegate authority for the planning of an institutional training program for staff
   B. on-the-job training is better than formalized training courses
   C. regularly scheduled training courses must be planned in advance
   D. staff training is the responsibility of higher levels of command

17. The one of the following that BEST describes the meaning of *in-service staff training* is:

   A. The training of personnel who are below average in performance
   B. The training given to each employee throughout his employment
   C. The training of staff only in their own specialized fields
   D. Classroom training where the instructor and employees develop a positive and productive relationship leading to improved efficiency on the job

18. All bureau personnel should be concerned about, and involved in, public relations. 18.____
Of the following, the MOST important reason for this statement is that

   A. an institution is an agency of the government supported by public funds and responsible to the public
   B. institutions are places of public business and, therefore, the public is interested in them
   C. some personnel need publicity in order to advance
   D. personnel sometimes need publicity in order to ensure that their grievances are acted upon by higher authority

19. The MOST important factor in establishing a disciplinary policy in an organization is 19.____

   A. consistency of application
   B. strict supervisors
   C. strong enforcement
   D. the degree of toughness or laxity

20. The FIRST step in planning a program is to 20.____

   A. clearly define the objectives
   B. estimate the costs
   C. hire a program director
   D. solicit funds

21. The PRIMARY purpose of control in an organization is to 21.____

   A. punish those who do not do their job well
   B. get people to do what is necessary to achieve an objective
   C. develop clearly stated rules and regulations
   D. regulate expenditures

22. The UNDERLYING principle of *sound* administration is to 22.____

   A. base administration on investigation of facts
   B. have plenty of resources available
   C. hire a strong administrator
   D. establish a broad policy

23. An IMPORTANT aspect to keep in mind during the decision-making process is that 23.____

   A. all possible alternatives for attaining goals should be sought out and considered
   B. considering various alternatives only leads to confusion
   C. once a decision has been made, it cannot be retracted
   D. there is only one correct method to reach any goal

24. Implementation of accountability requires 24.____

   A. a leader who will not hesitate to take punitive action
   B. an established system of communication from the bottom to the top
   C. explicit directives from leaders
   D. too much expense to justify it

25. The CHIEF danger of a decentralized control system is that
    A. excessive reports and communications will be generated
    B. problem areas may not be detected readily
    C. the expense will become prohibitive
    D. this will result in too many *chiefs*

KEY (CORRECT ANSWERS)

1.	D	11.	D
2.	C	12.	A
3.	B	13.	B
4.	A	14.	B
5.	B	15.	A
6.	A	16.	D
7.	C	17.	B
8.	A	18.	A
9.	A	19.	A
10.	C	20.	A

21.	B
22.	A
23.	A
24.	B
25.	B

TEST 2

DIRECTIONS: Each question or incomplete statement is followed by several suggested answers or completions. Select the one that BEST answers the question or completes the statement. *PRINT THE LETTER OF THE CORRECT ANSWER IN THE SPACE AT THE RIGHT.*

1. When giving orders to his subordinates, a certain supervisor often includes information as to why the work is necessary.
   This approach by the supervisor is *generally*

   A. *inadvisable,* since it appears that he is avoiding responsibility and wishes to blame his superiors
   B. *inadvisable,* since it creates the impression that he is trying to impress the subordinates with his importance
   C. *advisable,* since it serves to motivate the subordinates by giving them a reason for wanting to do the work
   D. *advisable,* since it shows that he is knowledgeable and is in control of his assignments

   1.____

2. Some supervisors often ask capable, professional subordinates to get some work done with questions such as: *Mary, would you try to complete that work today?*
   The use of such request orders *usually*

   A. gets results which are as good as or better than results from direct orders
   B. shows the supervisor to be weak and lowers the respect of his subordinates
   C. provokes resentment as compared to the use of direct orders
   D. leads to confusion as to the proper procedure to follow when carrying out orders

   2.____

3. Assume that a supervisor, because of an emergency when time was essential, and in the absence of his immediate superior, went out of the chain of command to get a decision from a higher level.
   It would consequently be MOST appropriate for the immediate superior to

   A. reprimand him for his action, since the long-range consequences are far more detrimental than the immediate gain
   B. encourage him to use this method, since the chain of command is an outmoded and discredited system which inhibits productive work
   C. order him to refrain from any repetition of this action in the future
   D. support him as long as he informed the superior of the action at the earliest opportunity

   3.____

4. A supervisor gave instructions which he knew were somewhat complex to a subordinate. He then asked the subordinate to repeat the instructions to him.
   The supervisor's decision to have the subordinate repeat the instructions was

   A. *good practice,* mainly because the subordinate would realize the importance of carefully following instructions
   B. *poor practice,* mainly because the supervisor should have given the employee time to ponder the instructions, and then, if necessary, to ask questions
   C. *good practice,* mainly because the supervisor could see whether the subordinate had any apparent problem in understanding the instructions
   D. *poor practice,* mainly because the subordinate should not be expected to have the same degree of knowledge as the supervisor

   4.____

5. Supervisors and subordinates must successfully communicate with each other in order to work well together.
Which of the following statements concerning communication of this type is CORRECT?

   A. When speaking to his subordinates, a supervisor should make every effort to appear knowledgeable about all aspects of their work.
   B. Written communications should be prepared by the supervisor at his own level of comprehension.
   C. The average employee tends to give meaning to communication according to his personal interpretation.
   D. The effective supervisor communicates as much information as he has available to anyone who is interested.

6. A supervisor should be aware of situations in which it is helpful to put his orders to his subordinates in writing.
Which of the following situations would MOST likely call for a WRITTEN order rather than an ORAL order? The order

   A. gives complicated instructions which vary from ordinary practice
   B. involves the performance of duties for which the subordinate is responsible
   C. directs subordinates to perform duties similar to those which they performed in the recent past
   D. concerns a matter that must be promptly completed or dealt with

7. Assume that a supervisor discovers that a false rumor about possible layoffs has spread among his subordinates through the grapevine.
Of the following, the BEST way for the supervisor to deal with this situation is to

   A. use the grapevine to leak accurate information
   B. call a meeting to provide information and to answer questions
   C. post a notice on the bulletin board denying the rumor
   D. institute procedures designed to eliminate the grapevine

8. Communications in an organization with many levels becomes subject to different interpretations at each level and have a tendency to become distorted. The more levels there are in an organization, the greater the likelihood that the final recipient of a communication will get the wrong message.
The one of the following statements which BEST supports the foregoing viewpoint is:

   A. Substantial communications problems exist at high management levels in organizations.
   B. There is a relationship in an organization between the number of hierarchical levels and interference with communications.
   C. An opportunity should be given to subordinates at all levels to communicate their views with impunity.
   D. In larger organizations, there tends to be more interference with downward communications than with upward communications.

9. A subordinate comes to you, his supervisor, to ask a detailed question about a new agency directive; however, you do not know the answer.
Of the following, the MOST helpful response to give the subordinate is to

   A. point out that since your own supervisor has failed to keep you informed of this matter, it is probably unimportant
   B. give the most logical interpretation you can, based on your best judgment
   C. ask him to raise the question with other supervisors until he finds one who knows the answer, then let you know also
   D. explain that you do not know and assure him that you will get the information for him

10. The traditional view of management theory is that communication in an organization should follow the table of organization. A newer theory holds that timely communication often requires bypassing certain steps in the hierarchical chain.
However, the MAIN advantage of using formal channels of communication within an organization is that

   A. an employee is thereby restricted in his relationships to his immediate superior and his immediate subordinates
   B. information is thereby transmitted to everyone who should be informed
   C. the organization will have an appeal channel, or a mechanism by which subordinates can go over their superior's head
   D. employees are thereby encouraged to exercise individual initiative

11. It is unfair to hold subordinates responsible for the performance of duties for which they do not have the requisite authority.
When this is done, it violates the principle that

   A. responsibility *cannot be greater* than that implied by delegated authority
   B. responsibility *should be greater* than that implied by delegated authority
   C. authority *cannot be greater* than that implied by delegated responsibility
   D. authority *should be greater* than that implied by delegated responsibility

12. Assume that a supervisor wishes to delegate some tasks to a capable subordinate.
It would be MOST in keeping with the principles of delegation for the supervisor to

   A. ask another supervisor who is experienced in the delegated tasks to evaluate the subordinate's work from time to time
   B. monitor continually the subordinate's performance by carefully reviewing his work at every step
   C. request experienced employees to submit peer ratings of the work of the subordinate
   D. tell the subordinates what problems are likely to be encountered and specify which problems to report on

13. There are *three* types of leadership: *autocratic*, in which the leader makes the decisions and seeks compliance from his subordinates; *democratic*, in which the leader consults with his subordinates and lets them help set policy; and *free rein*, in which the leader acts as an information center and exercises minimum control over his subordinates.
A supervisor can be MOST effective if he decides to

    A. use democratic leadership techniques exclusively
    B. avoid the use of autocratic leadership techniques entirely
    C. employ the three types of leadership according to the situation
    D. rely mainly on autocratic leadership techniques

14. During a busy period of work, Employee A asked his supervisor for leave in order to take an ordinary vacation. The supervisor denied the request. The following day, Employee B asked for leave during the same period because his wife had just gone to the hospital for an indeterminate stay and he had family matters to tend to.
Of the following, the BEST way for the supervisor to deal with Employee B's request is to

    A. grant the request and give the reason to the other employee
    B. suggest that the employee make his request to higher management
    C. delay the request immediately since granting it would show favoritism
    D. defer any decision until the duration of the hospital stay is determined

15. Assume that you are a supervisor and that a subordinate tells you he has a grievance. In general, you should FIRST

    A. move the grievance forward in order to get a prompt decision
    B. discourage this type of behavior on the part of subordinates
    C. attempt to settle the grievance
    D. refer the subordinate to the personnel office

16. A supervisor may have available a large variety of rewards he can use to motivate his subordinates. However, some supervisors choose the wrong rewards.
A supervisor is *most likely* to make such a mistake if he

    A. appeals to a subordinate's desire to be well regarded by his co-workers
    B. assumes that the subordinate's goals and preferences are the same as his own
    C. conducts in-depth discussions with a subordinate in order to discover his preference
    D. limits incentives to those rewards which he is authorized to provide or to recommend

17. Employee performance appraisal is open to many kinds of errors.
When a supervisor is preparing such an appraisal, he is *most likely* to commit an error if

    A. employees are indifferent to the consequences of their performance appraisals
    B. the entire period for which the evaluation is being made is taken into consideration
    C. standard measurement criteria are used as performance benchmarks
    D. personal characteristics of employees which are not job-related are given weight

18. Assume that a supervisor finds that a report prepared by an employee is unsatisfactory and should be done over. Which of the following should the supervisor do?

    A. Give the report to another employee who can complete it properly.
    B. Have the report done over by the same employee after successfully training him.
    C. Hold a meeting to train all the employees so as not to single out the employee who performed unsatisfactorily
    D. Accept the report so as not to discourage the employee and then make the corrections himself.

19. Employees sometimes wish to have personal advice and counseling, in confidence, about their job-related problems. These problems may include such concerns as health matters, family difficulties, alcoholism, debts, emotional disturbances, etc.
    Such assistance is BEST provided through

    A. maintenance of an exit interview program to find reasons for, and solutions to, turnover problems
    B. arrangements for employees to discuss individual problems informally outside normal administrative channels
    C. procedures which allow employees to submit anonymous inquiries to the personnel department
    D. special hearing committees consisting of top management in addition to immediate supervisors

20. An employee is always a member of some unit of the formal organization. He may also be a member of an informal work group.
    With respect to employee productivity and job satisfaction, the informal work group can MOST accurately be said to

    A. have no influence of any kind on its members
    B. influence its members negatively only
    C. influence its members positively only
    D. influence its members negatively or positively

21. In order to encourage employees to make suggestions, many public agencies have employee suggestion programs.
    What is the MAJOR benefit of such a program to the agency as a whole? It

    A. brings existing or future problems to management's attention
    B. reduces the number of minor accidents
    C. requires employees to share in decision-making responsibilities
    D. reveals employees who have inadequate job knowledge

22. Assume that you have been asked to interview a seemingly shy applicant for a temporary position in your department.
    For you to ask the kinds of questions that begin with *What, Where, Why, When, Who, and How,* is

    A. *good practice ;* it informs the applicant that he must conform to the requirements of the department
    B. *poor practice;* it exceeds the extent and purpose of an initial interview
    C. *good practice;* it encourages the applicant to talk to a greater extent
    D. *poor practice;* it encourages the applicant to dominate the discussion

23. In recent years, job enlargement or job enrichment has tended to replace job simplification.
Those who advocate job enrichment or enlargement consider it *desirable* CHIEFLY because

    A. it allows supervisors to control closely the activities of subordinates
    B. it produces greater job satisfaction through reduction of responsibility
    C. most employees prefer to avoid work which is new and challenging
    D. positions with routinized duties are unlikely to provide job satisfaction

24. Job rotation is a training method in which an employee temporarily changes places with another employee of equal rank.
What is usually the MAIN purpose of job rotation? To

    A. politely remove the person being rotated from an unsuitable assignment
    B. increase skills and provide broader experience
    C. prepare the person being rotated for a permanent change
    D. test the skills of the person being rotated

25. There are several principles that a supervisor needs to know if he is to deal adequately with his training responsibilities.
Which of the following is usually NOT a principle of training?

    A. People should be trained according to their individual needs.
    B. People can learn by being told or shown how to do work, but best of all by doing work under guidance.
    C. People can be easily trained even if they have no desire to learn.
    D. Training should be planned, scheduled, executed, and evaluated systematically.

KEY (CORRECT ANSWERS)

1. C
2. A
3. D
4. C
5. C

6. A
7. B
8. B
9. D
10. B

11. A
12. D
13. C
14. A
15. C

16. B
17. D
18. B
19. B
20. D

21. A
22. C
23. D
24. B
25. C

READING COMPREHENSION
UNDERSTANDING AND INTERPRETING WRITTEN MATERIAL
EXAMINATION SECTION
TEST 1

DIRECTIONS: Each question or incomplete statement is followed by several suggested answers or completions. Select the one that BEST answers the question or completes the statement. *PRINT THE LETTER OF THE CORRECT ANSWER IN THE SPACE AT THE RIGHT.*

Questions 1-3.

DIRECTIONS: Questions 1 through 3 are to be answered SOLELY on the basis of the following paragraph.

Every organization needs a systematic method of checking its operations as a means to increase efficiency and promote economy. Many successful private firms have instituted a system of audits or internal inspections to accomplish these ends. Law enforcement organizations, which have an extremely important service to *sell,* should be no less zealous in developing efficiency and economy in their operations. Periodic, organized, and systematic inspections are one means of promoting the achievement of these objectives. The necessity of an organized inspection system is perhaps greatest in those law enforcement groups which have grown to such a size that the principal officer can no longer personally supervise or be cognizant of every action taken. Smooth and effective operation demands that the head of the organization have at hand some tool with which he can study and enforce general policies and procedures and also direct compliance with day-to-day orders, most of which are put into execution outside his sight and hearing. A good inspection system can serve as that tool.

1. The central thought of the above paragraph is that a system of inspections within a police department

    A. is unnecessary for a department in which the principal officer can personally supervise all official actions taken
    B. should be instituted at the first indication that there is any deterioration in job performance by the force
    C. should be decentralized and administered by first-line supervisory officers
    D. is an important aid to the police administrator in the accomplishment of law enforcement objectives

2. The MOST accurate of the following statements concerning the need for an organized inspection system in a law enforcement organization is: It is

    A. never needed in an organization of small size where the principal officer can give personal supervision
    B. most needed where the size of the organization prevents direct supervision by the principal officer
    C. more needed in law enforcement organizations than in private firms
    D. especially needed in an organization about to embark upon a needed expansion of services

1.____

2.____

3. According to the above paragraph, the head of the police organization utilizes the internal inspection system

   A. as a tool which must be constantly re-examined in the light of changing demands for police service
   B. as an administrative technique to increase efficiency and promote economy
   C. by personally visiting those areas of police operation which are outside his sight and hearing
   D. to augment the control of local commanders over detailed field operations

Questions 4-10.

DIRECTIONS: Questions 4 through 10 are to be answered SOLELY on the basis of the following passage.

Job evaluation and job rating systems are intended to introduce scientific procedures. Any type of approach, when properly used, will give satisfactory results. The Point System, when properly validated by actual use, is more likely to be suitable for general use than the ranking system. In many aspects, the Factor Comparison Plan is a point system tied to money values. Of course, there may be another system that combines the ranking system with the point system, especially during the initial stages of the development of the program. After the program has been in use for some time, the tendency is to drop off the ranking phase and continue the use of the point system.

In the ranking system of rating of jobs, every job within the plant is arranged in some order, either from the one with the simplest qualifications to the one with maximum requirements, or in the reverse order. This system should be preceded by careful job analysis and the writing of accurate job descriptions before the rating process is undertaken. It is possible, of course, to take the jobs as they are found in the business enterprise and use the names as they are without any attempt at standardization, and merely rank them according to the general over-all impression of the raters. Such a procedure is certain to fall short of what may reasonably be expected of job rating. Another procedure that is in reality merely a modification of the simple rating described above is to establish a series of grades or zones and arrange all the jobs in the plant into groups within these grades and zones. The practice in most common use is to arrange all the jobs in the plant according to their requirements by rating them and then to establish the classifications or groups.

The actual ranking of jobs may be done by one individual, several individuals, or a committee. If several individuals are working independently on the task, it will usually be found that, in general, they agree but that their rankings vary in certain details. A conference between the individuals, with each person giving his reasons why he rated one way or another, usually produces agreement. The detailed job descriptions are particularly helpful when there is disagreement among raters as to the rating of certain jobs. It is not only possible but desirable to have workers participate in the construction of the job description and in rating the job.

4. The MAIN theme of this passage is

   A. the elimination of bias in job rating
   B. the rating of jobs by the ranking system

C. the need for accuracy in allocating points in the point system
D. pitfalls to avoid in selecting key jobs in the Factor Comparison Plan

5. The ranking system of rating jobs consists MAINLY of

   A. attaching a point value to each ratable factor of each job prior to establishing an equitable pay scale
   B. arranging every job in the organization in descending order and then following this up with a job analysis of the key jobs
   C. preparing accurate job descriptions after a job analysis and then arranging all jobs either in ascending or descending order based on job requirements
   D. arbitrarily establishing a hierarchy of job classes and grades and then fitting each job into a specific class and grade based on the opinions of unit supervisors

5.____

6. The above passage states that the system of classifying jobs MOST used in an organization is to

   A. organize all jobs in the organization in accordance with their requirements and then create categories or clusters of jobs
   B. classify all jobs in the organization according to the titles and rank by which they are currently known in the organization
   C. establish a pre-arranged series of grades or zones and then fit
   D. all jobs into one of the grades or zones
   E. determine the salary currently being paid for each job and then rank the jobs in order according to salary

6.____

7. According to the above passage, experience has shown that when a group of raters is assigned to the job evaluation task and each individual rates independently of the others, the raters GENERALLY

   A. agree with respect to all aspects of their rankings
   B. disagree with respect to all or nearly all aspects of the rankings
   C. disagree on overall ratings, but agree on specific rating factors
   D. agree on overall rankings, but have some variance in some details

7.____

8. The above passage states that the use of a detailed job description is of SPECIAL value when

   A. employees of an organization have participated in the preliminary step involved in actual preparation of the job description
   B. labor representatives are not participating in ranking of the jobs
   C. an individual rater who is unsure of himself is ranking the jobs
   D. a group of raters is having difficulty reaching unanimity with respect to ranking a certain job

8.____

9. A comparison of the various rating systems as described in the above passage shows that

   A. the ranking system is not as appropriate for general use as a properly validated point system
   B. the point system is the same as the Factor Comparison Plan except that it places greater emphasis on money

9.____

C. no system is capable of combining the point system and the Factor Comparison Plan
D. the point system will be discontinued last when used in combination with the Factor Comparison System

10. The above passage implies that the PRINCIPAL reason for creating job evaluation and rating systems was to help

    A. overcome union opposition to existing salary plans
    B. base wage determination on a more objective and orderly foundation
    C. eliminate personal bias on the part of the trained scientific job evaluators
    D. management determine if it was overpricing the various jobs in the organizational hierarchy

10.___

Questions 11-13.

DIRECTIONS: Questions 11 through 13 are to be answered SOLELY on the basis of the following paragraph.

The common sense character of the merit system seems so natural to most Americans that many people wonder why it should ever have been inoperative. After all, the American economic system, the most phenomenal the world has ever known, is also founded on a rugged selective process which emphasizes the personal qualities of capacity, industriousness, and productivity. The criteria may not have always been appropriate and competition has not always been fair, but competition there was, and the responsibilities and the rewards — with exceptions, of course — have gone to those who could measure up in terms of intelligence, knowledge, or perseverance. This has been true not only in the economic area, in the money-making process, but also in achievement in the professions and other walks of life.

11. According to the above paragraph, economic rewards in the United States have

    A. always been based on appropriate, fair criteria
    B. only recently been based on a competitive system
    C. not gone to people who compete too ruggedly
    D. usually gone to those people with intelligence, knowledge, and perseverance

11.___

12. According to the above passage, a merit system is

    A. an unfair criterion on which to base rewards
    B. unnatural to anyone who is not American
    C. based only on common sense
    D. based on the same principles as the American economic system

12.___

13. According to the above passage, it is MOST accurate to say that

    A. the United States has always had a civil service merit system
    B. civil service employees are very rugged
    C. the American economic system has always been based on a merit objective
    D. competition is unique to the American way of life

13.___

Questions 14-15.

DIRECTIONS: Questions 14 and 15 are to be answered SOLELY on the basis of the following paragraph.

In-basket tests are often used to assess managerial potential. The exercise consists of a set of papers that would be likely to be found in the in-basket of an administrator or manager at any given time, and requires the individuals participating in the examination to indicate how they would dispose of each item found in the in-basket. In order to handle the in-basket effectively, they must successfully manage their time, refer and assign some work to subordinates, juggle potentially conflicting appointments and meetings, and arrange for follow-up of problems generated by the items in the in-basket. In other words, the in-basket test is attempting to evaluate the participants' abilities to organize their work, set priorities, delegate, control, and make decisions.

14. According to the above paragraph, to succeed in an in-basket test, an administrator must   14._____

   A. be able to read very quickly
   B. have a great deal of technical knowledge
   C. know when to delegate work
   D. arrange a lot of appointments and meetings

15. According to the above paragraph, all of the following abilities are indications of manage-   15._____
    rial potential EXCEPT the ability to

   A. organize and control   B. manage time
   C. write effective reports   D. make appropriate decisions

Questions 16-19.

DIRECTIONS: Questions 16 through 19 are to be answered SOLELY on the basis of the following paragraph.

A personnel researcher has at his disposal various approaches for obtaining information, analyzing it, and arriving at conclusions that have value in predicting and affecting the behavior of people at work. The type of method to be used depends on such factors as the nature of the research problem, the available data, and the attitudes of those people being studied to the various kinds of approaches. While the experimental approach, with its use of control groups, is the most refined type of study, there are others that are often found useful in personnel research. Surveys, in which the researcher obtains facts on a problem from a variety of sources, are employed in research on wages, fringe benefits, and labor relations. Historical studies are used to trace the development of problems in order to understand them better and to isolate possible causative factors. Case studies are generally developed to explore all the details of a particular problem that is representative of other similar problems. A researcher chooses the most appropriate form of study for the problem he is investigating. He should recognize, however, that the experimental method, commonly referred to as the scientific method, if used validly and reliably, gives the most conclusive results.

16. The above paragraph discusses several approaches used to obtain information on par-   16._____
    ticular problems. Which of the following may be MOST reasonably concluded from the paragraph?
    A(n)

A. historical study cannot determine causative factors
B. survey is often used in research on fringe benefits
C. case study is usually used to explore a problem that is unique and unrelated to other problems
D. experimental study is used when the scientific approach to a problem fails

17. According to the above paragraph, all of the following are factors that may determine the type of approach a researcher uses EXCEPT

   A. the attitudes of people toward being used in control groups
   B. the number of available sources
   C. his desire to isolate possible causative factors
   D. the degree of accuracy he requires

17.___

18. The words *scientific method*, as used in the last sentence of the above paragraph, refer to a type of study which, according to the above paragraph

   A. uses a variety of sources
   B. traces the development of problems
   C. uses control groups
   D. analyzes the details of a representative problem

18.___

19. Which of the following can be MOST reasonably concluded from the above paragraph? In obtaining and analyzing information on a particular problem, a researcher employs the method which is the

   A. most accurate   B. most suitable
   C. least expensive   D. least time-consuming

19.___

Questions 20-25.

DIRECTIONS: Questions 20 through 25 are to be answered SOLELY on the basis of the following passage.

The quality of the voice of a worker is an important factor in conveying to clients and co-workers his attitude and, to some degree, his character. The human voice, when not consciously disguised, may reflect a person's mood, temper, and personality. It has been shown in several experiments that certain character traits can be assessed with better than chance accuracy through listening to the voice of an unknown person who cannot be seen.

Since one of the objectives of the worker is to put clients at ease and to present an encouraging and comfortable atmosphere, a harsh, shrill, or loud voice could have a negative effect. A client who displays emotions of anger or resentment would probably be provoked even further by a caustic tone. In a face-to-face situation, an unpleasant voice may be compensated for, to some degree, by a concerned and kind facial expression. However, when one speaks on the telephone, the expression on one's face cannot be seen by the listener. A supervising clerk who wishes to represent himself effectively to clients should try to eliminate as many faults as possible in striving to develop desirable voice qualities.

20. If a worker uses a sarcastic tone while interviewing a resentful client, the client, according to the above passage, would MOST likely

    A. avoid the face-to-face situation
    B. be ashamed of his behavior
    C. become more resentful
    D. be provoked to violence

21. According to the passage, experiments comparing voice and character traits have demonstrated that

    A. prospects for improving an unpleasant voice through training are better than chance
    B. the voice can be altered to project many different psychological characteristics
    C. the quality of the human voice reveals more about the speaker than his words do
    D. the speaker's voice tells the hearer something about the speaker's personality

22. Which of the following, according to the above passage, is a person's voice MOST likely to reveal?
    His

    A. prejudices
    B. intelligence
    C. social awareness
    D. temperament

23. It may be MOST reasonably concluded from the above passage that an interested and sympathetic expression on the face of a worker

    A. may induce a client to feel certain he will receive welfare benefits
    B. will eliminate the need for pleasant vocal qualities in the interviewer
    C. may help to make up for an unpleasant voice in the interviewer
    D. is desirable as the interviewer speaks on the telephone to a client

24. Of the following, the MOST reasonable implication of the above paragraph is that a worker should, when speaking to a client, control and use his voice to

    A. simulate a feeling of interest in the problems of the client
    B. express his emotions directly and adequately
    C. help produce in the client a sense of comfort and security
    D. reflect his own true personality

25. It may be concluded from the above passage that the PARTICULAR reason for a worker to pay special attention to modulating her voice when talking on the phone to a client is that, during a telephone conversation,

    A. there is a necessity to compensate for the way in which a telephone distorts the voice
    B. the voice of the worker is a reflection of her mood and character
    C. the client can react only on the basis of the voice and words she hears
    D. the client may have difficulty getting a clear under-standing over the telephone

KEY (CORRECT ANSWERS)

1.	D	11.	D
2.	B	12.	D
3.	B	13.	C
4.	B	14.	C
5.	C	15.	C
6.	A	16.	B
7.	D	17.	D
8.	D	18.	C
9.	A	19.	B
10.	B	20.	C

21. D
22. D
23. C
24. C
25. C

TEST 2

Questions 1-3.

DIRECTIONS: Questions 1 through 3 are to be answered SOLELY on the basis of the following paragraph.

Suppose you are given the job of printing, collating, and stapling 8,000 copies of a ten-page booklet as soon as possible. You have available one photo-offset machine, a collator with an automatic stapler, and the personnel to operate these machines. All will be available for however long the job takes to complete. The photo-offset machine prints 5,000 impressions an hour, and it takes about 15 minutes to set up a plate. The collator, including time for insertion of pages and stapling, can process about 2,000 booklets an hour. (Answers should be based on the assumption that there are no breakdowns or delays.)

1. Assuming that all the printing is finished before the collating is started, if the job is given to you late Monday and your section can begin work the next day and is able to devote seven hours a day, Monday through Friday, to the job until it is finished, what is the BEST estimate of when the job will be finished?   1.____

   A. Wednesday afternoon of the same week
   B. Thursday morning of the same week
   C. Friday morning of the same week
   D. Monday morning of the next week

2. An operator suggests to you that instead of completing all the printing and then beginning collating and stapling, you first print all the pages for 4,000 booklets, so that they can be collated and stapled while the last 4,000 booklets are being printed.
   If you accepted this suggestion, the job would be completed   2.____

   A. sooner but would require more man-hours
   B. at the same time using either method
   C. later and would require more man-hours
   D. sooner but there would be more wear and tear on the plates

3. Assume that you have the same assignment and equipment as described above, but 16,000 copies of the booklet are needed instead of 8,000.
   If you decided to print 8,000 complete booklets, then collate and staple them while you started printing the next 8,000 booklets, which of the following statements would MOST accurately describe the relationship between this new method and your original method of printing all the booklets at one time, and then collating and stapling them?
   The   3.____

   A. job would be completed at the same time regardless of the method used
   B. new method would result in the job's being completed 3 1/2 hours earlier
   C. original method would result in the job's being completed an hour later
   D. new method would result in the job's being completed 1 1/2 hours earlier.

Questions 4-6.

DIRECTIONS: Questions 4 through 6 are to be answered SOLELY on the basis of the following passage.

When using words like company, association, council, committee, and board in place of the full official name, the writer should not capitalize these short forms unless he intends them to invoke the full force of the institution's authority. In legal contracts, in minutes, or in formal correspondence where one is speaking formally and officially on behalf of the company, the term Company is usually capitalized, but in ordinary usage, where it is not essential to load the short form with this significance, capitalization would be excessive. (Example: The company will have many good openings for graduates this June.)

The treatment recommended for short forms of place names is essentially the same as that recommended for short forms of organizational names. In general, we capitalize the full form but not the short form. If Park Avenue is referred to in one sentence, then the *avenue* is sufficient in subsequent references. The same is true with words like building, hotel, station, and airport, which are capitalized when part of a proper name changed (Pan Am Building, Hotel Plaza, Union Station, O'Hare Airport), but are simply lower-cased when replacing these specific names.

4. The above passage states that USUALLY the short forms of names of organizations

    A. and places should not be capitalized
    B. and places should be capitalized
    C. should not be capitalized, but the short forms of names of places should be capitalized
    D. should be capitalized, but the short forms of names of places should not be capitalized

5. The above passage states that in legal contracts, in minutes, and in formal correspondence, the short forms of names of organizations should

    A. usually not be capitalized
    B. usually be capitalized
    C. usually not be used
    D. never be used

6. It can be INFERRED from the above passage that decisions regarding when to capitalize certain words

    A. should be left to the discretion of the writer
    B. should be based on generally accepted rules
    C. depend on the total number of words capitalized
    D. are of minor importance

Questions 7-10.

DIRECTIONS: Questions 7 through 10 are to be answered SOLELY on the basis of the following passage.

Use of the systems and procedures approach to office management is revolutionizing the supervision of office work. This approach views an enterprise as an entity which seeks to fulfill definite objectives. Systems and procedures help to organize repetitive work into a routine, thus reducing the amount of decision making required for its accomplishment. As a result, employees are guided in their efforts and perform only necessary work. Supervisors are relieved of any details of execution and are free to attend to more important work. Establishing work guides which require that identical tasks be performed the same way each time permits standardization of forms, machine operations, work methods, and controls. This approach also reduces the probability of errors. Any error committed is usually discovered quickly because the incorrect work does not meet the requirement of the work guides. Errors are also reduced through work specialization, which allows each employee to become thoroughly proficient in a particular type of work. Such proficiency also tends to improve the morale of the employees.

7. The above passage states that the accuracy of an employee's work is INCREASED by   7.____

    A. using the work specialization approach
    B. employing a probability sample
    C. requiring him to shift at one time into different types of tasks
    D. having his supervisor check each detail of work execution

8. Of the following, which one BEST expresses the main theme of the above passage? The   8.____

    A. advantages and disadvantages of the systems and procedures approach to office management
    B. effectiveness of the systems and procedures approach to office management in developing skills
    C. systems and procedures approach to office management as it relates to office costs
    D. advantages of the systems and procedures approach to office management for supervisors and office workers

9. Work guides are LEAST likely to be used when   9.____

    A. standardized forms are used
    B. a particular office task is distinct and different from all others
    C. identical tasks are to be performed in identical ways
    D. similar work methods are expected from each employee

10. According to the above passage, when an employee makes a work error, it USUALLY   10.____

    A. is quickly corrected by the supervisor
    B. necessitates a change in the work guides
    C. can be detected quickly if work guides are in use
    D. increases the probability of further errors by that employee

Questions 11-12.

DIRECTIONS: Questions 11 and 12 are to be answered SOLELY on the basis of the following passage.

The coordination of the many activities of a large public agency is absolutely essential. Coordination, as an administrative principle, must be distinguished from and is independent of cooperation. Coordination can be of either the horizontal or the vertical type. In large organizations, the objectives of vertical coordination are achieved by the transmission of orders and statements of policy down through the various levels of authority. It is an accepted generalization that the more authoritarian the organization, the more easily may vertical coordination be accomplished. Horizontal coordination is arrived at through staff work, administrative management, and conferences of administrators of equal rank. It is obvious that of the two types of coordination, the vertical kind is more important, for at best horizontal coordination only supplements the coordination effected up and down the line.

11. According to the above passage, the ease with which vertical coordination is achieved in a large agency depends upon

    A. the extent to which control is firmly exercised from above
    B. the objectives that have been established for the agency
    C. the importance attached by employees to the orders and statements of policy transmitted through the agency
    D. the cooperation obtained at the various levels of authority

12. According to the above passage,

    A. vertical coordination is dependent for its success upon horizontal coordination
    B. one type of coordination may work in opposition to the other
    C. similar methods may be used to achieve both types of coordination
    D. horizontal coordination is at most an addition to vertical coordination

Questions 13-17.

DIRECTIONS: Questions 13 through 17 are to be answered SOLELY on the basis of the following situation.

Assume that you are a newly appointed supervisor in the same unit in which you have been acting as a provisional for some time. You have in your unit the following workers:

WORKER I - He has always been an efficient worker. In a number of his cases, the clients have recently begun to complain that they cannot manage on the departmental budget.

WORKER II - He has been under selective supervision for some time as an experienced, competent worker. He now begins to be late for his supervisory conferences and to stress how much work he has to do.

WORKER III - He has been making considerable improvement in his ability to handle the details of his job. He now tells you, during an individual conference, that he does not need such close supervision and that he wants to operate more independently. He says that Worker II is always available when he needs a little information or help but, in general, he can manage very well by himself.

WORKER IV - He brings you a complex case for decision as to eligibility. Discussion of the case brings out the fact that he has failed to consider all the available resources adequately but has stressed the family's needs to include every extra item in the budget. This is the third case of a similar nature that this worker has brought to you recently. This worker and Worker I work in adjacent territory and are rather friendly.

In the following questions, select the option that describes the method of dealing with these workers that illustrates BEST supervisory practice.

13. With respect to supervision of Worker I, the assistant supervisor should   13._____

    A. discuss with the worker, in an individual conference, any problems that he may be having due to the increase in the cost of living
    B. plan a group conference for the unit around budgeting, as both Workers I and IV seem to be having budgetary difficulties
    C. discuss with Workers I and IV together the meaning of money as acceptance or rejection to the clients
    D. discuss with Worker I the budgetary data in each case in relation to each client's situation

14. With respect to supervision of Worker II, the supervisor should   14._____

    A. move slowly with this worker and give him time to learn that the supervisor's official appointment has not changed his attitudes or methods of supervision
    B. discuss the worker's change of attitude and ask him to analyze the reasons for his change in behavior
    C. take time to show the worker how he is avoiding his responsibility in the supervisor-worker relationship and that he is resisting supervision
    D. hold an evaluatory conference with the worker and show him how he is taking over responsibilities that are not his by providing supervision for Worker III

15. With respect to supervision of Worker III, the supervisor should discuss with this worker   15._____

    A. why he would rather have supervision from Worker II than from the supervisor
    B. the necessity for further improvement before he can go on selective supervision
    C. an analysis of the improvement that has been made and the extent to which the worker is able to handle the total job for which he is responsible
    D. the responsibility of the supervisor to see that clients receive adequate service

16. With respect to supervision of Worker IV, the supervisor should   16._____

    A. show the worker that resources figures are incomplete but that even if they were complete, the family would probably be eligible for assistance
    B. ask the worker why he is so protective of these families since there are three cases so similar
    C. discuss with the worker all three cases at the same time so that the worker may see his own role in the three situations
    D. discuss with the worker the reasons for departmental policies and procedures around budgeting

17. With respect to supervision of Workers I and IV, since these two workers are friends and would seem to be influencing each other, the supervisor should   17._____

    A. hold a joint conference with them both, pointing out how they should clear with the supervisor and not make their own rules together
    B. handle the problems of each separately in individual conferences
    C. separate them by transferring one to another territory or another unit
    D. take up the problem of workers asking help of each other rather than from the supervisor in a group meeting

Questions 18-20.

DIRECTIONS: Questions 18 through 20 are to be answered SOLELY on the basis of the following passage.

One of the key supervisory problems in a large municipal recreation department is that many leaders are assigned to isolated playgrounds or small centers, where it is difficult to observe their work regularly. Often their facilities are extremely limited. In such settings, as well as in larger recreation centers, where many recreation leaders tend to have other jobs as well, there tends to be a low level of morale and incentive. Still, it is the supervisor's task to help recreation personnel to develop pride in their work and to maintain a high level of performance. With isolated leaders, the supervisor may give advice or assistance. Leaders may be assigned to different tasks or settings during the year to maximize their productivity and provide new challenges. When it is clear that leaders are not willing to make a real effort to contribute to the department, the possibility of penalties must be considered, within the scope of departmental policy and the union contract. However, the supervisor should be constructive, encourage and assist workers to take a greater interest in their work, be innovative, and try to raise morale and to improve performance in positive ways.

18. The one of the following that would be the MOST appropriate title for the above passage is

    A. SMALL COMMUNITY CENTERS - PRO AND CON
    B. PLANNING BETTER RECREATION PROGRAMS
    C. THE SUPERVISOR'S TASK IN UPGRADING PERSONNEL PERFORMANCE
    D. THE SUPERVISOR AND THE MUNICIPAL UNION - RIGHTS AND OBLIGATIONS

19. The above passage makes clear that recreation leadership performance in ALL recreation playgrounds and centers throughout a large city is

    A. generally above average, with good morale on the part of most recreation leaders
    B. beyond description since no one has ever observed or evaluated recreation leaders
    C. a key test of the personnel department's effort to develop more effective hiring standards
    D. of mixed quality, with many recreation leaders having poor morale and a low level of achievement

20. According to the above passage, the supervisor's role is to

    A. use disciplinary action as his major tool in upgrading performance
    B. tolerate the lack of effort of individual employees since they are assigned to isolated playgrounds or small centers
    C. employ encouragement, advice, and, when appropriate, disciplinary action to improve performance
    D. inform the county supervisor whenever malfeasance or idleness is detected

Questions 21-25.

DIRECTIONS: Questions 21 through 25 are to be answered SOLELY on the basis of the following passage.

EMPLOYEE LEAVE REGULATIONS

Peter Smith, as a full-time permanent city employee under the Career and Salary Plan, earns an *annual leave allowance*. This consists of a certain number of days off a year with pay and may be used for vacation, personal business, and for observing religious holidays. As a newly appointed employee, during his first 8 years of city service, he will earn an annual leave allowance of 20 days off a year (an average of 1 2/3 days off a month). After he has finished 8 full years of working for the city, he will begin earning an additional 5 days off a year. His *annual leave allowance*, therefore, will then be 25 days a year and will remain at this amount for seven full years. He will begin earning an additional two days off a year after he has completed a total of 15 years of city employment. Therefore, in his sixteenth year of working for the city, Mr. Smith will be earning 27 days off a year as his *annual leave allowance* (an average of 2 1/4 days off a month).

A *sick leave allowance* of one day a month is also given to Mr. Smith, but it can be used only in cases of actual illness. When Mr. Smith returns to work after *using sick leave allowance*, he must have a doctor's note if the absence is for a total of more than 3 days, but he may also be required to show a doctor's note for absences of 1, 2, or 3 days.

21. According to the above passage, Mr. Smith's *annual leave allowance* consists of a certain number of days off a year which he

    A. does not get paid for
    B. gets paid for at time and a half
    C. may use for personal business
    D. may not use for observing religious holidays

22. According to the above passage, after Mr. Smith has been working for the city for 9 years, his *annual leave allowance* will be _____ days a year.

    A. 20   B. 25   C. 27   D. 37

23. According to the above passage, Mr. Smith will begin earning an average of 2 days off a month as his *annual leave allowance* after he has worked for the city for full years.

    A. 7   B. 8   C. 15   D. 17

24. According to the above passage, Mr. Smith is given a *sick leave allowance* of

    A. 1 day every 2 months   B. 1 day per month
    C. 1 2/3 days per month   D. 2 1/4 days a month

25. According to the above passage, when he uses *sick leave allowance*, Mr. Smith may be required to show a doctor's note

    A. even if his absence is for only 1 day
    B. only if his absence is for more than 2 days
    C. only if his absence is for more than 3 days
    D. only if his absence is for 3 days or more

KEY (CORRECT ANSWERS)

1. C
2. C
3. D
4. A
5. B

6. B
7. A
8. D
9. B
10. C

11. A
12. D
13. D
14. A
15. C

16. C
17. B
18. C
19. D
20. C

21. C
22. B
23. C
24. B
25. A

———

TEST 3

Questions 1-6.

DIRECTIONS: Questions 1 through 6 are to be answered SOLELY on the basis of the following passage.

A folder is made of a sheet of heavy paper (manila, kraft, pressboard, or red rope stock) that has been folded once so that the back is about one-half inch higher than the front. Folders are larger than the papers they contain in order to protect them. Two standard folder sizes are *letter size* for papers that are 8 1/2" x 11" and *legal cap* for papers that are 8 1/2" x 13".

Folders are cut across the top in two ways: so that the back is straight (straight-cut) or so that the back has a tab that projects above the top of the folder. Such tabs bear captions that identify the contents of each folder. Tabs vary in width and position. The tabs of a set of folders that are *one-half cut* are half the width of the folder and have only two positions.

One-third cut folders have three positions, each tab occupying a third of the width of the folder. Another standard tabbing is *one-fifth cut*, which has five positions. There are also folders with *two-fifths cut*, with the tabs in the third and fourth or fourth and fifth positions.

1. Of the following, the BEST title for the above passage is 1.____

   A. FILING FOLDERS B. STANDARD FOLDER SIZES
   C. THE USES OF THE FOLDER D. THE USE OF TABS

2. According to the above passage, one of the standard folder sizes is called 2.____

   A. Kraft cut B. legal cap
   C. one-half cut D. straight-cut

3. According to the above passage, tabs are GENERALLY placed along the _____ of the 3.____
   folder.

   A. back B. front
   C. left side D. right side

4. According to the above passage, a tab is GENERALLY used to 4.____

   A. distinguish between standard folder sizes
   B. identify the contents of a folder
   C. increase the size of the folder
   D. protect the papers within the folder

5. According to the above passage, a folder that is two-fifths cut has _____ tabs. 5.____

   A. no B. two C. three D. five

6. According to the above passage, one reason for making folders larger than the papers 6.____
   they contain is that

   A. only a certain size folder can be made from heavy paper
   B. they will protect the papers
   C. they will aid in setting up a tab system
   D. the back of the folder must be higher than the front

Questions 7-15.

DIRECTIONS: Questions 7 through 15 are to be answered SOLELY on the basis of the following passage.

The City University of New York traces its origins to 1847, when the Free Academy, which later became City College, was founded as the first tuition-free municipal college. City and Hunter Colleges were placed under the direction of the Board of Higher Education in 1926, and Brooklyn and Queens Colleges were subsequently added to the system of municipal colleges. In 1955, Staten Island Community College, the first of the two-year colleges sponsored by the Board of Higher Education under the program of the State University of New York, joined the system.

In 1961, the four senior colleges and three community colleges then under the jurisdiction of the Board of Higher Education became the City University of New York, and a University Graduate Division was organized to offer programs leading to the Ph.D. Since then, the university has undergone even more rapid growth. Today, it consists of nine senior colleges, an upper division college which admits students at the junior level, eight community colleges, a graduate division, and an affiliated medical center.

In the summer of 1969, the Board of Higher Education resolved that the time had come to commit the resources of the university to meeting an urgent social need—unrestricted access to higher education for all youths of the City. Determined to prevent the waste of human potential represented by the thousands of high school graduates whose limited educational opportunities left them unable to meet existing admission standards, the Board moved to adopt a policy of Open Admissions. It was their judgment that the best way of determining whether a potential student can benefit from college work is to admit him to college, provide him with the learning assistance he needs, and then evaluate his performance.

Beginning with the class of June 1970, every New York City resident who received a high school diploma from a public or private high school was guaranteed a place in one of the colleges of City University.

7. Of the following, the BEST title for the above passage is

    A. A BRIEF HISTORY OF THE CITY UNIVERSITY
    B. HIGH SCHOOLS AND THE CITY UNIVERSITY
    C. THE COMPONENTS OF THE UNIVERSITY
    D. TUITION-FREE COLLEGES

8. According to the above passage, which one of the following colleges of the City University was ORIGINALLY called the Free Academy?

    A. Brooklyn College   B. City College
    C. Hunter College   D. Queens College

9. According to the above passage, the system of municipal colleges became the City University of New York in

    A. 1926   B. 1955   C. 1961   D. 1969

10. According to the above passage, Staten Island Community College came under the jurisdiction of the Board of Higher Education

 A. 6 years after a Graduate Division was organized
 B. 8 years before the adoption of the Open Admissions Policy
 C. 29 years after Brooklyn and Queens Colleges
 D. 29 years after City and Hunter Colleges

10.____

11. According to the above passage, the Staten Island Community College is

 A. a graduate division center
 B. a senior college
 C. a two-year college
 D. an upper division college

11.____

12. According to the above passage, the TOTAL number of colleges, divisions, and affiliated branches of the City University is

 A. 18   B. 19   C. 20   D. 21

12.____

13. According to the above passage, the Open Admissions Policy is designed to determine whether a potential student will benefit from college by PRIMARILY

 A. discouraging competition for placement in the City University among high school students
 B. evaluating his performance after entry into college
 C. lowering admission standards
 D. providing learning assistance before entry into college

13.____

14. According to the above passage, the FIRST class to be affected by the Open Admissions Policy was the

 A. high school class which graduated in January 1970
 B. City University class which graduated in June 1970
 C. high school class when graduated in June 1970
 D. City University class which graduated in June 1970

14.____

15. According to the above passage, one of the reasons that the Board of Higher Education initiated the policy of Open Admissions was to

 A. enable high school graduates with a background of limited educational opportunities to enter college
 B. expand the growth of the City University so as to increase the number and variety of degrees offered
 C. provide a social resource to the qualified youth of the City
 D. revise admission standards to meet the needs of the City

15.____

Questions 16-18.

DIRECTIONS: Questions 16 through 18 are to be answered SOLELY on the basis of the following passage.

Hereafter, all probationary students interested in transferring to community college career programs (associate degrees) from liberal arts programs in senior colleges (bachelor degrees) will be eligible for such transfers if they have completed no more than three semesters.

For students with averages of 1.5 or above, transfer will be automatic. Those with 1.0 to 1.5 averages can transfer provisionally and will be required to make substantial progress during the first semester in the career program. Once transfer has taken place, only those courses in which passing grades were received will be computed in the community college grade-point average.

No request for transfer will be accepted from probationary students wishing to enter the liberal arts programs at the community college.

16. According to this passage, the one of the following which is the BEST statement concerning the transfer of probationary students is that a probationary student

    A. may transfer to a career program at the end of one semester
    B. must complete three semester hours before he is eligible for transfer
    C. is not eligible to transfer to a career program
    D. is eligible to transfer to a liberal arts program

17. Which of the following is the BEST statement of academic evaluation for transfer purposes in the case of probationary students?

    A. No probationary student with an average under 1.5 may transfer.
    B. A probationary student with an average of 1.3 may not transfer.
    C. A probationary student with an average of 1.6 may transfer.
    D. A probationary student with an average of .8 may transfer on a provisional basis.

18. It is MOST likely that, of the following, the next degree sought by one who already holds the Associate in Science degree would be a(n)

    A. Assistantship in Science degree
    B. Associate in Applied Science degree
    C. Bachelor of Science degree
    D. Doctor of Philosophy degree

Questions 19-20.

DIRECTIONS: Questions 19 and 20 are to be answered SOLELY on the basis of the following passage.

Auto: Auto travel requires prior approval by the President and/or appropriate Dean and must be indicated in the *Request for Travel Authorization* form. Employees authorized to use personal autos on official College business will be reimbursed at the rate of 28¢ per mile for the first 500 miles driven and 18¢ per mile for mileage driven in excess of 500 miles. The Comptroller's Office may limit the amount of reimbursement to the expenditure that would have been made if a less expensive mode of transportation (railroad, airplane, bus, etc.) had been utilized. If this occurs, the traveler will have to pick up the excess expenditure as a personal expense.

Tolls, Parking Fees, and Parking Meter Fees are not reimbursable and may not be claimed.

19. Suppose that Professor T. gives the office assistant the following memorandum:
Used car for official trip to Albany, New York, and return. Distance from New York to Albany is 148 miles. Tolls were $3.50 each way. Parking garage cost $3.00.
When preparing the Travel Expense Voucher for Professor T., the figure which should be claimed for transportation is

   A. $120.88   B. $113.88   C. $82.88   D. $51.44

20. Suppose that Professor V. gives the office assistant the following memorandum:
Used car for official trip to Pittsburgh, Pennsylvania, and return.
Distance from New York to Pittsburgh is 350 miles. Tolls were $3.30, $11.40 going, and $3.30, $2.00 returning.
When preparing the Travel Expense Voucher for Professor V., the figure which should be claimed for transportation is

   A. $225.40   B. $176.00   C. $127.40   D. $98.00

Questions 21-25.

DIRECTIONS: Questions 21 through 25 are to be answered SOLELY on the basis of the following passage.

For a period of nearly fifteen years, beginning in the mid-1950's, higher education sustained a phenomenal rate of growth. The factors principally responsible were continuing improvement in the rate of college entrance by high school graduates, a 50 percent increase in the size of the college-age (eighteen to twenty-one) group, and – until about 1967 – a rapid expansion of university research activity supported by the Federal government.

Today, as one looks ahead to the year 2010, it is apparent that each of these favorable stimuli will either be abated or turn into a negative factor. The rate of growth of the college-age group has already diminished; and from 2000 to 2005, the size of the college-age group has shrunk annually almost as fast as it grew from 1965 to 1970. From 2005 to 2010, this annual decrease will slow down so that by 2010 the age group will be about the same size as it was in 2009. This substantial net decrease in the size of the college-age group (from 1995 to 2010) will dramatically affect college enrollments since, currently, 83 percent of undergraduates are twenty-one and under, and another 11 percent are twenty-two to twenty-four.

21. Which one of the following factors is NOT mentioned in the above passage as contributing to the high rate of growth of higher education?

   A. A large increase in the size of the eighteen to twenty-one age group
   B. The equalization of educational opportunities among socio-economic groups
   C. The Federal budget impact on research and development spending in the higher education sector
   D. The increasing rate at which high school graduates enter college

22. Based on the information in the above passage, the size of the college-age group in 2010 will be

   A. larger than it was in 2009
   B. larger than it was in 1995
   C. smaller than it was in 2005
   D. about the same as it was in 2000

23. According to the above passage, the tremendous rate of growth of higher education started around

    A. 1950   B. 1955   C. 1960   D. 1965

24. The percentage of undergraduates who are over age 24 is MOST NEARLY

    A. 6%   B. 8%   C. 11%   D. 17%

25. Which one of the following conclusions can be substantiated by the information given in the above passage?
    A. The college-age group was about the same size in 2000 as it was in 1965.
    B. The annual decrease in the size of the college-age group from 2000 to 2005 is about the same as the annual increase from 1965 to 1970.
    C. The overall decrease in the size of the college-age group from 2000 to 2005 will be followed by an overall increase in its size from 2005 to 2010.
    D. The size of the college-age group is decreasing at a fairly constant rate from 1995 to 2010.

KEY (CORRECT ANSWERS)

1.	A		11.	C
2.	B		12.	C
3.	A		13.	B
4.	B		14.	C
5.	B		15.	A
6.	B		16.	A
7.	A		17.	C
8.	B		18.	C
9.	C		19.	C
10.	D		20.	B

21. B
22. C
23. B
24. A
25. B

PREPARING WRITTEN MATERIAL

PARAGRAPH REARRANGEMENT
COMMENTARY

The sentences which follow are in scrambled order. You are to rearrange them in proper order and indicate the letter choice containing the correct answer at the space at the right.

Each group of sentences in this section is actually a paragraph presented in scrambled order. Each sentence in the group has a place in that paragraph; no sentence is to be left out. You are to read each group of sentences and decide upon the best order in which to put the sentences so as to form as well-organized paragraph.

The questions in this section measure the ability to solve a problem when all the facts relevant to its solution are not given.

More specifically, certain positions of responsibility and authority require the employee to discover connections between events sometimes, apparently, unrelated. In order to do this, the employee will find it necessary to correctly infer that unspecified events have probably occurred or are likely to occur. This ability becomes especially important when action must be taken on incomplete information.

Accordingly, these questions require competitors to choose among several suggested alternatives, each of which presents a different sequential arrangement of the events. Competitors must choose the MOST logical of the suggested sequences.

In order to do so, they may be required to draw on general knowledge to infer missing concepts or events that are essential to sequencing the given events. Competitors should be careful to infer only what is essential to the sequence. The plausibility of the wrong alternatives will always require the inclusion of unlikely events or of additional chains of events which are NOT essential to sequencing the given events.

It's very important to remember that you are looking for the best of the four possible choices, and that the best choice of all may not even be one of the answers you're given to choose from.

There is no one right way to solve these problems. Many people have found it helpful to first write out the order of the sentences, as they would have arranged them, on their scrap paper before looking at the possible answers. If their optimum answer is there, this can save them some time. If it isn't, this method can still give insight into solving the problem. Others find it most helpful to just go through each of the possible choices, contrasting each as they go along. You should use whatever method feels comfortable, and works, for you.

While most of these types of questions are not that difficult, we've added a higher percentage of the difficult type, just to give you more practice. Usually there are only one or two questions on this section that contain such subtle distinctions that you're unable to answer confidently, and you then may find yourself stuck deciding between two possible choices, neither of which you're sure about.

EXAMINATION SECTION
TEST 1

DIRECTIONS: Each group of sentences in this section is actually a paragraph presented in scrambled order. Each sentence in the group has a place in that paragraph; no sentence is to be left out. You are to read each group of sentences, so as to form a well-organized paragraph. Before trying to answer the questions which follow each group of sentences, jot down the correct order of the sentences. Then answer each of the questions by printing the letter of the correct answer in the space at the right. Remember that you will receive credit only for answers marked.

- P. American divorce statutes derive principally from ecclesiastical law and embody certain moral concepts.
- Q. Divorces are granted under such statutes only to an innocent spouse where the other spouse has been guilty of statutorily-defined misconduct.
- R. All the states and territories of the United States grant divorces.
- S. If, therefore, both parties are guilty, there can be no divorce.
- T. The statutes of each territory and state determine the permissible grounds for the divorces granted in that territory and state.

1. Which sentence did you put after Sentence R? 1.____
   - A. P
   - B. Q
   - C. S
   - D. T
   - E. None of the above. Sentence R is last.

2. Which sentence did you put before Sentence Q? 2.____
   - A. P
   - B. R
   - C. S
   - D. T
   - E. None of the above. Sentence Q is first.

3. Which sentence did you put after Sentence S? 3.____
   - A. P
   - B. Q
   - C. R
   - D. T
   - E. None of the above. Sentence S is last.

4. Which sentence did you put last? 4.____
   - A. P   B. Q   C. R   D. S   E. T

5. Which sentence did you put before Sentence R? 5.___

    A. P
    B. Q
    C. S
    D. T
    E. None of the above. Sentence R is first.

KEY (CORRECT ANSWERS)

1. D
2. A
3. E
4. D
5. E

TEST 2

DIRECTIONS: Each group of sentences in this section is actually a paragraph presented in scrambled order. Each sentence in the group has a place in that paragraph; no sentence is to be left out. You are to read each group of sentences, so as to form a well-organized paragraph. Before trying to answer the questions which follow each group of sentences, jot down the correct order of the sentences. Then answer each of the questions by printing the letter of the correct answer in the space at the right. Remember that you will receive credit only for answers marked.

   P. Sporting dogs include pointers, setters, and retrievers.
   Q. Terriers include airedales, fox terriers, and schnauzers.
   R. Hounds include bloodhounds, greyhounds, and wolfhounds.
   S. Working dogs include collies, sheep dogs, and boxers.
   T. Four of the major classifications of dogs are sporting dogs, hounds, terriers, and working dogs.

1. Which sentence did you put before Sentence R? 1.____

   A. P
   B. Q
   C. S
   D. T
   E. None of the above. Sentence R is first.

2. Which sentence did you put after Sentence S? 2.____

   A. P
   B. Q
   C. R
   D. T
   E. None of the above. Sentence S is last.

3. Which sentence did you put before Sentence Q? 3.____

   A. P
   B. R
   C. S
   D. T
   E. None of the above. Sentence Q is first.

4. Which sentence did you put last? 4.____

   A. P   B. Q   C. R   D. S   E. T

5. Which sentence did you put after Sentence T? 5.____

   A. P
   B. Q
   C. R
   D. S
   E. None of the above. Sentence T is last.

KEY (CORRECT ANSWERS)

1. A
2. E
3. B
4. D
5. A

TEST 3

DIRECTIONS: Each group of sentences in this section is actually a paragraph presented in scrambled order. Each sentence in the group has a place in that paragraph; no sentence is to be left out. You are to read each group of sentences, so as to form a well-organized paragraph. Before trying to answer the questions which follow each group of sentences, jot down the correct order of the sentences. Then answer each of the questions by printing the letter of the correct answer in the space at the right. Remember that you will receive credit only for answers marked.

P. Dostoevsky came to be regarded as the most promising of Russia's young novelists.
Q. He continued, however, to write prolifically for the next three years, producing three novels in that period.
R. Unlike his later works, too, they betray intense interest in problems of form and show originality of verbal expression.
S. But his second novel, THE DOUBLE, disappointed critics, and his success began to wane.
T. These early works display the strong influence of Gogol.

1. Which sentence did you put before Sentence P?   1.____

   A. Q
   B. R
   C. S
   D. T
   E. None of the above. Sentence P is first.

2. Which sentence did you put third?   2.____

   A. P   B. Q   C. R   D. S   E. T

3. Which sentence did you put after Sentence Q?   3.____

   A. P
   B. R
   C. S
   D. T
   E. None of the above. Sentence Q is last.

4. Which sentence did you put last?   4.____

   A. P   B. Q   C. R   D. S   E. T

5. Which sentence did you put before Sentence S?   5.____

   A. P
   B. Q
   C. R
   D. T
   E. None of the above. Sentence S is first.

KEY (CORRECT ANSWERS)

1. E
2. B
3. D
4. C
5. A

TEST 4

DIRECTIONS: Each group of sentences in this section is actually a paragraph presented in scrambled order. Each sentence in the group has a place in that paragraph; no sentence is to be left out. You are to read each group of sentences, so as to form a well-organized paragraph. Before trying to answer the questions which follow each group of sentences, jot down the correct order of the sentences. Then answer each of the questions by printing the letter of the correct answer in the space at the right. Remember that you will receive credit only for answers marked.

P. Not every state of awareness in sleep is classifiable as a dream state.
Q. Dreams are ordinarily defined as states of consciousness taking place during sleep.
R. For example, people often hear a telephone ringing while asleep, and awaken to find that a telephone is, indeed, ringing.
S. And sleep is not invariably necessary to the manifestation of dream consciousness.
T. This definition is hardly adequate.

1. Which sentence did you put after Sentence T? 1.____

   A. P
   B. Q
   C. R
   D. S
   E. None of the above. Sentence T is last.

2. Which sentence did you put after Sentence R? 2.____

   A. P
   B. Q
   C. S
   D. T
   E. None of the above. Sentence R is last.

3. Which sentence did you put after Sentence Q? 3.____

   A. P
   B. R
   C. S
   D. T
   E. None of the above. Sentence Q is last.

4. Which sentence did you put after Sentence P? 4.____

   A. Q
   B. R
   C. S
   D. T
   E. None of the above. Sentence P is last.

5. Which sentence did you put before Sentence Q?
   A. P
   B. R
   C. S
   D. T
   E. None of the above. Sentence Q is first.

5.__

———

KEY (CORRECT ANSWERS)

1. A
2. C
3. D
4. B
5. E

———

TEST 5

DIRECTIONS: Each group of sentences in this section is actually a paragraph presented in scrambled order. Each sentence in the group has a place in that paragraph; no sentence is to be left out. You are to read each group of sentences, so as to form a well-organized paragraph. Before trying to answer the questions which follow each group of sentences, jot down the correct order of the sentences. Then answer each of the questions by printing the letter of the correct answer in the space at the right. Remember that you will receive credit only for answers marked.

P. Yet the long history of disarmament proposals and counterproposals is discouraging.
Q. It is also a wasteful mode of international competition.
R. Only those, therefore, who despair of the West's ability to compete constructively put their trust in the arms race.
S. It is now generally accepted that the arms race is too dangerous for any nation to continue pursuing without restraint or inhibition.
T. The fears and tensions it generates prevent East and West from competing constructively.

1. Which sentence did you put next to last?   1.____
   A. P   B. Q   C. R   D. S   E. T

2. Which sentence did you put before Sentence T?   2.____
   A. P
   B. Q
   C. R
   D. S
   E. None of the above. Sentence T is first.

3. Which sentence did you put before Sentence Q?   3.____
   A. P
   B. R
   C. S
   D. T
   E. None of the above. Sentence Q is first.

4. Which sentence did you put after Sentence R?   4.____
   A. P
   B. Q
   C. S
   D. T
   E. None of the above. Sentence R is last.

5. Which sentence did you put before Sentence S?

    A. P
    B. Q
    C. R
    D. T
    E. None of the above. Sentence S is first.

5.__

KEY (CORRECT ANSWERS)

1. C
2. B
3. C
4. A
5. E

PREPARING WRITTEN MATERIAL

EXAMINATION SECTION
TEST 1

DIRECTIONS: Each of the sentences in the tests that follow may be classified under one of the following four categories:

    A. *Incorrect* because of faulty grammar or sentence structure
    B. *Incorrect* because of faulty punctuation
    C. *Incorrect* because of faulty capitalization
    D. *Correct*

Examine each sentence carefully to determine under which of the above four options it is best classified. Then, in the space on the right, print the capital letter preceding the option which is the *BEST* of the four suggested above.

(Each incorrect sentence contains but one type of error. Consider a sentence to be correct if it contains none of the types of errors mentioned, even though there may be other correct ways of expressing the same thought.)

1. This fact, together with those brought out at the previous meeting, prove that the schedule is satisfactory to the employees.   1.____

2. Like many employees in scientific fields, the work of bookkeepers and accountants requires accuracy and neatness.   2.____

3. "What can I do for you," the secretary asked as she motioned to the visitor to take a seat.   3.____

4. Our representative, Mr. Charles will call on you next week to determine whether or not your claim has merit.   4.____

5. We expect you to return in the spring; please do not disappoint us.   5.____

6. Any supervisor, who disregards the just complaints of his subordinates, is remiss in the performance of his duty.   6.____

7. Because she took less than an hour for lunch is no reason for permitting her to leave before five o'clock.   7.____

8. "Miss Smith," said the supervisor, "Please arrange a meeting of the staff for two o'clock on Monday."   8.____

9. A private company's vacation and sick leave allowance usually differs considerably from a public agency.   9.____

10. Therefore, in order to increase the efficiency of operations in the department, a report on the recommended changes in procedures was presented to the departmental committee in charge of the program.   10.____

11. We told him to assign the work to whoever was available.   11.____

12. Since John was the most efficient of any other employee in the bureau, he received the highest service rating.   12.____

13. Only those members of the national organization who resided in the middle West attended the conference in Chicago. 13.__

14. The question of whether the office manager has as yet attained, or indeed can ever hope to secure professional status is one which has been discussed for years. 14.__

15. No one knew who to blame for the error which, we later discovered, resulted in a considerable loss of time. 15.__

KEY (CORRECT ANSWERS)

1. A
2. A
3. B
4. B
5. D
6. B
7. A
8. C
9. A
10. D
11. D
12. A
13. C
14. B
15. A

TEST 2

DIRECTIONS: Each of the sentences in the tests that follow may be classified under one of the following four categories:

    A. *Incorrect* because of faulty grammar or sentence structure
    B. *Incorrect* because of faulty punctuation
    C. *Incorrect* because of faulty capitalization
    D. *Correct*

1. The National alliance of Businessmen is trying to persuade private businesses to hire youth in the summertime.   1.____

2. The supervisor who is on vacation, is in charge of processing vouchers.   2.____

3. The activity of the committee at its conferences is always stimulating.   3.____

4. After checking the addresses again, the letters went to the mailroom.   4.____

5. The director, as well as the employees, are interested in sharing the dividends.   5.____

KEY (CORRECT ANSWERS)

1. C
2. B
3. D
4. A
5. A

TEST 3

DIRECTIONS: In each of the following groups of sentences, one of the four sentences is faulty in grammar, punctuation, or capitalization. Select the incorrect sentence in each case.

1. A. Sailing down the bay was a thrilling experience for me.
   B. He was not consulted about your joining the club.
   C. This story is different than the one I told you yesterday.
   D. There is no doubt about his being the best player.

   1.____

2. A. He maintains there is but one road to world peace.
   B. It is common knowledge that a child sees much he is not supposed to see.
   C. Much of the bitterness might have been avoided if arbitration had been resorted to earlier in the meeting.
   D. The man decided it would be advisable to marry a girl somewhat younger than him.

   2.____

3. A. In this book, the incident I liked least is where the hero tries to put out the forest fire.
   B. Learning a foreign language will undoubtedly give a person a better understanding of his mother tongue.
   C. His actions made us wonder what he planned to do next.
   D. Because of the war, we were unable to travel during the summer vacation.

   3.____

4. A. The class had no sooner become interested in the lesson than the dismissal bell rang.
   B. There is little agreement about the kind of world to be planned at the peace conference.
   C. "Today," said the teacher, "we shall read 'The Wind in the Willows.' I am sure you'll like it.
   D. The terms of the legal settlement of the family quarrel handicapped both sides for many years.

   4.____

5. A. I was so suprised that I was not able to say a word.
   B. She is taller than any other member of the class.
   C. It would be much more preferable if you were never seen in his company.
   D. We had no choice but to excuse her for being late.

   5.____

KEY (CORRECT ANSWERS)

1. C
2. D
3. A
4. C
5. C

TEST 4

DIRECTIONS: In each of the following groups of sentences, one of the four sentences is faulty in grammar, punctuation, or capitalization. Select the incorrect sentence in each case.

1. A. Please send me these data at the earliest opportunity.
   B. The loss of their material proved to be a severe handicap.
   C. My principal objection to this plan is that it is impracticable .
   D. The doll had laid in the rain for an hour and was ruined.

   1.____

2. A. The garden scissors, left out all night in the rain, were in a badly rusted condition.
   B. The girls felt bad about the misunderstanding which had arisen.
   C. Sitting near the campfire, the old man told John and I about many exciting adventures he had had.
   D. Neither of us is in a position to undertake a task of that magnitude.

   2.____

3. A. The general concluded that one of the three roads would lead to the besieged city.
   B. The children didn't, as a rule, do hardly anything beyond what they were told to do.
   C. The reason the girl gave for her negligence was that she had acted on the spur of the moment.
   D. The daffodils and tulips look beautiful in that blue vase.

   3.____

4. A. If I was ten years older, I should be interested in this work.
   B. Give the prize to whoever has drawn the best picture.
   C. When you have finished reading the book, take it back to the library.
   D. My drawing is as good as or better than yours.

   4.____

5. A. He asked me whether the substance was animal or vegetable.
   B. An apple which is unripe should not be eaten by a child.
   C. That was an insult to me who am your friend.
   D. Some spy must of reported the matter to the enemy.

   5.____

6. A. Limited time makes quoting the entire message impossible.
   B. Who did she say was going?
   C. The girls in your class have dressed more dolls this year than we.
   D. There was such a large amount of books on the floor that I couldn't find a place for my rocking chair.

   6.____

7. A. What with his sleeplessness and his ill health, he was unable to assume any responsibility for the success of the meeting.
   B. If I had been born in February, I should be celebrating my birthday soon.
   C. In order to prevent breakage, she placed a sheet of paper between each of the plates when she packed them.
   D. After the spring shower, the violets smelled very sweet.

   7.____

8. A. He had laid the book down very reluctantly before the end of the lesson.
   B. The dog, I am sorry to say, had lain on the bed all night.
   C. The cloth was first lain on a flat surface; then it was pressed with a hot iron.
   D. While we were in Florida, we lay in the sun until we were noticeably tanned.

   8.____

9.
   A. If John was in New York during the recent holiday season, I have no doubt he spent most of his time with his parents.
   B. How could he enjoy the television program; the dog was barking and the baby was crying.
   C. When the problem was explained to the class, he must have been asleep.
   D. She wished that her new dress were finished so that she could go to the party.

10.
   A. The engine not only furnishes power but light and heat as well.
   B. You're aware that we've forgotten whose guilt was established, aren't you?
   C. Everybody knows that the woman made many sacrifices for her children.
   D. A man with his dog and gun is a familiar sight in this neighborhood.

KEY (CORRECT ANSWERS)

1. D
2. C
3. B
4. A
5. D
6. D
7. B
8. C
9. B
10. A

TEST 5

DIRECTIONS: Each of Questions 1 to 15 consists of a sentence which may be classified appropriately under one of the following four categories:
  A. *Incorrect* because of faulty grammar
  B. *Incorrect* because of faulty punctuation
  C. *Incorrect* because of faulty spelling
  D. *Correct*

Examine each sentence carefully. Then, print, in the space on the right, the letter preceding the category which is the best of the four suggested above.

(Note: Each incorrect sentence contains only one type of error. Consider a sentence correct if it. contains no errors, although there may be other correct ways of writing the sentence.)

1. Of the two employees, the one in our office is the most efficient.   1.____
2. No one can apply or even understand, the new rules and regulations.   2.____
3. A large amount of supplies were stored in the empty office.   3.____
4. If an employee is occassionally asked to work overtime, he should do so willingly.   4.____
5. It is true that the new procedures are difficult to use but, we are certain that you will learn them quickly.   5.____
6. The office manager said that he did not know who would be given a large allotment under the new plan.   6.____
7. It was at the supervisor's request that the clerk agreed to postpone his vacation.   7.____
8. We do not believe that it is necessary for both he and the clerk to attend the conference.   8.____
9. All employees, who display perseverance, will be given adequate recognition.   9.____
10. He regrets that some of us employees are dissatisfied with our new assignments.   10.____
11. "Do you think that the raise was merited," asked the supervisor?   11.____
12. The new manual of procedure is a valuable supplament to our rules and regulations.   12.____
13. The typist admitted that she had attempted to pursuade the other employees to assist her in her work.   13.____
14. The supervisor asked that all amendments to the regulations be handled by you and I.   14.____
15. The custodian seen the boy who broke the window.   15.____

KEY (CORRECT ANSWERS)

1. A
2. B
3. A
4. C
5. B

6. D
7. D
8. A
9. B
10. D

11. B
12. C
13. C
14. A
15. A

INTERPRETING STATISTICAL DATA
GRAPHS, CHARTS AND TABLES
TEST 1

DIRECTIONS: Study the following graphs, charts, and/or tables. Base your answers to the questions that follow SOLELY on the information contained therein. *PRINT THE LETTER OF THE CORRECT ANSWER IN THE SPACE AT THE RIGHT.*

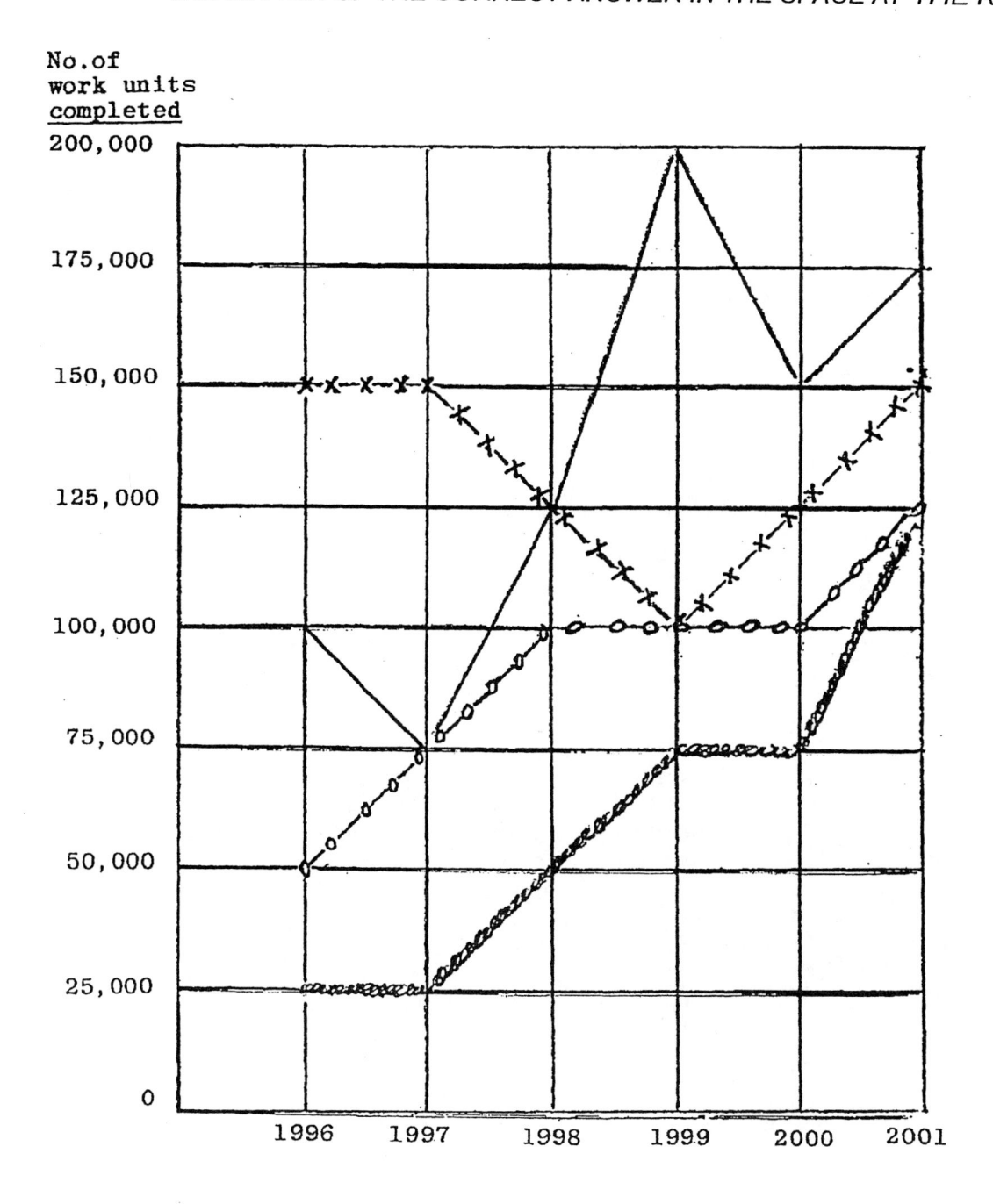

No. of work units completed

Units of each type of work completed by a public agency from 1996 to 2001.

```
Letters Written      _____
Documents Filed      ___X___X___X___X
Applications Processed ___0___0___0___0
Inspections Made     ooooooooooooooooooo
```

1. The year for which the number of units of one type of work completed was *less* than it was for the previous year while the number of each of the other types of work completed was *more* than it was for the previous year was

   A. 1997   B. 1998   C. 1999   D. 2000

2. The number of letters written EXCEEDED the number of applications processed by the *same* amount in

   A. two of the years
   B. three of the years
   C. four of the years
   D. five of the years

3. The YEAR in which the number of each type of work completed was *greater* than in the preceding year was

   A. 1998   B. 1999   C. 2000   D. 2001

4. The number of applications processed and the number of documents filed were the SAME in

   A. 1997   B. 1998   C. 1999   D. 2000

5. The *total number* of units of work completed by the agency

   A. increased in each year after 1996
   B. decreased from the prior year in two of the years after 1996
   C. was the same in two successive years from 1996 to 2001
   D. was less in 1996 than in any of the following years

6. For the year in which the number of letters written was twice as high as it was in 1996, the number of documents FILED was

   A. the same as it was in 1996
   B. two-thirds of what it was in 1996
   C. five-sixths of what it was in 1996
   D. one and one-half times what it was in 1996

7. The *variable* which was the MOST stable during the period 1996 through 2001 was

   A. Inspections Made   B. Letters Written
   C. Documents Filed   D. Applications Processed

KEY (CORRECT ANSWERS)

1. B   5. C
2. B   6. B
3. D   7. D
4. C

TEST 2

Questions 1-8.

GOVERNMENT PURCHASES OF GOODS AND SERVICE
(IN BILLIONS OF DOLLARS)

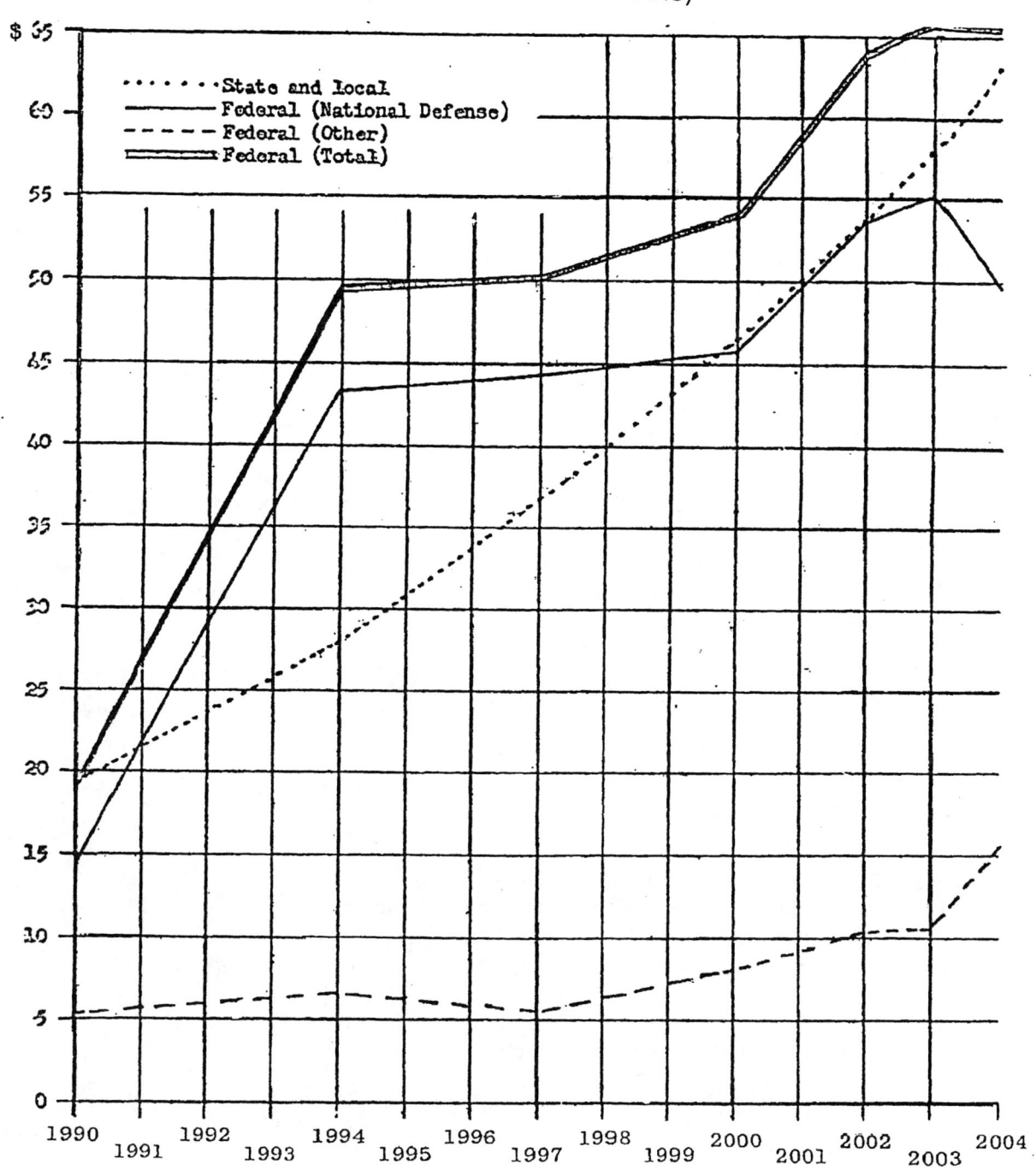

1. Purchases by the Federal government for non-defense purposes, and purchases by State and local governments comprised the smallest proportion of the total government purchases of goods and services for all purposes in which of the following years?

    A. 1990   B. 1994   C. 1997   D. 2000

1._____

2 (#2)

2. Which one of the following MOST closely approximates the percentage increase in State and local purchases of goods and services in 2004 as compared with 1990?

    A. 110%   B. 150%   C. 220%   D. 350%

3. Total government purchases of goods and services in 2004 was MOST NEARLY, billion dollars.

    A. 80   B. 110   C. 128   D. 144

4. In 2000, purchases made by State and local governments

    A. exceeded Federal government total purchases
    B. exceeded purchases made by them in 1994 by more than 50%
    C. increased less than 10% over 1997
    D. were less than 50% of purchases made by them in 2003

5. Purchases of goods and services for national defense in 1994 by the Federal government was, *MOST NEARLY,*

    A. 15% less than the total spent by Federal, State and local governments for all purposes in 1990
    B. 50% of the total spent by Federal, State and local governments for all purposes in 1997
    C. four times the amount spent in 1990 for national defense
    D. ten times the amount spent in 1994 by the Federal government for purposes other than national defense

6. In which one of the following years did State and local purchases of goods and services comprise the GREATEST proportion of the total spent by all government jurisdictions?

    A. 1990   B. 1994   C. 1997   D. 2002

7. The dollar increase in purchases of goods and services was LEAST for which one of the following?

    A. State and local governments between 1990 and 1994
    B. State and local governments between 1997 and 2000
    C. Total Federal government between 2000 and 2002
    D. Federal government other than national defense between 2000 and 2003

8. The rate of increase in Federal purchases of goods and services for national defense was GREATEST between which of the following periods?

    A. From 1994 to 1997   B. From 1997 to 2000
    C. From 2000 to 2002   D. From 2002 to 2004

KEY (CORRECT ANSWERS)

1. B   5. B
2. C   6. A
3. C   7. D
4. B   8. C

TEST 3

Questions 1-10.

DIRECTIONS: Questions 1-10 are to be answered SOLELY on the basis of the following table showing the amounts purchased by various purchasing units during 2000.

DOLLAR VOLUME PURCHASED BY EACH PURCHASING UNIT DURING EACH QUARTER OF 2000
(Figures Shown Represent Thousands of Dollars)

Purchasing Unit	First Quarter	Second Quarter	Third Quarter	Fourth Quarter
A	578	924	698	312
B	1,426	1,972	1,586	1,704
C	366	494	430	716
D	1,238	1,708	1,884	1,546
E	730	742	818	774
F	948	1,118	1,256	788

1. The TOTAL dollar volume purchased by *all* of the purchasing units during 2000 approximated, *most nearly,*

   A. $2,000,000   B. $4,000,000   C. $20,000,000   D. $40,000,000

2. During which quarter was the GREATEST total dollar amount of purchases made?

   A. First   B. Second   C. Third   D. Fourth

3. Assume that the dollar volume purchased by Unit F during 2000 exceeded the dollar volume purchased by Unit F during 1999 was 50%. Then the dollar volume purchased by Unit F during 1999 was

   A. $2,055,000   B. $2,550,000   C. $2,740,000   D. $6,165,000

4. Which *one* of the following purchasing units showed the SHARPEST decrease in the amount purchased during the *fourth* quarter as compared with the *third* quarter? Unit

   A. A   B. B   C. D   D. E

5. Comparing the dollar volume purchased in the *second* quarter with the dollar volume purchased in the *third* quarter, the *decrease* in the dollar volume during the third quarter was PRIMARILY due to the decrease in the dollar volume purchased by Units

   A. A and B   B. C and D   C. C and E   D. C and F

6. Of the following, the unit which had the LARGEST number of dollars of increased purchases from any one quarter to the next following quarter was Unit

   A. A   B. B   C. C   D. D

7. Of the following, the unit with the LARGEST dollar volume of purchases during the *second half* of 2000 was Unit

   A. A   B. B   C. D   D. F

8. Which one of the following *most closely* approximates the percentage which Unit B's total 2000 purchases represents of the total 2000 purchases of all units, including Unit B?

   A. 10% B. 15% C. 25% D. 45%

9. Assume that research showed that each ten thousand dollars ($10,000) of purchases by Unit D during 2000 required an average of thirteen (13) man-hours of buyers' staff time. On that basis, which *one* of the following *most closely* approximates the NUMBER OF MAN-HOURS of buyers' staff time required by Unit D during 2000? _____ man-hours.

   A. 1,800 B. 8,000 C. 68,000 D. 78,000

10. Assume that research showed that each ten thousand dollars ($10,000) of purchases by Unit C during 2000 required an average of ten (10) man-hours of buyers' staff time. This research also showed that during 2000 the average man-hours of buyers' staff time per ten thousand dollars of purchases required by Unit C exceeded by 25% the average man-hours of buyers' staff time per ten thousand dollars of purchases required by Unit E. On that basis, which *one* of the following *most closely* approximates the NUMBER OF BUYER'S STAFF MAN-HOURS required by Unit E during 2000? _____ man-hours

   A. 2,200 B. 2,400 C. 3,000 D. 3,700

KEY (CORRECT ANSWERS)

1. C
2. B
3. C
4. A
5. A

6. B
7. C
8. C
9. B
10. B

TEST 4

Questions 1-6.

DIRECTIONS: Questions 1 to 6 are to be answered SOLELY on the basis of the following table and graph and the accompanying notes.

CONSUMER PROTECTION DIVISION-METROPOLITAN CITY
Number and Kinds of Violations (2002-2004)

NATURE OF VIOLATION	2002 District A	B	C	D		Total	2003 District A	B	c	D	E	Total	2004 District A	B	C	D	E	Total
Scales	27	31	42	16	12	128	18	34	36	15	19	122	20	28	31	12	10	101
Gasoline sales	12	9	17	6	3	47	9	4	19			32	6	5	16	3	6	36
Illegal meat coloring	9	8	13	4		34	10	12	21	9	2	54	8	6	5	2	1	22
Fat content-chopped meat	21	19	40	7	1	88	20	17	31	3	3	74	16	12	18	4	3	53
Checkout counter errors	12	9	10	2		33	12	8	21			41	16	21	9	2	2	50
Fuel oil sales	6	5	4		16	31			2		6	8	5	6	6		18	35
Fraudulent labels	18	29	39	14	14	114	21	36	31	12	18	118	12	25	19	15	25	96
TOTALS	105	110	165	49	46	475	90	111	161	39	48	449	83	103	104	38	65	393

CONSUMER PROTECTION DIVISION-METROPOLITAN CITY
Number of Inspections Performed (2002-2004)

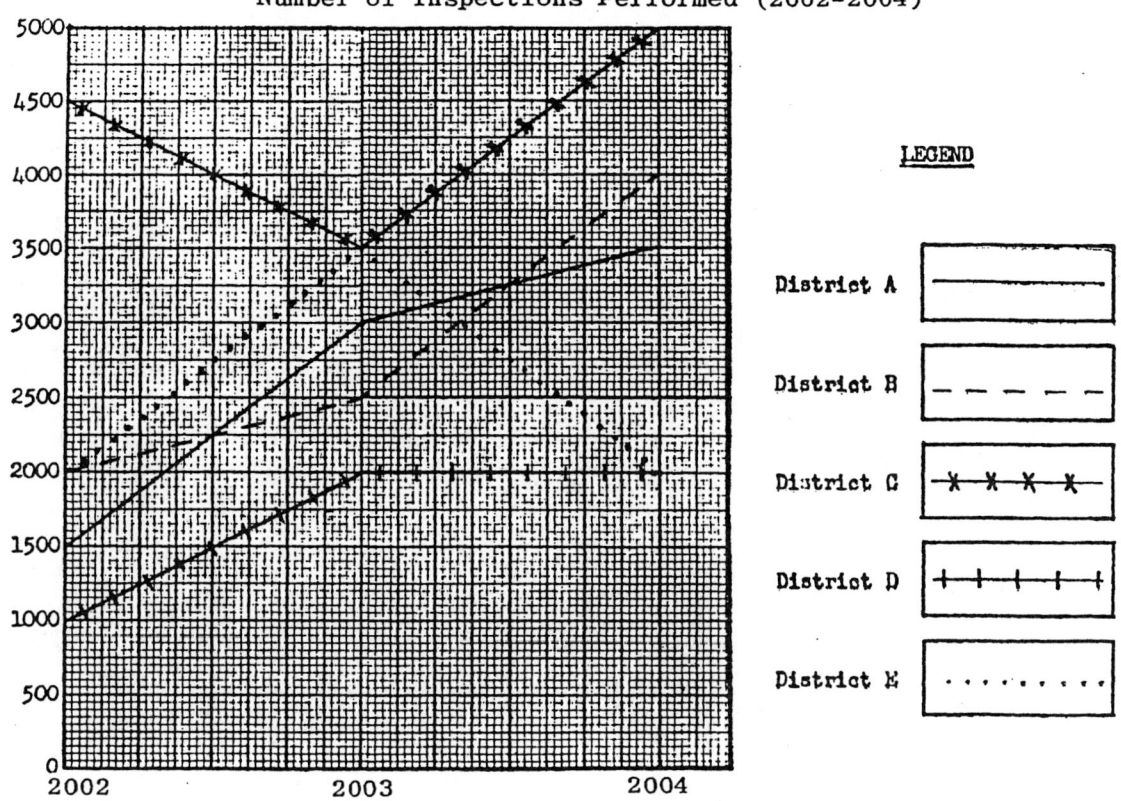

LEGEND

District A ———
District B — — —
District C —x—x—x—
District D —+—+—+—
District E ·········

NOTES: The Consumer Protection Division of Metropolitan City is divided into five districts designated A, B, C, D and E.

Number of establishments in each district:

District A - 26,000   District C - 27,000   District E - 12,000
District B - 30,000   District D - 15,000

Number of field inspectors assigned to each district in 2002 and 2003

District A - 20   District C - 25   District # - 11
District B - 24   District D - 21

At the beginning of 2004 there was a general reassignment of field inspectors and the staff of field inspectors was increased. This resulted in assignments of field inspectors as follows:

District A - 20   District C - 32   District E - 16
District B - 26   District D - 16

1. Of the following districts, the one in which the ratio of meat coloring violations to total number of violations in the district was GREATEST in 2003 is District

   A. A   B. B   C. C   D. D

2. In 2003, the number of violations uncovered per field inspector for the entire city was, *most nearly*,

   A. 3.9   B. 4.1   C. 4.4   D. 4.8

3. In 2002, the number of violations per 1,000 establishments in District C was, *most nearly*,

   A. 3.9   B. 6.1   C. 10.4   D. 16.5

4. The number of inspections performed by the Consumer Protection Division in 2003 was, *most nearly*,

   A. 449   B. 12,000   C. 13,500   D. 14,500

5. In 2002, the number of violations uncovered per 100 inspections for the entire city was, *most nearly*,

   A. .23   B. 3.2   C. 4.3   D. 48.0

6. If it had been decided at the beginning of 2004 to assign inspectors so that the ratio of the number of inspectors in each district to the total number of inspectors would be the same as the ratio of the number of establishments in the district to the total number of establishments in the city, the number of inspectors assigned to District A would have been

   A. 24   B. 25   C. 26   D. 27

KEY (CORRECT ANSWERS)

1. D
2. C
3. B
4. D
5. C
6. C

TEST 5

Questions 1-4.

DIRECTIONS: Questions 1 to 4 are to be answered SOLELY on the basis of the following graph and the accompanying notes. (Graph appears on the following page.)

NOTES: The graph shows space allocation in three municipal food markets in a certain city. The five columns for each market represent the total amount of each market's space. The miscellaneous column accounts for all non-rental space allocated to shopping aisles, loading facilities, etc.

Assume that during 2004 there was no tenant turnover and that the amount of space rented and unrented remained constant.
The rental charges in 2004 for all types of business were as follows:
Jefferson Market - $10.00 per square foot
Jackson Market - $17.50 per square foot
Lincoln Market - $15.00 per square foot

2004 SPACE ALLOCATIONS IN THE JEFFERSON, JACKSON AND LINCOLN MUNICIPAL FOOD MARKETS
(According to Type of Business)

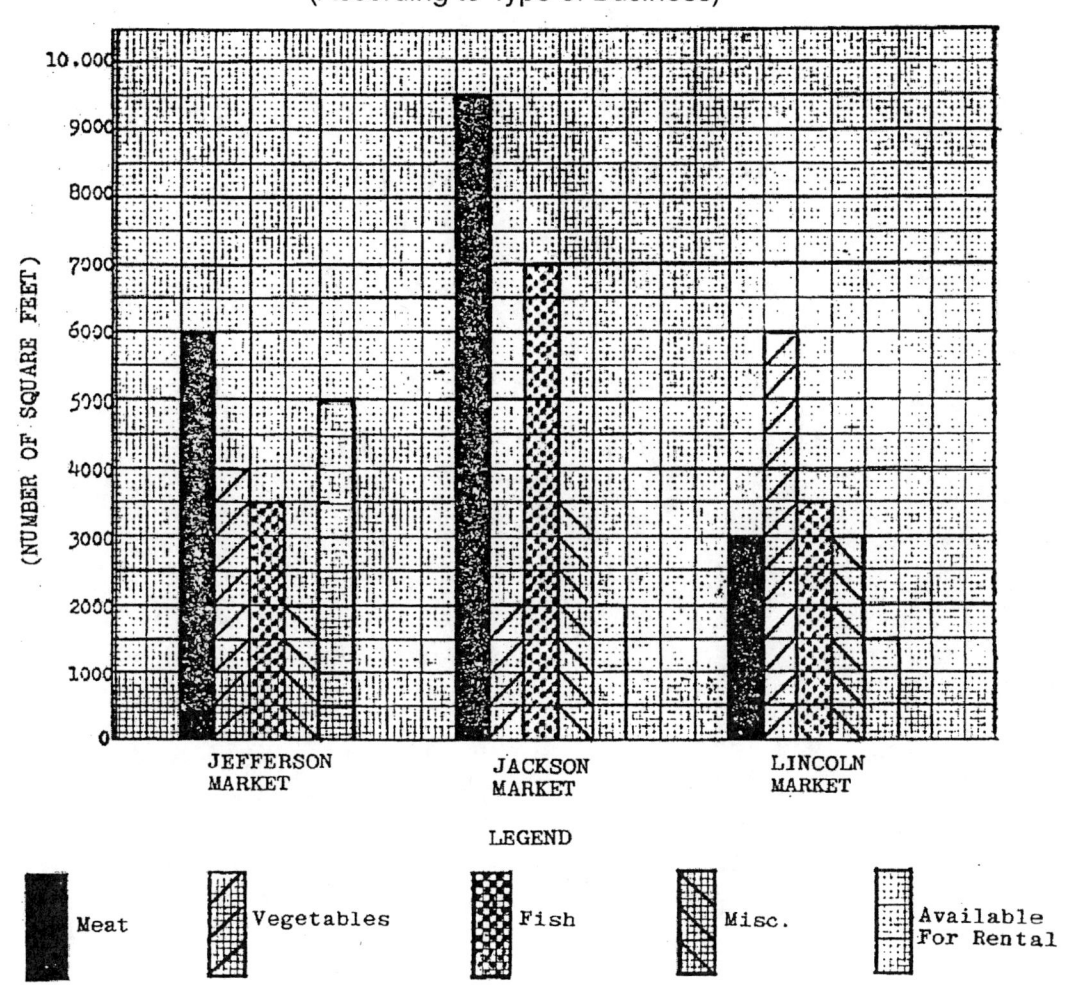

1. The percentage of over-all space in the Lincoln Market leased to fish dealers in 2004 is, most nearly,

   A. 17%   B. 19%   C. 21%   D. 23%

2. The total amount of space in all three municipal food markets devoted to the *meat business* EXCEEDED the amount of space in these markets devoted to the *fish business* by _____ square feet.

   A. 2,500   B. 4,500   C. 14,000   D. 18,500

3. If all of the space in the Lincoln Market available for rental in 2004 had been rented, the income received from this market would have INCREASED by

   A. 6%   B. 12%   C. 18%   D. 24%

4. Approximately what percent of the 2004 rental income of the Jackson Market was derived from vegetable dealers?

   A. 8.3%
   B. 9.1%
   C. 10.8%
   D. a percent which cannot be determined from the data given

---

KEY (CORRECT ANSWERS)

1. C
2. B
3. B
4. C

TEST 6

Questions 1-5.

DIRECTIONS: Questions 1 to 5 involve calculation of annual grade averages for college students who have just completed their junior year. These averages are to be based on the following table showing the number of credit hours for each student during the year at each of the grade levels: A,B,C,D,and F. How these letter grades may be translated into numerical grades is indicated in the first column of the table.

Grade Value	Credit hours - Junior Year					
	King	Lewis	Martin	Norris	Ott	Perry
A = 95	12	12	9	15	6	3
B = 85	9	12	9	12	18	6
C = 75	6	6	9	3	3	21
D = 65	3	3	3	3	-	-
F = 0	-	-	3	-	-	-

NOTES: Calculating a grade average for an individual student is a 4-step process:
I. Multiply each grade value by the number of credit hours for which the student received that grade.
II. Add these multiplication products for each student.
III. Add the student's total credit hours.
IV. Divide the multiplication product total by the total number of credit hours.
V. Round the result, if there is a decimal place, to the nearest whole number. A number ending in .5 would be rounded to the next higher number.

EXAMPLE: Using student King's grades as an example, his grade average can be calculated by going through the following four steps:

```
I.     95 x 12 = 1140       III.    12
       85 x  9 =  765                9
       75 x  6 =  450                6
       65 x  3 =  195                3
        0 x  0 =    0                0
II.        TOTAL = 2550              30   TOTAL credit hours
                             IV.   Divide 2550 by 30: 2550 / 30 = 85
```

King's grade average is 85.
Now answer questions 1 through 5 on the basis of the information given above.

1. The grade average of Lewis is
   A. 83   B. 84   C. 85   D. 86

2. The grade average of Martin is
   A. 72   B. 73   C. 74   D. 75

3. The grade average of Norris is
   A. 85   B. 86   C. 87   D. 88

4. Student Ott must attain a grade average of 90 in each of his years in college to be accepted into the graduate school of his choice. If, in summer school during his junior year, he takes two 3-credit courses and receives a grade of 95 in each one, his grade average for his junior year will then be, *most nearly.*

    A. 87   B. 88   C. 89   D. 90

5. If Perry takes an additional 3-credit course during the year and receives a grade of 95, his grade average will be increased to *approximately*

    A. 79   B. 80   C. 81   D. 82

KEY (CORRECT ANSWERS)

1. C
2. D
3. C
4. B
5. B

TEST 7

Questions 1-5.

DIRECTIONS: Questions 1 to 5 are to be answered SOLELY on the basis of the chart below which relates to the increase in taxes.

Increase In State and Local Taxes Per Person

	1987	1999	Percent Increase		1987	1999	Percent Increase
Delaware	$138	$372	170	Iowa	$180	9389	116
Maryland	161	411	156	Tennessee	118	252	114
New York	227	576	153	Arkansas	103	221	114
Nebraska	144	362	151	Wyoming	193	414	114
Kentucky	111	278	150	New Mexico	151	324	114
Rhode bland	153	379	148	Idaho	156	328	110
Virginia	128	314	145	Pennsylvania	162	340	109
Arizona	163	387	13S	South Dakota	169	353	108
Indiana	141	334	137	Illinois	179	373	108
New Jersey	173	406	135	South Carolina	108	225	108
Wisconsin	187	439	135	Maine	149	308	106
California	232	540	133	Ohio.	149	306	105
Michigan	184	428	132	Colorado	189	386	104
Missouri	132	301	128	Nevada	232	466	101
North Carolina	115	259	125	Connecticut	196	392	100
Vermont	173	384	123	Kansas	173	346	100
Minnesota	183	406	122	Texas	139	276	99
West Virginia	119	263	120	Utah	166	327	98
Massachusetts	206	453	119	New Hampshire	152	299	97
Alabama	103	224	118	North Dakota	176	338	92
Washington	189	410	117	Oregon	204	387	90
Florida	153	330	116	Oklahoma	152	287	89
Georgia	125	270	116	Louisiana	160	298	86
Mississippi	112	242	116	Montana	189	351	86

1. The dollar increase per person in taxes between 1987-1999 was GREATEST in which state?   1._____

   A. New York   B. California   C. Wisconsin
   D. New Jersey   E. Delaware

2. The state whose people paid the LOWEST amount per person in taxes in 1999 was   2._____

   A. Montana   B. Mississippi   C. Alabama
   D. Arkansas   E. South Carolina

3. Which of the following states DOUBLED its taxes from 1987 to 1999?

   A. Kentucky
   B. North Carolina
   C. Kansas
   D. Texas
   E. None of these

4. Which state had the SMALLEST $ increase in taxes from 1987 to 1999?

   A. Montana
   B. Alabama
   C. Arkansas
   D. Mississippi
   E. South Carolina

5. In which of the following states was the per capita tax the GREATEST in 1987?

   A. Massachusetts
   B. New York
   C. Nevada
   D. Delaware
   E. Oregon

KEY (CORRECT ANSWERS)

1. A
2. D
3. C
4. E
5. C

TEST 8

Questions 1-6.

DIRECTIONS: Questions 1 to 6 are to be answered SOLELY on the basis of the chart below which relates to the Distribution of Minority Groups by Pay Category.

TABLE 1-- DISTRIBUTION OF ALL MINORITY GROUPS COMBINED, BY PAY CATEGORY AS OF NOVEMBER 30, 1999 AND MAY 31, 2000

Pay System	November 1999 Number	November 1999 Percent	May 2000 Number	May 2000 Percent	Percent Change
All Pay Systems	500,508	100.0	501,871	100.0	0.3
General Schedule and Similar	181,725	36.3	186,170	37.1	2.4
Wage Systems	155,744	31.1	151,919	30.3	-2.5
Postal Field Service	158,945	31.8	159,211	31.7	0.2
All Other	4,094	0.8	4,571	0.9	11.7

1. From the table, what was the TOTAL of government workers in *all* pay systems in November, 1999?

    A. 155,744   B. 181,725   C. 186,170
    D. 500,508   E. None of these

2. What was the percentage difference between Wage Systems and All Pay Systems in November, 1999, and Postal Field Service and All Pay Systems in May, 2000?

    A. .2%   B. .6%   C. 1.1%   D. 1.7%   E. 2.5%

3. How many more minority group members were employed by the Postal Field Service in May, 2000 than in November, 1999?

    A. .2%   B. 256   C. 266   D. 1256   E. 1266

4. In which of the pay systems did the percentage of minority workers decline?

    A. General Schedule and Similar   B. Wage Systems
    C. Postal Field Service   D. All Other
    E. None of these

5. In which system was the percentage gain of minority members from 1999 to 2000 the greatest?

    A. General Schedule and similar   B. Wage Systems
    C. Postal Field Service   D. All Other systems
    E. One cannot tell from the information given

6. Which system reflects the GREATEST percentage increase from 1999 to 2000 to the total minority work force?

    A. General Schedule and similar   B. Wage systems
    C. Postal Field Service   D. All Other
    E. One cannot tell from the information given

KEY (CORRECT ANSWERS)

1. E
2. B
3. C
4. B
5. D
6. A

PRINCIPLES AND PRACTICES OF ADMINISTRATION, SUPERVISION & MANAGEMENT

TABLE OF CONTENTS

	Page
GENERAL ADMINISTRATION	1
SEVEN BASIC FUNCTIONS OF THE SUPERVISOR	2
1. Planning	2
2. Organizing	3
3. Staffing	3
4. Directing	3
5. Coordinating	3
6. Reporting	3
7. Budgeting	3
PLANNING TO MEET MANAGEMENT GOALS	4
I. What is Planning?	4
II. Who Should Make Plans?	4
III. What are the Results of Poor Planning?	4
IV. Principles of Planning	4
MANAGEMENT PRINCIPLES	5
I. Management	5
II. Management Principles	5
III. Organization Structure	6
ORGANIZATION	8
PRINCIPLES OF ORGANIZATION	9
1. Definition	9
2. Purpose of Organization	9
3. Basic Considerations in Organizational Planning	9
4. Bases for Organization	10
5. Assignment of Functions	10
6. Delegation of Authority and Responsibility	10
7. Employee Relationships	10
DELEGATING	11
REPORTS	11

MANAGEMENT CONTROLS	12
1. Control	12
2. Basis for Control	13
3. Policy	13
4. Procedure	13
5. Basis of Control	14
FRAMEWORK OF MANAGEMENT	14
PROBLEM SOLVING	16
1. Identify the Problem	16
2. Gather Data	17
3. List Possible Solutions	17
4. Test Possible Solutions	17
5. Select the Best Solution	18
6. Put the Solution Into Actual Practice	18
COMMUNICATION	19
1. What is Communication?	19
2. Why is Communication Needed?	19
3. How is Communication Achieved?	19
4. Why Does Communication Fail?	20
5. How to Improve Communication?	20
6. How to Determine if You Are Getting Across	21
7. The Key Attitude	21
FUNCTIONS OF A DEPARTMENT PERSONNEL OFFICE	22
SUPERVISION	23
1. The Authoritarian Approach	23
2. The Laissez-Faire Approach	23
3. The Democratic Approach	24
EMPLOYEE MORALE	25
MOTIVATION	25
EMPLOYEE PARTICIPATION	26
STEPS IN HANDLING A GRIEVANCE	27
DISCIPLINE	28

PRINCIPLES AND PRACTICES OF ADMINISTRATION, SUPERVISION & MANAGEMENT

Most people are inclined to think of administration as something that only a few persons are responsible for in a large organization. Perhaps this is true if you are thinking of Administration with a capital A, but administration with a lower case a is a responsibility of supervisors at all levels each working day.

All of us feel we are pretty good supervisors and that we do a good job of administering the workings of our agency. By and large, this is true, but every so often it is good to check up on ourselves. Checklists appear from time to time in various publications which psychologists say, tell whether or not a person will make a good wife, husband, doctor, lawyer, or supervisor.

The following questions are an excellent checklist to test yourself as a supervisor and administrator.

Remember, Administration gives direction and points the way but administration carries the ideas to fruition. Each is dependent on the other for its success. Remember, too, that no unit is too small for these departmental functions to be carried out. These statements apply equally as well to the Chief Librarian as to the Department Head with but one or two persons to supervise.

GENERAL ADMINISTRATION - General Responsibilities of Supervisors

1. Have I prepared written statements of functions, activities, and duties for my organizational unit?

2. Have I prepared procedural guides for operating activities?

3. Have I established clearly in writing, lines of authority and responsibility for my organizational unit?

4. Do I make recommendations for improvements in organization, policies, administrative and operating routines and procedures, including simplification of work and elimination of non-essential operations?

5. Have I designated and trained an understudy to function in my absence?

6. Do I supervise and train personnel within the unit to effectively perform their assignments?

7. Do I assign personnel and distribute work on such a basis as to carry out the organizational unit's assignment or mission in the most effective and efficient manner?

8. Have I established administrative controls by:

   a. Fixing responsibility and accountability on all supervisors under my direction for the proper performance of their functions and duties.

b. Preparing and submitting periodic work load and progress reports covering the operations of the unit to my immediate superior.

c. Analysis and evaluation of such reports received from subordinate units.

d. Submission of significant developments and problems arising within the organizational unit to my immediate superior.

e. Conducting conferences, inspections, etc., as to the status and efficiency of unit operations.

9. Do I maintain an adequate and competent working force?

10. Have I fostered good employee-department relations, seeing that established rules, regulations, and instructions are being carried out properly?

11. Do I collaborate and consult with other organizational units performing related functions to insure harmonious and efficient working relationships?

12. Do I maintain liaison through prescribed channels with city departments and other governmental agencies concerned with the activities of the unit?

13. Do I maintain contact with and keep abreast of the latest developments and techniques of administration (professional societies, groups, periodicals, etc.) as to their applicability to the activities of the unit?

14. Do I communicate with superiors and subordinates through prescribed organizational channels?

15. Do I notify superiors and subordinates in instances where bypassing is necessary as soon thereafter as practicable?

16. Do I keep my superior informed of significant developments and problems?

SEVEN BASIC FUNCTIONS OF THE SUPERVISOR

1. <u>PLANNING</u>
This means working out goals and means to obtain goals. <u>What</u> needs to be done, <u>who</u> will do it, <u>how</u>, <u>when</u>, and <u>where</u> it is to be done.

<u>SEVEN STEPS IN PLANNING</u>

1. Define job or problem clearly.
2. Consider priority of job.
3. Consider time-limit - starting and completing.
4. Consider minimum distraction to, or interference with, other activities.
5. Consider and provide for contingencies - possible emergencies.
6. Break job down into components.
7. Consider the 5 W's and H:

WHY	...	is it necessary to do the job? (Is the purpose clearly defined?)
WHAT	...	needs to be done to accomplish the defined purpose?
	...	is needed to do the job? (money, materials, etc.)
WHO	...	is needed to do the job?
	...	will have responsibilities?
WHERE	...	is the work to be done?
WHEN	...	is the job to begin and end? (schedules, etc.)
HOW	...	is the job to be done? (methods, controls, records, etc.)

2. **ORGANIZING**
   This means dividing up the work, establishing clear lines of responsibility and authority and coordinating efforts to get the job done.

3. **STAFFING**
   The whole personnel function of bringing in and <u>training</u> staff, getting the right man and fitting him to the right job - the job to which he is best suited.
   In the normal situation, the supervisor's responsibility regarding staffing normally includes providing accurate job descriptions, that is, duties of the jobs, requirements, education and experience, skills, physical, etc.; assigning the work for maximum use of skills; and proper utilization of the probationary period to weed out unsatisfactory employees.

4. **DIRECTING**
   Providing the necessary leadership to the group supervised. Important work gets done to the supervisor's satisfaction.

5. **COORDINATING**
   The all-important duty of inter-relating the various parts of the work.
   The supervisor is also responsible for controlling the coordinated activities. This means measuring performance according to a time schedule and setting quotas to see that the goals previously set are being reached. Reports from workers should be analyzed, evaluated, and made part of all future plans.

6. **REPORTING**
   This means proper and effective communication to your superiors, subordinates, and your peers (in definition of the job of the supervisor). Reports should be read and information contained therein should be used not be filed away and forgotten. Reports should be written in such a way that the desired action recommended by the report is forthcoming.

7. **BUDGETING**
   This means controlling current costs and forecasting future costs. This forecast is based on past experience, future plans and programs, as well as current costs.

   You will note that these seven functions can fall under three topics:

Planning	)	
Organizing	)	Make a Plan
Staffing	)	
Directing	)	Get things done
Controlling	)	

Reporting)
Budgeting) Watch it work

PLANNING TO MEET MANAGEMENT GOALS

I. <u>WHAT IS PLANNING</u>?
   A. Thinking a job through before new work is done to determine the best way to do it
   B. A method of doing something
   C. Ways and means for achieving set goals
   D. A means of enabling a supervisor to deliver with a minimum of effort, all details involved in coordinating his work

II. <u>WHO SHOULD MAKE PLANS</u>?
   Everybody!
   All levels of supervision must plan work. (Top management, heads of divisions or bureaus, first line supervisors, and individual employees.) The higher the level, the more planning required.

III. <u>WHAT ARE THE RESULTS OF POOR PLANNING</u>?
   A. Failure to meet deadline
   B. Low employee morale
   C. Lack of job coordination
   D. Overtime is frequently necessary
   E. Excessive cost, waste of material and manhours

IV. <u>PRINCIPLES OF PLANNING</u>
   A. Getting a clear picture of your objectives. What exactly are you trying to accomplish?
   B. Plan the whole job, then the parts, in proper sequence.
   C. Delegate the planning of details to those responsible for executing them.
   D. Make your plan flexible.
   E. Coordinate your plan with the plans of others so that the work may be processed with a minimum of delay.
   F. Sell your plan before you execute it.
   G. Sell your plan to your superior, subordinate, in order to gain maximum participation and coordination.
   H. Your plan should take precedence. Use knowledge and skills that others have brought to a similar job.
   I. Your plan should take account of future contingencies; allow for future expansion.
   J. Plans should include minor details. Leave nothing to chance that can be anticipated.
   K. Your plan should be simple and provide standards and controls. Establish quality and quantity standards and set a standard method of doing the job. The controls will indicate whether the job is proceeding according to plan.
   L. Consider possible bottlenecks, breakdowns, or other difficulties that are likely to arise.

V. Q. WHAT ARE THE *YARDSTICKS* BY WHICH PLANNING SHOULD BE MEASURED?
   A. Any plan should:
   - Clearly state a definite course of action to be followed and goal to be achieved, with consideration for emergencies.
   - Be realistic and practical.

- State what's to be done, when it's to be done, where, how, and by whom.
- Establish the most efficient sequence of operating steps so that more is accomplished in less time, with the least effort, and with the best quality results.
- Assure meeting deliveries without delays.
- Establish the standard by which performance is to be judged.

Q. WHAT KINDS OF PLANS DOES EFFECTIVE SUPERVISION REQUIRE?
A. Plans should cover such factors as:
- Manpower - right number of properly trained employees on the job.
- Materials - adequate supply of the right materials and supplies.
- Machines - full utilization of machines and equipment, with proper maintenance.
- Methods - most efficient handling of operations.
- Deliveries - making deliveries on time.
- Tools - sufficient well-conditioned tools
- Layout - most effective use of space.
- Reports - maintaining proper records and reports.
- Supervision - planning work for employees and organizing supervisor's own time.

I. <u>MANAGEMENT</u>

Question: *What do we mean by management?*

Answer: *Getting work done through others.*

Management could also be defined as planning, directing, and controlling the operations of a bureau or division so that all factors will function properly and all persons cooperate efficiently for a common objective.

II. <u>MANAGEMENT PRINCIPLES</u>

1. There should be a hierarchy - wherein authority and responsibility run upward and downward through several levels - with a broad base at the bottom and a single head at the top.

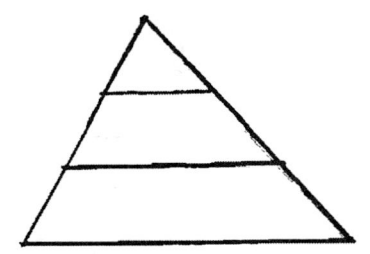

2. Each and every unit or person in the organization should be answerable ultimately to the manager at the apex. In other words, *The buck stops here!*

3. Every necessary function involved in the bureau's objectives is assigned to a unit in that bureau.

4. Responsibilities assigned to a unit are specifically clear-cut and understood.

5. Consistent methods of organizational structure should be applied at each level of the organization.

6. Each member of the bureau from top to bottom knows:
   to whom he reports
   who reports to him.

7. No member of one bureau reports to more than one supervisor.
   No dual functions

8. Responsibility for a function is matched by authority necessary to perform that function.
   Weight of authority

9. Individuals or units reporting to a supervisor do not exceed the number which can be feasibly and effectively coordinated and directed.
   Concept of *span of control*

10. Channels of command (management) are not violated by staff units, although there should be staff services to facilitate and coordinate management functions.

11. Authority and responsibility should be decentralized to units and individuals who are responsible for the actual performance of operations.
    Welfare - down to Welfare Centers
    Hospitals - down to local hospitals

12. Management should exercise control through attention to policy problems of exceptional importance, rather than through review of routine actions of subordinates.

13. Organizations should never be permitted to grow so elaborate as to hinder work accomplishments.
    Empire building

II. <u>ORGANIZATION STRUCTURE</u>
    <u>Types of Organizations.</u>
    The purest form is a leader and a few followers, such as:

```
                    | Supervisor |
    _____
    | Worker |   | Worker |   | Worker |   | Worker |
```

(Refer to organization chart) from supervisor to workers.

The line of authority is direct, The workers know exactly where they stand in relation to their boss, to whom they report for instructions and direction.

Unfortunately, in our present complex society, few organizations are similar to this example of a pure line organization. In this era of specialization, other people are often needed in the simplest of organizations. These specialists are known as staff. The sole purpose for their existence (staff) is to assist, advise, suggest, help or counsel line organizations. Staff has no authority to direct line people - nor do they give them direct instructions.

```
                          ┌─────────────┐
                          │ SUPERVISOR  │
                          └─────────────┘
    ┌──────────────┬──────────────┬──────────────┐
┌───────────┐ ┌────────────┐ ┌────────────┐ ┌─────────┐
│ Personnel │ │ Accounting │ │ Inspection │ │  Legal  │
└───────────┘ └────────────┘ └────────────┘ └─────────┘
┌──────────┐  ┌──────────┐   ┌──────────┐   ┌──────────┐
│  Worker  │  │  Worker  │   │  Worker  │   │  Worker  │
└──────────┘  └──────────┘   └──────────┘   └──────────┘
```

Line Functions	Staff Functions
1. Directs	1. Advises
2. Orders	2. Persuades and sells
3. Responsibility for carrying out activities from beginning to end	3. Staff studies, reports, recommends but does not carry out
4. Follows chain of command	4. May advise across department lines
5. Is identified with what it does	5. May find its ideas identified with others
6. Decides when and how to use staff advice	6. Has to persuade line to want its advice
7. Line executes	7. Staff - Conducts studies and research. Provides advice and instructions in technical matters. Serves as technical specialist to render specific services

Types and Functions of Organization Charts.
An organization chart is a picture of the arrangement and inter-relationship of the subdivisions of an organization.

1. Types of Charts:
   a. Structural - basic relationships only
   b. Functional - includes functions or duties
   c. Personnel - positions, salaries, status, etc.
   d. Process Chart - work performed
   e. Gantt Chart - actual performance against planned
   f. Flow Chart - flow and distribution of work

2. Functions of Charts:
   a. Assist in management planning and control
   b. Indicate duplication of functions
   c. Indicate incorrect stressing of functions
   d. Indicate neglect of important functions
   e. Correct unclear authority
   f. Establish proper span of control

3. Limitations of Charts:
   a. Seldom maintained on current basis

    b. Chart is oversimplified
    c. Human factors cannot adequately be charted

4. Organization Charts should be:
    a. Simple
    b. Symmetrical
    c. Indicate authority
    d. Line and staff relationship differentiated
    e. Chart should be dated and bear signature of approving officer
    f. Chart should be displayed, not hidden

ORGANIZATION

There are four basic principles of organization:

1. Unity of command
2. Span of control
3. Uniformity of assignment
4. Assignment of responsibility and delegation of authority

Unity of Command

Unity of command means that each person in the organization should receive orders from one, and only one, supervisor. When a person has to take orders from two or more people, (a) the orders may be in conflict and the employee is upset because he does not know which he should obey, or, (b) different orders may reach him at the same time and he does not know which he should carry out first.

Equally as bad as having two bosses is the situation where the supervisor is by-passed. Let us suppose you are a supervisor whose boss by-passes you (deals directly with people reporting to you). To the worker, it is the same as having two bosses; but to you, the supervisor, it is equally serious. By-passing on the part of your boss will undermine your authority, and the people under you will begin looking to your boss for decisions and even for routine orders.

You can prevent by-passing by telling the people you supervise that if anyone tries to give them orders, they should direct that person to you.

Span of Control

Span of control on a given level involves:

    a. The number of people being supervised
    b. The distance
    c. The time involved in supervising the people. (One supervisor cannot supervise too many workers effectively.)

Span of control means that a supervisor has the right number (not too many and not too few) of subordinates that he can supervise well.

Uniformity of Assignment

In assigning work, you as the supervisor should assign to each person jobs that are similar in nature. An employee who is assigned too many different types of jobs will waste time in going from one kind of work to another. It takes time for him to get to top production in one kind of task and, before he does so, he has to start on another.

When you assign work to people, remember that:

a. Job duties should be definite. Make it clear from the beginning <u>what</u> they are to do, <u>how</u> they are to do it, and <u>why</u> they are to do it. Let them know how much they are expected to do and how well they are expected to do it.

b. Check your assignments to be certain that there are no workers with too many unrelated duties, and that no two people have been given overlapping responsibilities. Your aim should be to have every task assigned to a specific person with the work fairly distributed and with each person doing his part.

Assignment of Responsibility and Delegation of Authority

A supervisor cannot delegate his final responsibility for the work of his department. The experienced supervisor knows that he gets his work done through people. He can't do it all himself. So he must assign the work and the responsibility for the work to his employees. Then they must be given the authority to carry out their responsibilities.

By assigning responsibility and delegating authority to carry out the responsibility, the supervisor builds in his workers initiative, resourcefulness, enthusiasm, and interest in their work. He is treating them as responsible adults. They can find satisfaction in their work, and they will respect the supervisor and be loyal to the supervisor.

PRINCIPLES OF ORGANIZATION

1. <u>Definition</u>
   Organization is the method of dividing up the work to provide the best channels for coordinated effort to get the agency's mission accomplished.

2. <u>Purpose of Organization</u>
   a. To enable each employee within the organization to clearly know his responsibilities and relationships to his fellow employees and to organizational units.
   b. To avoid conflicts of authority and overlapping of jurisdiction.
   c. To ensure teamwork.

3. <u>Basic Considerations in Organizational Planning</u>
   a. The basic plans and objectives of the agency should be determined, and the organizational structure should be adapted to carry out effectively such plans and objectives.
   b. The organization should be built around the major functions of the agency and not individuals or groups of individuals.
   c. The organization should be sufficiently flexible to meet new and changing conditions which may be brought about from within or outside the department.
   d. The organizational structure should be as simple as possible and the number of organizational units kept at a minimum.
   e. The number of levels of authority should be kept at a minimum. Each additional management level lengthens the chain of authority and responsibility and increases the time for instructions to be distributed to operating levels and for decisions to be obtained from higher authority.

    f.   The form of organization should permit each executive to exercise maximum initiative within the limits of delegated authority.

4. <u>Bases for Organization</u>
    a. Purpose (Examples: education, police, sanitation)
    b. Process (Examples: accounting, legal, purchasing)
    c. Clientele (Examples: welfare, parks, veteran)
    d. Geographic (Examples: borough offices, precincts, libraries)

5. <u>Assignments of Functions</u>
    a. Every function of the agency should be assigned to a specific organizational unit. Under normal circumstances, no single function should be assigned to more than one organizational unit.
    b. There should be no overlapping, duplication, or conflict between organizational elements.
    c. Line functions should be separated from staff functions, and proper emphasis should be placed on staff activities.
    d. Functions which are closely related or similar should normally be assigned to a single organizational unit.
    e. Functions should be properly distributed to promote balance, and to avoid overemphasis of less important functions and underemphasis of more essential functions.

6. <u>Delegation of Authority and Responsibility</u>
    a. Responsibilities assigned to a specific individual or organizational unit should carry corresponding authority, and all statements of authority or limitations thereof should be as specific as possible.
    b. Authority and responsibility for action should be decentralized to organizational units and individuals responsible for actual performance to the greatest extent possible, without relaxing necessary control over policy or the standardization of procedures. Delegation of authority will be consistent with decentralization of responsibility but such delegation will not divest an executive in higher authority of his overall responsibility.
    c. The heads of organizational units should concern themselves with important matters and should delegate to the maximum extent details and routines performed in the ordinary course of business.
    d. All responsibilities, authorities, and relationships should be stated in simple language to avoid misinterpretation.
    e. Each individual or organizational unit charged with a specific responsibility will be held responsible for results.

7. <u>Employee Relationships</u>
    a. The employees reporting to one executive should not exceed the number which can be effectively directed and coordinated. The number will depend largely upon the scope and extent of the responsibilities of the subordinates.
    b. No person should report to more than one supervisor. Every supervisor should know who reports to him, and every employee should know to whom he reports. Channels of authority and responsibility should not be violated by staff units.
    c. Relationships between organizational units within the agency and with outside organizations and associations should be clearly stated and thoroughly understood to avoid misunderstanding.

DELEGATING

1. <u>What is Delegating?</u>
   Delegating is assigning a job to an employee, giving him the authority to get that job done, and giving him the responsibility for seeing to it that the job is done.

   a. <u>What to Delegate</u>
      (1) Routine details
      (2) Jobs which may be necessary and take a lot of time, but do not have to be done by the supervisor personally (preparing reports, attending meetings, etc.)
      (3) Routine decision-making (making decisions which do not require the supervisor's personal attention)

   b. <u>What Not to Delegate</u>
      (1) Job details which are *executive functions* (setting goals, organizing employees into a good team, analyzing results so as to plan for the future)
      (2) Disciplinary power (handling grievances, preparing service ratings, reprimands, etc.)
      (3) Decision-making which involves large numbers of employees or other bureaus and departments
      (4) Final and complete responsibility for the job done by the unit being supervised

   c. <u>Why Delegate?</u>
      (1) To strengthen the organization by developing a greater number of skilled employees
      (2) To improve the employee's performance by giving him the chance to learn more about the job, handle some responsibility, and become more interested in getting the job done
      (3) To improve a supervisor's performance by relieving him of routine jobs and giving him more time for *executive functions* (planning, organizing, controlling, etc.) which cannot be delegated

2. <u>To Whom to Delegate</u>
   People with abilities not being used. Selection should be based on ability, not on favoritism.

REPORTS

<u>Definition</u>
   A report is an orderly presentation of factual information directed to a specific reader for a specific purpose.

<u>Purpose</u>
   The general purpose of a report is to bring to the reader useful and factual information about a condition or a problem. Some specific purposes of a report may be:

1. To enable the reader to appraise the efficiency or effectiveness of a person or an operation
2. To provide a basis for establishing standards
3. To reflect the results of expenditures of time, effort, and money
4. To provide a basis for developing or altering programs

Types
1. Information Report - Contains facts arranged in sequence
2. Summary (Examination) Report - Contains facts plus an analysis or discussion of the significance of the facts. Analysis may give advantages and disadvantages or give qualitative and quantitative comparisons
3. Recommendation Report - Contains facts, analysis, and conclusion logically drawn from the facts and analysis, plus a recommendation based upon the facts, analysis, and conclusions

Factors to Consider Before Writing Report

1. <u>Why</u> write the report - The purpose of the report should be clearly defined.
2. <u>Who</u> will read the report - What level of language should be used? Will the reader understand professional or technical language?
3. <u>What</u> should be said - What does the reader need or want to know about the subject?
4. <u>How</u> should it be said - Should the subject be presented tactfully? Convincingly? In a stimulating manner?

Preparatory Steps

1. Assemble the facts - Find out who, why, what, where, when, and how.
2. Organize the facts - Eliminate unnecessary information.
3. Prepare an outline - Check for orderliness, logical sequence.
4. Prepare a draft - Check for correctness, clearness, completeness, conciseness, and tone.
5. Prepare it in final form - Check for grammar, punctuation, appearance.

Outline For a Recommendation Report
Is the report:

1. Correct in information, grammar, and tone?
2. Clear?
3. Complete?
4. Concise?
5. Timely?
6. Worth its cost?

Will the report accomplish its purpose?

MANAGEMENT CONTROLS

1. <u>Control</u>
   What is control? What is controlled? Who controls?

   The essence of control is action which adjusts operations to predetermined standards, and its basis is information in the hands of managers. Control is checking to determine whether plans are being observed and suitable progress toward stated objectives is being made, and action is taken, if necessary, to correct deviations.

We have a ready-made model for this concept of control in the automatic systems which are widely used for process control in the chemical and petroleum industries. A process control system works this way. Suppose, for example, it is desired to maintain a constant rate of flow of oil through a pipe at a predetermined or set-point value. A signal, whose strength represents the rate of flow, can be produced in a measuring device and transmitted to a control mechanism. The control mechanism, when it detects any deviation of the actual from the set-point signal, will reposition the value regulating flow rate.

2. Basis For Control
A process control mechanism thus acts to adjust operations to predetermined standards and does so on the basis of information it receives. In a parallel way, information reaching a manager gives him the opportunity for corrective action and is his basis for control. He cannot exercise control without such information, and he cannot do a complete job of managing without controlling.

3. Policy
What is policy?

Policy is simply a statement of an organization's intention to act in certain ways when specified types of circumstances arise. It represents a general decision, predetermined and expressed as a principle or rule, establishing a normal pattern of conduct for dealing with given types of business events - usually recurrent. A statement is therefore useful in economizing the time of managers and in assisting them to discharge their responsibilities equitably and consistently.

Policy is not a means of control, but policy does generate the need for control.

Adherence to policies is not guaranteed nor can it be taken on faith. It has to be verified. Without verification, there is no basis for control. Policy and procedures, although closely related and interdependent to a certain extent, are not synonymous. A policy may be adopted, for example, to maintain a materials inventory not to exceed one million dollars. A procedure for inventory control would interpret that policy and convert it into methods for keeping within that limit, with consideration, too, of possible but foreseeable expedient deviation.

4. Procedure
What is procedure?

A procedure specifically prescribes:

    a. What work is to be performed by the various participants
    b. Who are the respective participants
    c. When and where the various steps in the different processes are to be performed
    d. The sequence of operations that will insure uniform handling of recurring transactions
    e. The *paper* that is involved, its origin, transition, and disposition

Necessary appurtenances to a procedure are:

    a. Detailed organizational chart

      b. Flow charts
      c. Exhibits of forms, all presented in close proximity to the text of the procedure

5. <u>Basis of Control - Information in the Hands of Managers</u>
   If the basis of control is information in the hands of managers, then <u>reporting</u> is elevated to a level of very considerable importance.

   Types of reporting may include:

       a. Special reports and routine reports
       b. Written, oral, and graphic reports
       c. Staff meetings
       d. Conferences
       e. Television screens
       f. Non-receipt of information, as where management is by exception
       g. Any other means whereby information is transmitted to a manager as a basis for control action

FRAMEWORK OF MANAGEMENT

<u>Elements</u>

1. <u>Policy</u> - It has to be verified, controlled.

2. <u>Organization</u> - is part of the giving of an assignment. The organizational chart gives to each individual in his title, a first approximation of the nature of his assignment and orients him as being accountable to a certain individual. Organization is not in a true sense a means of control. Control is checking to ascertain whether the assignment is executed as intended and acting on the basis of that information.

3. <u>Budgets</u> - perform three functions:

   a. They present the objectives, plans, and programs of the organization in financial terms.
   b. They report the progress of actual performance against these predetermined objectives, plans, and programs.
   c. Like organizational charts, delegations of authority, procedures and job descriptions, they define the assignments which have flowed from the Chief Executive. Budgets are a means of control in the respect that they report progress of actual performance against the program. They provide information which enables managers to take action directed toward bringing actual results into conformity with the program.

4. <u>Internal Check</u> - provides in practice for the principle that the same person should not have responsibility for all phases of a transaction. This makes it clearly an aspect of organization rather than of control. Internal Check is static, or built-in.

5. <u>Plans, Programs, Objectives</u>
   People must know what they are trying to do. <u>Objectives</u> fulfill this need. Without them, people may work industriously and yet, working aimlessly, accomplish little.

Plans and Programs complement Objectives, since they propose how and according to what time schedule the objectives are to be reached.
6. <u>Delegations of Authority</u>
Among the ways we have for supplementing the titles and lines of authority of an organizational chart are delegations of authority. Delegations of authority clarify the extent of authority of individuals and in that way serve to define assignments. That they are not means of control is apparent from the very fact that wherever there has been a delegation of authority, the need for control increases. This could hardly be expected to happen if delegations of authority were themselves means of control.

<u>Manager's Responsibility</u>

Control becomes necessary whenever a manager delegates authority to a subordinate because he cannot delegate and then simply sit back and forget all about it. A manager's accountability to his own superior has not diminished one whit as a result of delegating part of his authority to a subordinate. The manager must exercise control over actions taken under the authority so delegated. That means checking serves as a basis for possible corrective action.

Objectives, plans, programs, organizational charts, and other elements of the managerial system are not fruitfully regarded as either <u>controls</u> or <u>means of control</u>. They are pre-established <u>standards</u> or <u>models of performance</u> to which operations are adjusted by the exercise of management control. These standards or models of performance are dynamic in character for they are constantly altered, modified, or revised. Policies, organizational set-up, procedures, delegations, etc. are constantly altered but, like objectives and plans, they remain in force until they are either abandoned or revised. All of the elements (or standards or models of performance), objectives, plans and prpgrams, policies, organization, etc. can be regarded as a *framework of management.*

<u>Control Techniques</u>

Examples of control techniques:
1. Compare against established standards
2. Compare with a similar operation
3. Compare with past operations
4. Compare with predictions of accomplishment

<u>Where Forecasts Fit</u>

Control is after-the-fact while forecasts are before. Forecasts and projections are important for setting objectives and formulating plans.

Information for aiming and planning does not have to before-the-fact. It may be an after-the-fact analysis proving that a certain policy has been impolitic in its effect on the relation of the company or department with customer, employee, taxpayer, or stockholder; or that a certain plan is no longer practical, or that a certain procedure is unworkable.

The prescription here certainly <u>would not be in control</u> (in these cases, control would simply bring operations into conformity with obsolete standards) but the establishment of new standards, a new policy, a new plan, and a new procedure to be controlled too.

<u>Information</u> is, of course, the basis for all <u>communication</u> in addition to furnishing evidence to management of the need for reconstructing the framework of management.

PROBLEM SOLVING

The accepted concept in modern management for problem solving is the utilization of the following steps:

1. Identify the problem
2. Gather data
3. List possible solutions
4. Test possible solutions
5. Select the best solution
6. Put the solution into actual practice

Occasions might arise where you would have to apply the second step of gathering data before completing the first step.

You might also find that it will be necessary to work on several steps at the same time.

1. <u>Identify the Problem</u>

    Your first step is to define as precisely as possible the problem to be solved. While this may sound easy, it is often the most difficult part of the process.

    It has been said of problem solving that you are halfway to the solution when you can write out a clear statement of the problem itself.

    Our job now is to get below the surface manifestations of the trouble and pinpoint the problem. This is usually accomplished by a logical analysis, by going from the general to the particular; from the obvious to the not-so-obvious cause.
    Let us say that production is behind schedule. WHY? Absenteeism is high. Now, is absenteeism the basic problem to be tackled, or is it merely a symptom of low morale among the workforce? Under these circumstances, you may decide that production is not the problem; the problem is *employee morale.*

    In trying to define the problem, remember there is seldom one simple reason why production is lagging, or reports are late, etc.

    Analysis usually leads to the discovery that an apparent problem is really made up of several subproblems which must be attacked separately.

    Another way is to limit the problem, and thereby ease the task of finding a solution, and concentrate on the elements which are within the scope of your control.

    When you have gone this far, write out a tentative statement of the problem to be solved.

2. Gather Data

In the second step, you must set out to collect all the information that might have a bearing on the problem. Do not settle for an assumption when reasonable fact and figures are available.

If you merely go through the motions of problem-solving, you will probably shortcut the information-gathering step. Therefore, do not stack the evidence by confining your research to your own preconceived ideas.

As you collect facts, organize them in some form that helps you make sense of them and spot possible relationships between them. For example: Plotting cost per unit figures on a graph can be more meaningful than a long column of figures.

Evaluate each item as you go along. Is the source material: absolutely reliable, probably reliable, or not to be trusted.

One of the best methods for gathering data is to go out and look the situation over carefully. Talk to the people on the job who are most affected by this problem.

Always keep in mind that a primary source is usually better than a secondary source of information.

3. List Possible Solutions

This is the creative thinking step of problem solving. This is a good time to bring into play whatever techniques of group dynamics the agency or bureau might have developed for a joint attack on problems.

Now the important thing for you to do is: Keep an open mind. Let your imagination roam freely over the facts you have collected. Jot down every possible solution that occurs to you. Resist the temptation to evaluate various proposals as you go along. List seemingly absurd ideas along with more plausible ones. The more possibilities you list during this step, the less risk you will run of settling for merely a workable, rather than the best, solution.

Keep studying the data as long as there seems to be any chance of deriving additional - ideas, solutions, explanations, or patterns from it.

4. Test Possible Solutions

Now you begin to evaluate the possible solutions. Take pains to be objective. Up to this point, you have suspended judgment but you might be tempted to select a solution you secretly favored all along and proclaim it as the best of the lot.

The secret of objectivity in this phase is to test the possible solutions separately, measuring each against a common yardstick. To make this yardstick try to enumerate as many specific criteria as you can think of. Criteria are best phrased as questions which you ask of each possible solution. They can be drawn from these general categories:

        Suitability   -   Will this solution do the job?
                                Will it solve the problem completely or partially?

Is it a permanent or a stopgap solution?

Feasibility - Will this plan work in actual practice?
Can we afford this approach?
How much will it cost?

Acceptability - Will the boss go along with the changes required in the plan?
Are we trying to drive a tack with a sledge hammer?

5. <u>Select the Best Solution</u>

This is the area of executive decision.

Occasionally, one clearly superior solution will stand out at the conclusion of the testing process. But often it is not that simple. You may find that no one solution has come through all the tests with flying colors.

You may also find that a proposal, which flunked miserably on one of the essential tests, racked up a very high score on others.

The best solution frequently will turn out to be a combination.

Try to arrange a marriage that will bring together the strong points of one possible solution with the particular virtues of another. The more skill and imagination that you apply, the greater is the likelihood that you will come out with a solution that is not merely adequate and workable, but is the best possible under the circumstances.

6. <u>Put the Solution Into Actual Practice</u>
As every executive knows, a plan which works perfectly on paper may develop all sorts of bugs when put into actual practice.

Problem-solving does not stop with selecting the solution which looks best in theory. The next step is to put the chosen solution into action and watch the results. The results may point towards modifications.

If the problem disappears when you put your solution into effect, you know you have the right solution.

If it does not disappear, even after you have adjusted your plan to cover unforeseen difficulties that turned up in practice, work your way back through the problem-solving solutions.

Would one of them have worked better?
Did you overlook some vital piece of data which would have given you a different slant on the whole situation? Did you apply all necessary criteria in testing solutions? If no light dawns after this much rechecking, it is a pretty good bet that you defined the problem incorrectly in the first place.

You came up with the wrong solution because you tackled the wrong problem.

Thus, step six may become step one of a new problem-solving cycle.

COMMUNICATION

1. <u>What is Communication?</u>
   We communicate through writing, speaking, action or inaction. In speaking to people face-to-face, there is opportunity to judge reactions and to adjust the message. This makes the supervisory chain one of the most, and in many instances the most, important channels of communication.

   In an organization, communication means keeping employees informed about the organization's objectives, policies, problems, and progress. Communication is the free interchange of information, ideas, and desirable attitudes between and among employees and between employees and management.

2. <u>Why is Communication Needed</u>?
   a. People have certain social needs
   b. Good communication is essential in meeting those social needs
   c. While people have similar basic needs, at the same time they differ from each other
   d. Communication must be adapted to these individual differences

   An employee cannot do his best work unless he knows why he is doing it. If he has the feeling that he is being kept in the dark about what is going on, his enthusiasm and productivity suffer.

   Effective communication is needed in an organization so that employees will understand what the organization is trying to accomplish; and how the work of one unit contributes to or affects the work of other units in the organization and other organizations.

3. <u>How is Communication Achieved?</u>
   Communication flows downward, upward, sideways.

   a. Communication may come from top management down to employees. This is <u>downward communication</u>.

      Some means of downward communication are:
      (1) Training (orientation, job instruction, supervision, public relations, etc.)
      (2) Conferences
      (3) Staff meetings
      (4) Policy statements
      (5) Bulletins
      (6) Newsletters
      (7) Memoranda
      (8) Circulation of important letters

      In downward communication, it is important that employees be informed in advance of changes that will affect them.

   b. Communications should also be developed so that the ideas, suggestions, and knowledge of employees will flow <u>upward</u> to top management.

Some means of upward communication are:
(1) Personal discussion conferences
(2) Committees
(3) Memoranda
(4) Employees suggestion program
(5) Questionnaires to be filled in giving comments and suggestions about proposed actions that will affect field operations

Upward communication requires that management be willing to listen, to accept, and to make changes when good ideas are present. Upward communication succeeds when there is no fear of punishment for speaking out or lack of interest at the top. Employees will share their knowledge and ideas with management when interest is shown and recognition is given.

   c. The *advantages* of downward communication:
      (1) It enables the passing down of orders, policies, and plans necessary to the continued operation of the station.
      (2) By making information available, it diminishes the fears and suspicions which result from misinformation and misunderstanding.
      (3) It fosters the pride people want to have in their work when they are told of good work.
      (4) It improves the morale and stature of the individual to be *in the know*.
      (5) It helps employees to understand, accept, and cooperate with changes when they know about them in advance.

   d. The *advantages* of upward communication:
      (1) It enables the passing upward of information, attitudes, and feelings.
      (2) It makes it easier to find out how ready people are to receive downward communication.
      (3) It reveals the degree to which the downward communication is understood and accepted.
      (4) It helps to satisfy the basic *social* needs.
      (5) It stimulates employees to participate in the operation of their organization.
      (6) It encourages employees to contribute ideas for improving the efficiency and economy of operations.
      (7) It helps to solve problem situations before they reach the explosion point.

4. <u>Why Does Communication Fail</u>?
   a. The technical difficulties of conveying information clearly
   b. The emotional content of communication which prevents complete transmission
   c. The fact that there is a difference between what management needs to say, what it wants to say, and what it does say
   d. The fact that there is a difference between what employees would like to say, what they think is profitable or safe to say, and what they do say

5. <u>How to Improve Communication.</u>
As a supervisor, you are a key figure in communication. To improve as a communicator, you should:
   a. <u>Know</u> - Knowing your subordinates will help you to recognize and work with individual differences.

b. <u>Like</u> - If you like those who work for you and those for whom you work, this will foster the kind of friendly, warm, work atmosphere that will facilitate communication.
  c. <u>Trust</u> - Showing a sincere desire to communicate will help to develop the mutual trust and confidence which are essential to the free flow of communication.
  d. <u>Tell</u> - Tell your subordinates and superiors *what's doing*. Tell your subordinates *why* as well as *how*.
  e. <u>Listen</u> - By listening, you help others to talk and you create good listeners. Don't forget that listening implies action.
  f. <u>Stimulate</u> - Communication has to be stimulated and encouraged. Be receptive to ideas and suggestions and motivate your people so that each member of the team identifies himself with the job at hand.
  g. <u>Consult</u> - The most effective way of consulting is to let your people participate, insofar as possible, in developing determinations which affect them or their work.

6. <u>How to Determine Whether You are Getting Across</u>.
   a. Check to see that communication is received and understood
   b. Judge this understanding by actions rather than words
   c. Adapt or vary communication, when necessary
   d. Remember that good communication cannot cure all problems

7. <u>The Key Attitude</u>.
   Try to see things from the other person's point of view. By doing this, you help to develop the permissive atmosphere and the shared confidence and understanding which are essential to effective two-way communication.

   Communication is a two-way process.
   a. The basic purpose of any communication is to get action.
   b. The only way to get action is through acceptance.
   c. In order to get acceptance, communication must be humanly satisfying as well as technically efficient.

HOW ORDERS AND INSTRUCTIONS SHOULD BE GIVEN

<u>Characteristics of Good Orders and Instructions</u>

1. <u>Clear</u>
   Orders should be definite as to
   - <u>What</u> is to be done
   - <u>Who</u> is to do it
   - <u>When</u> it is to be done
   - <u>Where</u> it is to be done
   - <u>How</u> it is to be done

2. <u>Concise</u>
   Avoid wordiness. Orders should be brief and to the point.

3. <u>Timely</u>
   Instructions and orders should be sent out at the proper time and not too long in advance of expected performance.

4. <u>Possibility of Performance</u>
   Orders should be feasible:
   a. Investigate before giving orders
   b. Consult those who are to carry out instructions before formulating and issuing them

5. <u>Properly Directed</u>
   Give the orders to the people concerned. Do not send orders to people who are not concerned. People who continually receive instructions that are not applicable to them get in the habit of neglecting instructions generally.

6. <u>Reviewed Before Issuance</u>
   Orders should be reviewed before issuance:
   a. Test them by putting yourself in the position of the recipient
   b. If they involve new procedures, have the persons who are to do the work review them for suggestions

7. <u>Reviewed After Issuance</u>
   Persons who receive orders should be allowed to raise questions and to point out unforeseen consequences of orders.

8. <u>Coordinated</u>
   Orders should be coordinated so that work runs smoothly.

9. <u>Courteous</u>
   Make a request rather than a demand. There is no need to continually call attention to the fact that you are the boss.

10. <u>Recognizable as an Order</u>
    Be sure that the order is recognizable as such.

11. <u>Complete</u>
    Be sure recipient has knowledge and experience sufficient to carry out order. Give illustrations and examples.

A DEPARTMENTAL PERSONNEL OFFICE IS RESPONSIBLE FOR THE FOLLOWING FUNCTIONS

1. Policy
2. Personnel Programs
3. Recruitment and Placement
4. Position Classification
5. Salary and Wage Administration
6. Employee Performance Standards and Evaluation
7. Employee Relations
8. Disciplinary Actions and Separations
9. Health and Safety
10. Staff Training and Development
11. Personnel Records, Procedures, and Reports
12. Employee Services
13. Personnel Research

SUPERVISION

<u>Leadership</u>

All leadership is based essentially on authority. This comes from two sources: it is received from higher management or it is earned by the supervisor through his methods of supervision. Although effective leadership has always depended upon the leader's using his authority in such a way as to appeal successfully to the motives of the people supervised, the conditions for making this appeal are continually changing. The key to today's problem of leadership is flexibility and resourcefulness on the part of the leader in meeting changes in conditions as they occur.

Three basic approaches to leadership are generally recognized:

1. <u>The Authoritarian Approach</u>
    a. The methods and techniques used in this approach emphasize the *I* in leadership and depend primarily on the formal authority of the leader. This authority is sometimes exercised in a hardboiled manner and sometimes in a benevolent manner, but in either case the dominating role of the leader is reflected in the thinking, planning, and decisions of the group.
    b. Group results are to a large degree dependent on close supervision by the leader. Usually, the individuals in the group will not show a high degree of initiative or acceptance of responsibility and their capacity to grow and develop probably will not be fully utilized. The group may react with resentment or submission, depending upon the manner and skill of the leader in using his authority
    c. This approach develops as a natural outgrowth of the authority that goes with the leader's job and his feeling of sole responsibility for getting the job done. It is relatively easy to use and does not require much resourcefulness.
    d. The use of this approach is effective in times of emergencies, in meeting close deadlines as a final resort, in settling some issues, in disciplinary matters, and with dependent individuals and groups.

2. <u>The Laissez-Faire or *Let 'em Alone* Approach</u>
    a. This approach generally is characterized by an avoidance of leadership responsibility by the leader. The activities of the group depend largely on the choice of its members rather than the leader.
    b. Group results probably will be poor. Generally, there will be disagreements over petty things, bickering, and confusion. Except for a few aggressive people, individuals will not show much initiative and growth and development will be retarded. There may be a tendency for informal leaders to take over leadership of the group.
    c. This approach frequently results from the leader's dislike of responsibility, from his lack of confidence, from failure of other methods to work, from disappointment or criticism. It is usually the easiest of the three to use and requires both understanding and resourcefulness on the part of the leader.
    d. This approach is occasionally useful and effective, particularly in forcing dependent individuals or groups to rely on themselves, to give someone a chance to save face by clearing his own difficulties, or when action should be delayed temporarily for good cause.

3. The Democratic Approach
   a. The methods and techniques used in this approach emphasize the *we* in leadership and build up the responsibility of the group to attain its objectives. Reliance is placed largely on the earned authority of the leader.
   b. Group results are likely to be good because most of the job motives of the people will be satisfied. Cooperation and teamwork, initiative, acceptance of responsibility, and the individual's capacity for growth probably will show a high degree of development.
   c. This approach grows out of a desire or necessity of the leader to find ways to appeal effectively to the motivation of his group. It is the best approach to build up inside the person a strong desire to cooperate and apply himself to the job.
   It is the most difficult to develop, and requires both understanding and resourcefulness on the part of the leader.
   d. The value of this approach increases over a long period where sustained efficiency and development of people are important. It may not be fully effective in all situations, however, particularly when there is not sufficient time to use it properly or where quick decisions must be made.

All three approaches are used by most leaders and have a place in supervising people. The extent of their use varies with individual leaders, with some using one approach predominantly. The leader who uses these three approaches, and varies their use with time and circumstance, is probably the most effective. Leadership which is used predominantly with a democratic approach requires more resourcefulness on the part of the leader but offers the greatest possibilities in terms of teamwork and cooperation.

The one best way of developing democratic leadership is to provide a real sense of participation on the part of the group, since this satisfies most of the chief job motives. Although there are many ways of providing participation, consulting as frequently as possible with individuals and groups on things that affect them seems to offer the most in building cooperation and responsibility. Consultation takes different forms, but it is most constructive when people feel they are actually helping in finding the answers to the problems on the job.

There are some requirements of leaders in respect to human relations which should be considered in their selection and development. Generally, the leader should be interested in working with other people, emotionally stable, self-confident, and sensitive to the reactions of others. In addition, his viewpoint should be one of getting the job done through people who work cooperatively in response to his leadership. He should have a knowledge of individual and group behavior, but, most important of all, he should work to combine all of these requirements into a definite, practical skill in leadership.

Nine Points of Contrast Between *Boss* and *Leader*

1. The boss drives his men; the leader coaches them.
2. The boss depends on authority; the leader on good will.
3. The boss inspires fear; the leader inspires enthusiasm.
4. The boss says *J*; the leader says *We*.
5. The boss says *Get here on time;* the leader gets there ahead of time.
6. The boss fixes the blame for the breakdown; the leader fixes the breakdown.
7. The boss knows how it is done; the leader shows how.
8. The boss makes work a drudgery; the leader makes work a game.
9. The boss says *Go*; the leader says *Let's go*.

EMPLOYEE MORALE

Employee morale is the way employees feel about each other, the organization or unit in which they work, and the work they perform.

Some Ways to Develop and Maintain Good Employee Morale

1. Give adequate credit and praise when due.
2. Recognize importance of all jobs and equalize load with proper assignments, always giving consideration to personality differences and abilities.
3. Welcome suggestions and do not have an *all-wise* attitude. Request employees' assistance in solving problems and use assistants when conducting group meetings on certain subjects.
4. Properly assign responsibilities and give adequate authority for fulfillment of such assignments.
5. Keep employees informed about matters that affect them.
6. Criticize and reprimand employees privately.
7. Be accessible and willing to listen.
8. Be fair.
9. Be alert to detect training possibilities so that you will not miss an opportunity to help each employee do a better job, and if possible with less effort on his part.
10. Set a good example.
11. Apply the golden rule.

Some Indicators of Good Morale
1. Good quality of work
2. Good quantity
3. Good attitude of employees
4. Good discipline
5. Teamwork
6. Good attendance
7. Employee participation

MOTIVATION

Drives

A *drive,* stated simply, is a desire or force which causes a person to do or say certain things. These are some of the most usual drives and some of their identifying characteristics recognizable in people motivated by such drives:

1. Security (desire to provide for the future)
   Always on time for work
   Works for the same employer for many years
   Never takes unnecessary chances Seldom resists doing what he is told

2. Recognition (desire to be rewarded for accomplishment)
   Likes to be asked for his opinion
   Becomes very disturbed when he makes a mistake
   Does things to attract attention

Likes to see his name in print

3. <u>Position</u> (desire to hold certain status in relation to others)
   Boasts about important people he knows
   Wants to be known as a key man
   Likes titles
   Demands respect
   Belongs to clubs, for prestige

4. <u>Accomplishment</u> (desire to get things done)
   Complains when things are held up
   Likes to do things that have tangible results
   Never lies down on the job
   Is proud of turning out good work

5. <u>Companionship</u> (desire to associate with other people)
   Likes to work with others
   Tells stories and jokes
   Indulges in horseplay
   Finds excuses to talk to others on the job

6. <u>Possession</u> (desire to collect and hoard objects)
   Likes to collect things
   Puts his name on things belonging to him
   Insists on the same work location

Supervisors may find that identifying the drives of employees is a helpful step toward motivating them to self-improvement and better job performance. For example: An employee's job performance is below average. His supervisor, having previously determined that the employee is motivated by a drive for security, suggests that taking training courses will help the employee to improve, advance, and earn more money. Since earning more money can be a step toward greater security, the employee's drive for security would motivate him to take the training suggested by the supervisor. In essence, this is the process of charting an employee's future course by using his motivating drives to positive advantage.

EMPLOYEE PARTICIPATION

<u>What is Participation?</u>

Employee participation is the employee's giving freely of his time, skill and knowledge to an extent which cannot be obtained by demand.

<u>Why is it Important</u>?

The supervisor's responsibility is to get the job done through people. A good supervisor gets the job done through people who work willingly and well. The participation of employees is important because:
1. Employees develop a greater sense of responsibility when they share in working out operating plans and goals.
2. Participation provides greater opportunity and stimulation for employees to learn, and to develop their ability.

3. Participation sometimes provides better solutions to problems because such solutions may combine the experience and knowledge of interested employees who want the solutions to work.
4. An employee or group may offer a solution which the supervisor might hesitate to make for fear of demanding too much.
5. Since the group wants to make the solution work, they exert *pressure* in a constructive way on each other.
6. Participation usually results in reducing the need for close supervision.

<u>How May Supervisors Obtain It?</u>

Participation is encouraged when employees feel that they share some responsibility for the work and that their ideas are sincerely wanted and valued. Some ways of obtaining employee participation are:

1. Conduct orientation programs for new employees to inform them about the organization and their rights and responsibilities as employees.
2. Explain the aims and objectives of the agency. On a continuing basis, be sure that the employees know what these aims and objectives are.
3. Share job successes and responsibilities and give credit for success.
4. Consult with employees, both as individuals and in groups, about things that affect them.
5. Encourage suggestions for job improvements. Help employees to develop good suggestions. The suggestions can bring them recognition. The city's suggestion program offers additional encouragement through cash awards.

The supervisor who encourages employee participation is not surrendering his authority. He must still make decisions and initiate action, and he must continue to be ultimately responsible for the work of those he supervises. But, through employee participation, he is helping his group to develop greater ability and a sense of responsibility while getting the job done faster and better.

STEPS IN HANDLING A GRIEVANCE

1. <u>Get the facts</u>
   a. Listen sympathetically.
   b. Let him talk himself out.
   c. Get his story straight.
   d. Get his point of view.
   e. Don't argue with him.
   f. Give him plenty of time.
   g. Conduct the interview privately.
   h. Don't try to shift the blame or pass the buck.

2. <u>Consider the facts</u>
   a. Consider the employee's viewpoint.
   b. How will the decision affect similar cases.
   c. Consider each decision as a possible precedent.
   d. Avoid snap judgments - don't jump to conclusions.

3. <u>Make or get a decision</u>
   a. Frame an effective counter-proposal.
   b. Make sure it is fair to all.
   c. Have confidence in your judgment.
   d. Be sure you can substantiate your decision.

4. <u>Notify the employee of your decision</u>
   Be sure he is told; try to convince him that the decision is fair and just.

5. <u>Take action when needed and if within your authority</u>
   Otherwise, tell employee that the matter will be called to the attention of the proper person or that nothing can be done, and why it cannot.

6. <u>Follow through</u> to see that the desired result is achieved.

7. <u>Record key facts</u> concerning the complaint and the action taken.

8. <u>Leave the way open to him to appeal your decision</u> to a higher authority.

9. <u>Report all grievances to your superior</u>, whether they are appealed or not.

DISCIPLINE

Discipline is training that develops self-control, orderly conduct, and efficiency.

To discipline does not necessarily mean to punish.

To discipline does mean to train, to regulate, and to govern conduct.

The Disciplinary Interview

Most employees sincerely want to do what is expected of them. In other words, they are self-disciplined. Some employees, however, fail to observe established rules and standards, and disciplinary action by the supervisor is required.

The primary purpose of disciplinary action is to improve conduct without creating dissatisfaction, bitterness, or resentment in the process.

Constructive disciplinary action is more concerned with causes and explanations of breaches of conduct than with punishment. The disciplinary interview is held to get at the causes of apparent misbehavior and to motivate better performance in the future.

It is important that the interview be kept on as impersonal a basis as possible. If the supervisor lets the interview descend to the plane of an argument, it loses its effectiveness.

Planning the Interview

Get all pertinent facts concerning the situation so that you can talk in specific terms to the employee.

Review the employee's record, appraisal ratings, etc.

Consider what you know about the temperament of the employee. Consider your attitude toward the employee. Remember that the primary requisite of disciplinary action is fairness.

Don't enter upon the interview when angry.

Schedule the interview for a place which is private and out of hearing of others.

Conducting the Interview

1. Make an effort to establish accord.

2. Question the employee about the apparent breach of discipline. Be sure that the question is not so worded as to be itself an accusation.

3. Give the employee a chance to tell his side of the story. Give him ample opportunity to talk.

4. Use understanding-listening except where it is necessary to ask a question or to point out some details of which the employee may not be aware. If the employee misrepresents facts, make a plain, accurate statement of the facts, but don't argue and don't engage in personal controversy.

5. Listen and try to understand the reasons for the employee's (mis)conduct. First of all, don't assume that there has been a breach of discipline. Evaluate the employee's reasons for his conduct in the light of his opinions and feelings concerning the consistency and reasonableness of the standards which he was expected to follow. Has the supervisor done his part in explaining the reasons for the rules? Was the employee's behavior unintentional or deliberate? Does he think he had real reasons for his actions? What new facts is he telling? Do the facts justify his actions? What causes, other than those mentioned, could have stimulated the behavior?

6. After listening to the employee's version of the situation, and if censure of his actions is warranted, the supervisor should proceed with whatever criticism is justified. Emphasis should be placed on future improvement rather than exclusively on the employee's failure to measure up to expected standards of job conduct.

7. Fit the criticism to the individual. With one employee, a word of correction may be all that is required.

8. Attempt to distinguish between unintentional error and deliberate misbehavior. An error due to ignorance requires training and not censure.

9. Administer criticism in a controlled, even tone of voice, never in anger. Make it clear that you are acting as an agent of the department. In general, criticism should refer to the job or the employee's actions and not to the person. Criticism of the employee's work is not an attack on the individual.

10. Be sure the interview does not destroy the employee's self-confidence. Mention his good qualities and assure him that you feel confident that he can improve his performance.
11. Wherever possible, before the employee leaves the interview, satisfy him that the incident is closed, that nothing more will be said on the subject unless the offense is repeated.

PROGRAM EVALUATION

Table of Contents

	Pages
Program Evaluation Strategy	1
Managing for Success	1
Types of Program Evaluation	1
Judging vs. Coaching	1
Conducting a Program Evaluation	3
The Need for Planning	3
Stage 1 - Evaluability Assessment	3
Performance Measurement	4
Mission, Goals and Objectives	4
Performance Indicators	5
Stage 2 - Designing the Evaluation	6
Stage 3 - Conducting the Study	8
Developing Data Measurement System	8
Determine Data Availability	9
Collecting Data	9
Analyzing Data	10
Data Presentation	10
Refining Measures	10
Stage 4 - Reporting Evaluation Findings	11
Stage 5 - Program Offices Implement Improvement Activities	12
Stage 6 - On-Going Consultation	13

PROGRAM EVALUATION

Program Evaluation Strategy

MANAGING FOR SUCCESS

An essential component of any successful organization is its ability to continually assess and evaluate its performance. To establish effective and efficient programs, managers need fundamental information regarding the position and progress of their programs, and what improvements can be made to enhance the overall quality of their operations.

In identifying this need, the PTO's Office of Planning and Evaluation (P&E) has developed an evaluation strategy for the Patent and Trademark Office. Our goal is to support PTO in planning, assessing, and improving its program activities, so that managers have the information and support they need to continually develop and advance their programs.

TYPES OF PROGRAM EVALUATION

Program evaluation is based on the fundamental idea that programs should have a demonstrable benefit.

In its simplest terms, program evaluation is defined as a systematic approach to assessing the performance of a program or service. Program evaluations are most commonly referred to as either summative or formative in nature. Summative evaluations make a judgment about a program's operations and usefulness, whereas formative evaluations describe a program's operations in order to improve the way in which it functions.

In recent years, the formative approach to evaluating has evolved into what has come to be called "evaluation research."

Evaluation research includes:
- Design of programs
- Ongoing monitoring of how well programs are functioning
- Assessment of program impact
- Analysis of benefits relative to costs.

This approach seems to be the most productive. As internal evaluators, our goal is not only to report to managers on their program's current situation, but also assist them in developing and enhancing the resources they need for continual operational improvement.

JUDGING VS. COACHING

In conducting formative evaluations, the goal is not to judge a program's worth or usefulness, rather the goal is to provide recommendations for program improvements in addition to assessing impacts and results.

A program evaluation trainer, uses the example of a world-class figure-skating champion to differentiate the roles of a coach and judge. As a skater performs, both the judge and the coach are meticulously assessing the skaters every move; however, each has a different motive for evaluating the performance. The judge looks at the performance and impassively scores the skater against the competition, providing little, if any, feedback to the skater. The coach on the other hand, goes a step beyond assessing the performance by actually working with the skater to improve his or her performance. The judge's objective is to score the skater's single performance, whereas the coach's objective is to help the skater achieve his or her fullest potential for future performances.

The coaching perspective helps programs become as efficient and effective as possible, while reaching their fullest potential. Using the example, the coach can work with and recommend improvements to the skater, but it is the skater who is responsible for making the improvements and for eventually becoming a guide and example for others that follow. By diagnosing, consulting and informing programs on their performance, we not only help programs gain a better understanding of what works well within their organization, we also maintain PTO's strategic goal of providing our customers with the highest level of quality and service in all aspects of PTO operations.

Conducting a Program Evaluation

In order to be effective, every evaluation must be tailored to the individual program or organization.

The following are stages in conducting a program evaluation. These stages are designed to adapt to individual needs, interests and the stage of development of the organization or program being evaluated.

THE NEED FOR PLANNING

Ideally, a successful evaluation will provide the best information possible on all key issues within a given set of constraints, such as available time, staff and budget resources. This makes it important to consider at the outset that the design of the evaluation needs to be done carefully, since criticism of the findings will likely focus on the methodology used.

Given the constraints we are all under these days, you may very well ask why you should spend precious resources on planning and designing your evaluation. The answer is precisely because of those constraints. In addition to increasing credibility in the product, a careful and sound design:

- increases overall quality,
- contains costs,
- ensures timeliness of findings,
- increases the strength and specificity of findings and recommendations,
- decreases criticism of methodology,
- improves customer satisfaction, and
- results in less resources required to carry out the evaluation.

STAGE 1: EVALUABILITY ASSESSMENT

Program evaluation is essentially a process in which questions are asked about a program or activity and answers are actively sought. In order to have an effective evaluation--which will result in improved program performance--first, the right questions must be asked, and second, the evaluation team must assure that the questions can be accurately answered.

Before conducting any formal evaluation, an evaluability assessment is conducted. The purpose of the evaluability assessment is to identify the program's goals, performance indicators and data sources, which will be used to conduct the evaluation. The evaluability assessment not only answers the question of whether a program can be meaningfully evaluated, but whether the evaluation is likely to contribute to improved program performance.

During the evaluability assessment there is usually a clear indication of whether a program is ready to be evaluated. If the necessary information (goals, objectives, performance measurements, etc.) is available and is identified by the evaluators and intended users as clear, concise and realistic (given resource allocations and restrictions), the evaluation can proceed. However, if the goals, objectives and performance indicators are found to be either underdeveloped or undefined, the program office is advised to first focus on developing or redefining their performance measurements before continuing with the evaluation.

The foremost question is whether or not the program can be evaluated in a meaningful way based on what currently exists.

Program evaluations are generally concerned with whether a program or policy is achieving its intended goal or purpose. Frequently though, the goals and purposes were to attract as much support as possible for the proposed project, but may lack consistency or be too ambitious given the realities of program functions. Programs and policies that do not have clear and consistent goals can not be evaluated for their effectiveness. Thus, uncovering those goals and purposes is generally the starting point of most evaluations. This first stage of an evaluation is necessary to determine whether they can be evaluated.

> Program Evaluation Criteria
> - Program goals and objectives, important side effects, and priority information needs are well defined.
> - Program goals and objectives are plausible.
> - Relevant performance data can be obtained.
> - The intended users of the evaluation results have agreed on how they will use the information.

Performance Measurement

Performance measurement is a process by which a program objectively measures how it is accomplishing its mission through the delivery of its products, services, or processes. It is a self-assessment, goal-setting, and progress monitoring tool, which provides on-going performance feedback to both management and staff. A good performance measurement system is designed to provide information which helps clarify goals and motivates performance, solves problems, and corrects deviations or alters planned directions.

> Performance Measurement is crucial to the overall management of programs because of one basic principle: "What gets measured, gets done."

Mission, Goals and Objectives

The first step in performance measurement is identifying the mission, goals and objectives. The following is a brief description of each:

The mission is the purpose for which a program or organization was created. A mission answers the following questions:

- Who are we?
- What do we do?
- For whom do we do it?
- Why do we do it?

Goals are statements, usually general and abstract, about how the program expects to accomplish its mission. Goals may be quantitative ("Increase production") or qualitative ("Improve worker morale").

> **Tips on Goal Setting**
> - Goals may be general or specific and may encompass time spans ranging from a few months to several years.
> - Goals may be set for the entire organization, programs, and individuals.
> - Goals at the various organizational levels must be coordinated if the organization is to achieve its intended overall purpose.
> - There must be coordination of the long-term goals of the organization with the short term goals of departments and programs, and of both of these with the personal goals of workers
> - Involve both management and staff when developing goals.

Objectives are the means for accomplishing goals. They must be quantifiable containing specific statements detailing the desired accomplishments of a program's goals.

> **Rules for Writing Objectives**
> - Use a single issue per objective.
> - Define measurable objectives using a verb-noun structure ("Increase productivity by 15 percent by fiscal year 2015").
> - Specify an expected time for achievement.

Performance Indicators

Once goals and objectives have been established, performance indicators are developed. Performance indicators track and measure whether the goals and objectives have been reached, or how well the program is progressing toward achieving them.

In the classical sense, a performance indicator is defined as a ratio where the output of an effort is divided by the inputs (labor, energy, time, etc.) required to produce it. . For example:

$$\frac{\text{\# of customers helped}}{\text{\# of service reps}}$$

$$\frac{\text{\# of acceptable documents produced}}{\text{hours expanded for documents}}$$

> **Customer Requirements and Stakeholder Requirements** are the Building Blocks for Measurement Ratios. When designing indicators ask the question: How Do We Know We Met Customer Requirements?

Two integral components of performance indicators are effectiveness and efficiency. Effective production is defined as producing the desired results, whereas efficient production is defined as producing the desired outputs with a minimum level of input. Simply stated, effectiveness is doing the right things, and efficiency is doing things right.

Effectiveness and efficiency are both critical measures of performance and success. Organizations can temporarily survive without perfect efficiency, but would most likely die if they were ineffective. When designing performance measurements, it is essential that an organization considers both effectiveness and efficiency. Omitting either would result in performance measurements that provide inaccurate and often costly productivity information.

It bears repeating that if a program has not clearly identified its goals and objectives and set effectiveness and efficiency measures, it will be difficult to evaluate.

Four Criteria for Measurement Effectiveness and Efficiency

1. **Quality-** The measure must define and reflect quality of production or services as well as quantity. A measure that assesses only quantity outputs can lead to reduced productivity.

2. **Mission and goals-** The measure must define and assess only outputs and services that are integrated with the organizational mission and strategic goals. Measures directed to products and services that are not consistent with mission and goals threaten productivity.

3. **Rewards and Incentives-** Measures must be integrated with performance incentives, reward systems and practices. Measures that have no important contingencies will not work to improve productivity.

4. **Employee Involvement-** There must be involvement of employees and other direct stakeholders in the definition and construction of productivity measures. When lack of involvement has not resulted in commitment and buy-in, results from the measures are not likely to be received favorably or to have any impact on future productivity.

STAGE 2: DESIGNING THE EVALUATION

What's worth knowing?
How will we get it?
How will it be used?

By the time you have an idea of the evaluation capacity of your program, you may have the answers to many of the questions that lead to the design. Every question asked by an evaluation can be looked at with varying levels of intensity and thoroughness. When great precision is needed and resources are available, the most powerful of evaluations may be conducted, on the other hand when time and resources are limited and only approximate answers are needed, the level of the evaluation will differ. Given the diversity of programs, policies and projects to be evaluated, the number of questions to be answered, and the differing availability of resources, there can be no single recipe for a successful evaluation. However, these simple guidelines, once tailored, should provide a solid framework for conducting an evaluation.

In determining the design of an evaluation, the following questions are answered and an Evaluation Design Proposal is drafted.

1. Why are we doing this evaluation?

Clarify what the overall purpose of the evaluation is and what specific objectives will be accomplished. Focus not only on what the evaluation will do, but also identify what the evaluation will NOT do.

2. For whom are we doing this evaluation?

It is essential to identify who the audience is so that their needs, perspectives and constraints can be assessed. Identify both the primary audience and secondary audiences.

Who is sponsoring the evaluation? Who is authorizing the expenditure of funds and human resources? Who will be approving the report?

3. What are we evaluating?

Discuss the issues of the evaluation. Are we studying the need for a program or activity? The operations of a program or activity? The effects of a program or activity? Define the specific questions to be answered during the evaluation.

4. How are we doing this evaluation?

Make a list of the information needed to conduct the evaluation. Once the information needs are defined, identify the data collection techniques. Examples of Data Collection Techniques:

- Surveys
- Interviews
- Focus Group Sessions
- Case Studies
- Tests
- Observations
- Document Reviews
- Production Reports
- Computerized databases

5. When are we doing this evaluation?

Establish both the beginning and completion dates and interim deadlines. It may be helpful to set up a project plan to track the dates and resources.

6. Where are we doing this evaluation?

Determine the location of the evaluation. Will a special staff be pulled together? Will they need space for meetings? For working? For storage of files?

7. Who is doing this evaluation?

Assess the skills and resources needed to conduct the evaluation. Identify possible training needs and establish roles and responsibilities for each team member (Hendricks, 1994).

Tips on Building an Effective Study Team
- Keep teams small.
- Acknowledge team members' need for high performance.
- Reward both team leaders and team members.
- Focus on people, not methodology.
- Keep a skills inventory of team members.
- Make use of project management tools to create benchmarks of success.
- Form a policy group and a work group to involve policy makers, managers, and key staff in the evaluation.

Consider whether the skills and resources are available internally, or whether it might be more economical or beneficial to hire an external contractor to conduct the evaluation. Depending on the nature of the program or project, it may be critical that the results of the evaluation come from an outside, objective source.

One More Thing

After the design is completed, it is helpful to take an overall look at the design.

A well-designed evaluation can usually be recognized by the way it has:

1. Defined and posed questions for study.
2. Developed the methodological strategies for answering those questions.
3. Formulated a data collection plan that anticipates and addresses problems and obstacles that are likely to be encountered.
4. Provided a detailed analysis plan that will ensure that the questions posed will be answered with the appropriate data in the best possible fashion.
5. Established and maintained focus on the usefulness of the product for the intended user.

A sound design reduces downtime deciding what to do next, reduces time spent on collecting and analyzing irrelevant data and strengthens the relevance of the evaluation.

STAGE 3: CONDUCTING THE STUDY

Once the evaluation proposal is drafted and agreed upon by the evaluation team and the evaluation users, the process of collecting and analyzing the relevant data can begin.

DATA COLLECTION AND ANALYSIS

Developing A Data Measurement System

There are two methods of evaluation studies: qualitative and quantitative. Qualitative data collection systems permit the evaluator to study selected issues, cases, or events in depth and detail; data collection is not constrained by predetermined categories of analysis. Quantitative methods use standardized measures that fit diverse opinions and experiences into predetermined response categories. Considering evaluation design alternatives leads directly to consideration of the relative strengths and weaknesses of qualitative and quantitative studies, and the time and resources available for the study.

The advantage of the quantitative approach is that it measures the reactions of a great many people to a limited set of questions, thus facilitating comparison and statistical aggregation of the data. It gives a broad, generalized set of findings. Qualitative methods typically produce a wealth of detailed data about a much smaller number of people and cases. Qualitative data provide depth and detail through direct quotation and careful description of program situations, events, people, interactions, and observed behaviors.

Purposes and functions of qualitative and quantitative data are different, yet can be complementary. The statistics from standardized items make summaries, comparisons, and generalizations quite easy and precise. The narrative comments from open-ended questions are typically meant to provide a forum for elaboration, explanations, meanings, and new ideas.

It is recommended that an evaluation team engage stakeholders early because they have a different perspective, have data the evaluator needs, and can influence the evaluation positively if they are engaged, or negatively if they are ignored or threatened.

Categorizing research questions into major categories can help refine the research agenda of almost any study. Time spent in developing a detailed research design, data collection and analysis plan may improve the quality of the overall results.

Stakeholders include potential users of evaluation information and those with an investment in the organization or unit involved in the study.

Determine Data Availability

Once it has been established what to measure, it must be determined if the data for those measures is available and how to get it. If data is not available, alternative indicators must be identified.

The evaluation team should try to keep its indicators simple and use existing data whenever possible. However, do not compromise the evaluation by discarding indicators the team thinks are meaningful and important before weighing their obtainability.

> Data Availability Concerns
>
> 1. Does the data currently exist ? If not, can it be developed, and at what effort and cost?
> 2. If the data exists, what will it cost to retrieve the data?
> 3. What will it take to get the data converted into the established measurement values?
> 4. Will a system investment be required? At what cost?
> 5. Will management support this level of cost? Can a limited version be used?
> 6. When will data be produced?

Collecting Data

The collection of data addresses the critical issues of making sure the correct data is identified, and a baseline is collected. The baseline data reflects the initial status of the program or process. During this phase, in addition to documenting the method of collection of the data, document any problems with the process, and work to resolve any process problems regularly. Meet with management at the end of an established trial period to evaluate results.

Analyzing Data

Once we have collected the data and before we meet with management, we must analyze the data to make sure that it will provide us with enough information and the right type of information on which to base an evaluation. We must ensure that the data fits the indicators identified to analyze. Agree to finalize the current indicators or revise them as needed, and analyze the baseline data collected for the purpose of setting goals.

DATA PRESENTATION

Once the data has been collected and analyzed, it must be decided how the data and results will be presented. Numbers by themselves are often difficult to understand, they cannot explain circumstances, and they may not easily lead to conclusions. Therefore, it is important to present the information in ways that make it easy to understand, that show relationships to other data, and that allow the information to be used to support decision-making processes. Whenever possible, use graphical tools to present data.

Measures must be shown in context. The most frequent evaluation contexts are: (1) goals compared to actual results, (2) trends in relation to previous periodic results, and (3) comparison of results to other relevant data. Using one or more of these contexts, meaningful conclusions should be drawn about the measurement result with little or no explanation.

REFINING MEASURES

Indicators may need some slight modifications or adjustment to better meet performance information needs of program or executive management. Continually check the usefulness of measurement data and adjust data collection methods if necessary.

Adjusting Measures

Are the measures working well?
What are the measures indicating?
Are additional indicators necessary?
Is data not really available (too difficult or expensive to acquire)?
Is data too difficult to use?

Balance Types Of Measures

One consideration of performance indicator development is that measures are interrelated and cannot be viewed in isolation. Timeliness, quality and cost are always in contention with each other, and the impact of improving any one or two must be weighed in relation to the expense of the third. A balance must be reached between the effectiveness and the economy and efficiency.

Consider Weighting Measures

Not all indicators are equally important. To reflect importance or priorities within measures or categories of measures, weight or index the measures. Weighting or indexing measures is an involved and advanced process and may not be necessary or appropriate for every program. However, weighting measures can provide some valuable insights into program outcomes.

Integrating with Management Process

Once performance results become available, the challenge shifts to presenting and using them effectively.

Establish Goals

Goals should be established based on: (1) policy or administrative priorities, (2) mission (3) customer feedback, (4) past history, (5) forecasted demand and (6) benchmark information.

Determine What The Measurements Say

It is extremely important to understand what the measurements say, as well as what they do not say. The measurements must be compared to performance goals, benchmarks, or past performance. Then variances or changes must be analyzed, and subsequent actions must be planned. In addition to program performance evaluation, the measurement results in the evaluation process can be used for external reporting, planning and budgeting activities and performance appraisal evaluation.

STAGE 4: REPORTING EVALUATION RESULTS

Reporting evaluation results is more of a process than a stage. Beginning on the first day of the evaluation, the evaluators should be continually reporting and discussing their findings with the evaluation users. It is not only important to keep them updated on the evaluation's progress, but also, it is important to keep them informed of any findings and recommendations that can be implemented before the full completion of the evaluation. Remember, the reason for doing an evaluation is to help an organization or program become as effective and efficient as possible. The sooner an organization can implement changes or improvements, the better.

Action-Oriented Reporting

As stated previously, the purpose of an evaluation is to improve a program or an organization's performance. The way in which evaluators do this is by providing recommendations for improvement to management and staff.

The majority of an evaluation report should be devoted to communicating the findings and specific recommendations. Reports should be action-oriented, centered mostly around the findings, but also around the recommendations and suggestions for implementation.

Action-oriented reports are often structured as a series of short reports targeted to specific audiences, rather than one all inclusive document.

Findings and recommendations should be presented clearly and concisely, in a way that meets the informational needs of the audience. In order for recommendations to be accepted by an organization, it must first understand what is being recommended and why it is relevant to their concerns. Evaluation studies are only useful if they are used.

Program Evaluation Report

Generally, an evaluation report should include:
- Executive Summary
  Purpose of Evaluation
  Program Background
  Evaluation Methodology
- Analysis of the Findings
- Recommendations

Tips for Reporting Evaluation Results

- Remember that the burden for effectively reporting results is on the evaluators, not the audience.
- Be aggressive. Instead of waiting for audiences to request information, actively look for opportunities to report results. Report regularly and frequently, appear in person if at all possible, and target multiple reports and briefings to specific audiences and /or issues.
- Simplify, simplify! Audiences are usually busy and their interest is pulled in different directions, so determine and report on the key points. If the core message creates interest, quickly follow up with more details.
- Study the audience. Learn about their backgrounds, interests, concerns, plans, pet peeves, etc.
- Focus on actions. Audiences are rarely interested in general information; they usually want guidance that will help them decide what to do next.
- Report in many different ways. Rather than using only one reporting technique or another, produce several different types of reports. Use written reports, personal briefings, screen show presentations, etc.

STAGE 5: PROGRAM OFFICES IMPLEMENT IMPROVEMENT ACTIVITIES

In this phase of the evaluation process, program office managers implement and monitor the recommendations and action plans originating from the evaluation study. The program manager facilitates the solution of problems by motivating staff and providing technical support. Particular attention must be given to customer and stakeholder requirements.

All employees should be trained in the process improvement recommendations so that they will possess the skills needed to recommend solutions to future problems. Decisions made closer to the customer and occurrence of events save time, reduce errors, and improve morale and service.

STAGE 6: ON-GOING CONSULTATION

Program evaluation is a continuous process of measuring, analyzing and refining an organization or program's performance.

A program evaluation is not an end in itself, rather it is the beginning of a continuous self-evaluation mechanism. With an effective evaluation comes additional data, refined measurements and new initiatives. In order to remain effective, organizations must continually evaluate this information to ensure the achievement of their mission, goals, and objectives.

ANSWER SHEET

TEST NO. _____ PART _____ TITLE OF POSITION _____
(AS GIVEN IN EXAMINATION ANNOUNCEMENT - INCLUDE OPTION, IF ANY)

PLACE OF EXAMINATION _____ DATE _____
(CITY OR TOWN)   (STATE)

RATING

USE THE SPECIAL PENCIL. MAKE GLOSSY BLACK MARKS.

Make only ONE mark for each answer. Additional and stray marks may be counted as mistakes. In making corrections, erase errors COMPLETELY.

ANSWER SHEET

APR – – 2017

TEST NO. _____ PART _____ TITLE OF POSITION _____
(AS GIVEN IN EXAMINATION ANNOUNCEMENT - INCLUDE OPTION, IF ANY)

PLACE OF EXAMINATION _____ DATE _____
(CITY OR TOWN)   (STATE)

RATING

USE THE SPECIAL PENCIL.   MAKE GLOSSY BLACK MARKS.

Questions 1–25, 26–50, 51–75, 76–100, 101–125 (answer grid with columns A B C D E)

Make only ONE mark for each answer. Additional and stray marks may be counted as mistakes. In making corrections, erase errors COMPLETELY.